ST. HELENA LIBRARY

How to Travel
Practically Anywhere

How to Travel Practically Anywhere

....

The Ultimate Travel Guide

SUSAN STELLIN

HOUGHTON MIFFLIN COMPANY

BOSTON • NEW YORK

For information about permission to reproduce selections
from this book, write to Permissions, Houghton Mifflin Company,
215 Park Avenue South, New York, New York 10003.

Visit our Web site: www.houghtonmifflinbooks.com.

Library of Congress Cataloging-in-Publication Data
Stellin, Susan.
How to travel practically anywhere / Susan Stellin.
p. cm.
ISBN-13: 978-0-618-60753-2
ISBN-10: 0-618-60753-6
1. Travel — Guidebooks. 1. Title.
G153.4.S736 2006
910'.2'02 — dc22   2005022728

Book design by Robert Overholtzer

PRINTED IN THE UNITED STATES OF AMERICA

QUM 14 13 12 11 10 9 8 7 6 5 4

To my parents, for staying put . . . and for letting me go when I first got the urge to wander.

Contents

Part II
BOOKING

5. LODGING........123

Part III
NAVIGATING

10. WHAT TO DO IF . . . 269

Introduction

AT FIRST, it seemed like such a revolution when we all began using the Internet to make our own travel plans. No more waiting on hold while a travel agent clicked a keyboard in the background, finally announcing "the best you can do": $469 to fly from New York to Los Angeles. Sure, you could try calling a few airlines yourself, to see whether you could find a better deal. But that meant more time on the phone — not even cordless back then.

But then, there was the Internet and on-line travel agencies like Expedia, Orbitz, and Travelocity. Before long, every airline, car rental company, cruise line, and hotel had a Web site, and even the most cautious shoppers relaxed their vigilance over their credit cards and began booking their own travel on line.

This fundamental shift in the way we plan and book travel certainly has many benefits. Price-comparison sites have made it easier to hunt down the best deals — which has helped lower fares — and on-line message boards have created more opportunities to trade tips with other travelers (even if contradictory opinions sometimes leave you scratching your head). And search engines like Google can help you find just about anything you might be looking for, whether that's a tour guide in Tanzania or a map of downtown Berlin.

There's just one catch: All this clicking and comparing takes some know-how, not to mention time — one thing most of us don't have to spare. Also, as "self-service" replaces "customer service" in the travel industry, being in the driver's seat takes on a whole new meaning if something goes wrong: You're on your own.

Welcome to the brave new world of do-it-yourself travel. There ought to be a guidebook for this.

How to Travel Practically Anywhere aims to be that resource. Not how to travel to a specific destination but how to travel, no matter where you're going. This book offers practical advice on the entire process of planning, booking, and navigating a trip, as well as strategies for dealing with situations that threaten to ruin even the best-laid plans.

The first part of the book walks you through the planning process, with tips on figuring out where to go, researching your destination, or finding an organized trip — say, a culinary tour or a rafting excursion through the Grand Canyon. Part II offers booking advice, covering everything from flights, lodging, car rentals, and cruises to other travel-related purchases, like insurance or train tickets. The last part of the book helps you get ready for your trip and then handle situations that might come up during your travels, like a delayed flight or a stomach virus that requires a doctor's attention.

Think of this book as a reference guide, which you can flip through as needed to find answers to specific questions, like how to decide whether you need car rental insurance or where to find a house to rent. To make all this information easier to digest, there are lots of sidebars highlighting useful Web sites and key advice.

But this book is not meant to be solely a guide to planning a vacation, since for most of us, travel is often simply a way to get from here to there — to see family, go to a wedding, meet a client, or visit friends. It's essentially a guidebook for the *logistics* of travel, whatever the reason for your trip. The goal is to help you save money and time and, I hope, avoid disappointment and stress.

On that note, there's no doubt that travel in the twenty-first century involves some new sources of anxiety, not to mention challenges that have plagued travelers as long as people have been exploring the planet. (Christopher Columbus's journey across the Atlantic was fraught with delays, and he really didn't know how he was going to pay for that trip until shortly before he left.)

But travel is still one of life's greatest pleasures — and for many of us, for both business and personal reasons, a necessity. *How to Travel Practically Anywhere* is really about making sure that you have the best trip possible — or as they say in Spanish, *que te vaya bien,* which, loosely translated, means "may it all go well for you": wherever, however, and whenever you travel.

PART I

PLANNING

1 Researching Your Destination

IF YOUR DAYS OFF aren't already set aside for your best friend's wedding in Denver, Christmas with your parents in Atlanta, or a family reunion in Montana, you have the luxury of planning an actual vacation — a rare opportunity when so much of our leisure travel involves visiting friends or relatives. Not that there's anything wrong with those trips: They certainly account for most of the travel charges on my credit card. But to paraphrase someone I once overheard on the subway, "Visiting family is a *trip*; going to Tahiti is a *vacation.*"

Of course, there is one thing that makes visiting loved ones easier than traveling somewhere new and exotic: There's much less planning involved. (As far as I'm concerned, whoever said, "Planning a trip is half the fun!" made that comment when travel agents still did most of the work.) But if you know where to look, the planning process *can* be part of the fun, and doing it right can make or break the trip itself.

This chapter guides you through the research phase, whether you already have a destination in mind or are still deciding where to go. Among the topics covered: how to find articles about your destination in back issues of travel publications, choose a guidebook that fits your style and budget, and track down tourist bureaus and other local sources of advice. There's also a list of Web sites where travelers trade tips — often, the best source of information about where to go and what to do all over the world.

As you're deciding where to go, it's also wise to consider *when* to go, another issue this chapter covers. Hurricanes, spring-break revelers, and local festivals and holidays are just a few things you should factor into your decision, and if you're traveling abroad, State Department advisories are worth checking for other timely concerns. There's more planning advice in chapter 8 ("Pretrip Preparations"), which covers the types of things most of us put off until after we've booked a trip — and some of us, until just before it's time to go.

Sources of Inspiration: A Week Off and No Idea Where to Go

Some people seem to know exactly where they want to go on their next vacation, their dream destinations stored in a mental must-see list like titles of movies to rent. Other people are more likely to ask a friend at a Memorial Day barbecue, "I've got a week off in August — where should I go?"

Twenty or thirty years ago, that question would have been directed at a travel agent, and the options would have been limited to certain predictable parts of the globe. But these days, adventure travel means trekking in Tibet, and once-inaccessible places like China, Eastern Europe, and Vietnam have become popular places to travel. So figuring out where to go on your next trip can literally be a matter of spinning the globe.

Search the archives, on line

Newspapers and magazines that cover travel are a great source of ideas when you're planning a trip, highlighting places you may not have considered or giving advice on what to do and where to stay if you know where you want to go. The problem is, there's a slim chance that you're planning to visit one of the current month's featured destinations, and the article you remember reading about a place that *is* on your short list has probably been recycled by the time you're ready to book.

Fortunately, back issues of most newspapers and magazines are now easily accessible on the Web, saving you the trouble of searching for a page you tore out or flipping through dusty periodicals. Even better, many publications have set up their on-line archives so you can choose a destination and see all the articles that have

BEST SOURCES FOR TRAVEL ARTICLES

These publications are all useful when you're looking for ideas or researching a destination. Their Web sites are among the easiest to search for past articles, and they all have comprehensive archives covering places all over the world. But pay attention to the publication date when you go exploring in archive territory; articles that are more than a year or two old may steer you toward a restaurant that's closed or a resort that's gone downhill. (For tips on finding local publications, including English-language newspapers abroad, see page 21.)

TRAVEL MAGAZINES

Budget Travel (budgettravelonline.com)
Condé Nast Traveler (cntraveler.com)
National Geographic Traveler (nationalgeographic.com/traveler)
Travel + Leisure (travelandleisure.com)

NEWSPAPERS

Boston Globe (boston.com/travel)
Chicago Tribune (chicagotribune.com/travel)
Los Angeles Times (latimes.com/travel)
New York Times (nytimes.com/travel)
San Francisco Chronicle (sfgate.com/travel)
USA Today (usatoday.com/travel)
Washington Post (washingtonpost.com/travel)

been published about that place in recent years — usually for free, though sometimes you have to register first.

Browsing the archives of travel publications can be somewhat hit or miss. For instance, you may click on a headline about Lake Como, Italy, only to find out that the article is really about how George Clooney decorated his home there — great if you're choosing rugs for your own villa but not if you're looking for a hotel. But with a little digging, you can find useful features on topics like the fifty best beaches in the Caribbean or where to go in France if you've already been to Paris and Provence, so don't give up if your mouse ends up at a few digital dead ends. (See the sidebar above for sites to check out.)

Hit the books

Of course, you can also hit the magazine rack of your local bookstore for current issues of travel publications — and while you're there, the travel section offers plenty of ways to dream about your next vacation during your lunch hour.

Although guidebooks tend to be more useful once you've got a destination in mind, publishers are starting to catch on that travelers also want help deciding where to go. One book that literally outlines a road map for a lifetime of travel is *1,000 Places to See Before You Die*, by Patricia Schultz. Organized by country, the book is nearly 1,000 pages itself, offering encyclopedic entries on must-see cities, towns, attractions, and experiences all over the world. Another option is *The Travel Book*, published by Lonely Planet. This A to Z guide to more than 230 countries is mostly a pictorial book, but there's also a description of each country.

Travel narratives are another source of inspiration for many people — evoking a place so artfully that you're motivated to follow in the author's footsteps. So don't overlook this section of the bookstore if you're searching for ideas, especially if you're looking for a more exotic place to explore.

Word of mouth

One of the best sources of advice on where to go is other travelers — often, a neighbor, relative, or coworker who just got back from a trip and can't wait for you to make the pilgrimage yourself. Of course, most of us have a pretty good sense of whom we trust for travel advice: Uncle Lou always knows the best undiscovered resorts, but beware Aunt Sally's preference for high-rise hotels.

So when it comes to relying on the opinions of strangers — available on countless travelogues all over the Web — you have to be somewhat savvy about the source. The on-line communities described later in this chapter can be great for generating ideas, with travel journals you can browse and message boards where you can post questions like, "I'm planning a trip to New Zealand. If I can spend only ten days there, where should I go?" These Web sites are also helpful once you've decided on a destination and want advice on topics like where to eat or how to get from the airport to your hotel.

WHAT TO CONSIDER WHEN YOU SPIN THE GLOBE

Here are some factors to think about when you're deciding where to go. At first glance, they may seem obvious, but I've talked to enough travelers who were disappointed by their destinations to conclude that it's easy to overlook the obvious. So consider these *reminders* about things you might forget in the rush to snap up a bargain.

- *Your traveling companions.* Yes, of course you're thoughtfully considering your fellow travelers' interests as you make your plans . . . but then again, if you're doing all the work, shouldn't you get to decide? A word of caution: Resist the temptation to exert your priorities over a reluctant traveling companion. More often than not, someone who hates the beach won't change his or her mind just because there's also a pool nearby.

- *Where you're coming from.* After I moved to New York City, it took me a long time to realize that I don't really enjoy vacationing in big cities anymore. My parents, who live in a town with one traffic light, *love* to visit me in New York. You may have less extreme travel preferences, but often the vacations people enjoy the most are the ones that offer the biggest contrast to what's familiar.

- *Your energy level.* If you've been working seven days a week on a big project or you're taking your first vacation without a toddler in tow, your priorities are probably R&R. Needing a break doesn't necessarily mean going to a beach or a spa, but it may make a road trip along California's coast less appealing than choosing one destination and staying put.

- *The climate.* Having a general sense that it's going to be hot or cold at your destination is one thing; enjoying your trip when the thermometer registers outside your comfort zone is another story. You may not be able to predict the actual temperature, but look into the average highs and lows, what time of year it tends to rain nonstop, and when the mosquitoes usually arrive (see page 24 for more weather advice).

- *Your budget.* Certain destinations are tough to visit on a limited budget, but if you're creative, you may be able to find an off-season bargain or go when the exchange rate fluctuates in the dollar's favor. But don't forget to factor in other costs besides your flight and hotel; that way, you won't end up ruining the whole trip because you can't afford to eat out.

- *Travel time.* A friend once mentioned that she was planning a trip to the Caribbean but would consider only places reachable on a nonstop flight. I thought that was a smart way to narrow the field, not to mention avoid the stress of changing planes or spending two full days of the trip in transit.

As you're planning, think carefully about how long you want to be on a plane or in the car.

- *Language issues.* Sometimes, you're just not in the mood to watch a movie with subtitles, and the same goes for negotiating a foreign language when you travel. But English is widely spoken in a lot more places than you might imagine, so don't assume that you'll have to struggle simply because your destination requires a passport.

- *Your gut.* If food is really important to you, think twice about vacationing in an isolated town or resort, where your restaurant choices will probably be limited and the food may not be much to write home about. Also, some destinations are dominated by one type of cuisine — often, seafood — so if you don't like fish, beware vacationing in a small coastal village.

Choosing a Guidebook: Which Series Fits Your Style — And Budget

One of the first places most people turn to when they're planning a trip is the travel section of their local bookstore, where you can always find plenty of customers leaning against the shelves, paging through books about places they may never go. (I'm certainly guilty of being one of those loiterers.)

This can be a pleasant way to kill time while a friend is searching for a present in the cookbook section, but if you're in the market for a guidebook, the number of choices can be daunting. Going to London? You'd better find a place to sit down. I once counted seventy-three guidebooks just about London in my local bookstore — and that's not including guides covering the rest of the United Kingdom.

What's new

With people traveling more — and to more places — it's not surprising that more guidebooks are being published. But people are also traveling differently, so guidebooks have started to reflect some of those trends. For instance, with travelers taking more short trips, publishers have created more miniguides that focus on one city. Among the options: Dorling Kindersley's Top 10 series, Fodor's City

Packs, Frommer's Portable Guides, Lonely Planet's *Best of* books, Insight's City Guides, and Rough Guides' Directions series. These pocket guides are smaller and lighter than their country cousins — and cheaper, too — but they generally maintain the writing style of the brand.

Travel publishers are also selling more specialty guides, either targeting a specific segment of the population — such as families, women, gay travelers, or people who won't leave home without their pets — or a certain type of trip, from camping, hiking, or biking getaways to spa vacations and road trips. Guidebooks also tend to have more of a "best of" focus these days, so you'll often find a list of must-see attractions at the beginning of a book, as well as books about the best spas worldwide, the best cruise vacations, or the best hotels.

Deciding which guide to buy

So what's the best guidebook? There's no one-guide-fits-all answer to that question, but here are some tips on choosing a series that's right for you, which will probably vary from trip to trip. Much as publishers insist that their customers are loyal to a particular brand, I've snooped around lots of home bookshelves and found a wide range of travel titles sharing shelf space. (By the way, if you live in a big city, there may be a travel bookstore nearby, where you can often get more personal advice from the staff.)

Look at the publication date. Guidebooks aren't always updated yearly, so before you head to the register, check the publication date. It's usually on the page with the copyright information, at either the front or the back of the book, though some publishers make this detail difficult to find. If the book was printed two years ago, the research was done at least three years ago, so that "undiscovered bistro" the writer mentions may be a shoe store by now. In general, guidebooks don't improve with age.

Get to know the writer. It's important to read not only about the author's qualifications (the author should get bonus points for having lived in the destination and for understanding the language and culture) but also enough of the text to see whether the author's tone is a good match. Some guidebooks are completely devoid of opinion, whereas others aren't shy about saying that a certain hotel or restaurant is overrated, and occasionally, the author's judgments get in the way. As a well-traveled friend once said, "Sometimes the writer will just irritate you to no end and you think, 'I have to get a different guide, because I can't have this person with me on vacation.'"

Read about a place you've been. If you haven't been to the place you're planning to visit, it can be tough to tell whether the guidebooks you're considering recommend restaurants or hotels you'd like. One solution: Check other books in the series about destinations you know pretty well. If one raves about a resort you think is a dud and the other highlights a hole-in-the-wall bistro you love, you know which guide to buy.

Check the prices. No, not the prices of the books — the prices listed inside. You may be seduced by the color photographs and the glossy paper in a well-designed guidebook, but if all the hotels and restaurants it recommends are beyond your budget and there's no information about public transportation, you may need to rethink your choice.

Look at the maps. Besides your guidebook, no doubt you'll also take along a fold-out map of the city you're visiting, but you probably won't buy a map for *every* city you pass through and certainly not for every one-horse town. There are also times when it's easier or more discreet to consult a map in a guidebook rather than a document the size of a coffee table. All good reasons to check out a guidebook's maps: how many there are, how well they're labeled, and whether you need a magnifying glass to read the street names.

Don't be afraid to stray. Just because you've always bought the same guidebook series doesn't necessarily mean that you have to be a customer for life. People change, and sometimes so do travel guides. Some brands that were previously known as backpacker favorites have been broadening their focus to appeal to kids now grown up and staying at nice hotels; others have updated their look with more photos or a different layout. Shop around; you may discover a new series you like.

A GUIDE TO THE TOP TRAVEL GUIDES

Here's an overview of the major travel guidebooks and where you can find them on line. Some publishers offer free information from their books on the Web and have lively message boards where you can trade tips with other travelers; other publishers simply give basic information about their guides. (Frommer's and Lonely Planet tend to have the most robust Web sites.) Many publishers also sell their books on the Web, so if the pickings are slim at your local bookstore, do your browsing and buying on line.

- **Access Guides** (accessguides.com). Access Guides cover mostly U.S. cities and are known for their annotated maps. Numbers on each neighborhood map correspond to color-coded listings highlighting hotels, restaurants, stores, and attractions in the area, which makes it easy to get around a city and find places to visit, eat, or shop.

- **Bradt Guides** (bradtguides.com). A British guidebook series started in the 1970s, Bradt specializes in destinations that are off the beaten path, like Antarctica, Croatia, the Falkland Islands, the Maldives, Rwanda, and even Iraq. Most of the company's roughly one hundred guides emphasize history and a culturally sensitive style of travel, but Bradt approaches more well-trodden places with a twist; for instance, its *Eccentric America* guide explores offbeat events and places across the United States.

- **DK Eyewitness Travel Guides** (dk.com). DK's tag line ("The guides that show you what others only tell you") accurately describes what you'll find inside: lots of color photographs, illustrations, and maps. So rather than simply describing a museum with four paragraphs of text, DK guides include a drawing of the floor plan, with callouts pointing to photos of major works of art. Although these guides are heavier than average and don't have as much practical information, they're great for sightseeing — especially DK's Top 10 city guides.

- **Fodor's** (fodors.com). Fodor's got its start in 1936, when Eugene Fodor wrote his first guide to Europe, *On the Continent — The Entertaining Travel Annual*. Covering destinations around the world, the company now publishes more than four hundred titles, including its flagship Gold Guides and a newer See It series of city guides, with color, glossy paper, and photos (a departure from Fodor's traditional text-on-newsprint approach). Fodor's was once considered more high end than Frommer's, but both series now offer comparable guides for middle-of-the-road travelers: people traveling on their own but not necessarily to Tibet.

- **Footprint Travel Guides** (footprintbooks.com). Footprint guides tend to appeal to the same types of travelers who buy Lonely Planet or Rough

Guides, though one reason to opt for the lesser-known Footprint books is that you won't cross paths with as many fellow readers during your travels. The British company publishes more than eighty guidebooks to cities and countries all over the world, with an emphasis on covering the history and culture of destinations in Africa, Asia, Australia, Europe, and Latin America.

- **Frommer's** (frommers.com). Arthur Frommer published his first guidebook, *Europe on $5 a Day*, in 1957, and the company still publishes a series in that same budget-minded vein — though now it's more like *Italy from $90 a Day*. Frommer's more than three hundred guidebooks cover mostly well-traveled cities and countries around the world, as well as niches like traveling with kids and driving tours. Frommer's guides are comprehensive and easy to use but not as adventurous as some of the younger brands.

- **Insiders' Guides** (insiders.com). These guidebooks cover more than sixty regional destinations in the United States, offering a local, or "insider's," perspective on each area. The series skips big cities in favor of places that provide an escape from urban life — the Outer Banks of North Carolina, the Olympic Peninsula in Washington, and Cape Cod and Nantucket in Massachusetts — and the writing style matches the leisurely pace of life in the areas described.

- **Insight Guides** (insightguides.com). Insight bills its books as "visual travel guides," and there's no doubt that its guides are among the most beautiful on the market, with glossy, high-quality paper and color photos on practically every page. That means these books are heavier than most other travel guides; they also focus more on sightseeing, culture, and shopping than on practical topics like where to eat or where to stay.

- **Let's Go** (letsgo.com). The Let's Go series was started in 1960 by a group of students at Harvard University, and its forty-five guidebooks are still written by Harvard students, with an emphasis on budget travel. Let's Go covers destinations all over the world but focuses mostly on the countries college students tend to explore, as opposed to places that are really off the beaten path. The series got a makeover in 2003, with a new design and more information about politics and culture.

- **Lonely Planet** (lonelyplanet.com). A bestseller among backpackers and independent travelers, Lonely Planet guidebooks still follow the same philosophy of exploration embraced by Maureen and Tony Wheeler in the early 1970s when they wrote the first *On a Shoestring* guide. With more than 650 guidebooks covering nearly every corner of the globe, the company has expanded beyond its early emphasis on longer trips with a series of city guides for shorter jaunts. Its books now cover a wider price range of accommodations and restaurants, an attempt to hang on to readers who have grown up and have more money to spend on travel.

- **Michelin** (viamichelin.com). The French publisher specializes in European destinations, and its star rating system is considered the gold standard in Europe. Michelin's Green Guides focus on what to do and see at your destination (a few also list hotels and restaurants); the Red Guides recommend where to eat and where to stay. Although the Red Guides are written in the language of the country covered, there's an introduction in English, and symbols next to each listing are easy to decipher.

- **Moon Handbooks** (moon.com). Moon has been publishing guidebooks for more than thirty years but has gained a following lately among independent, budget-minded travelers. The company specializes in the Americas and Asia and also publishes the more compact Moon Metro guides to cities in Canada, Europe, and the United States. Moon tends to allow more personality and opinion in its writing style, making the text less dry than you might find in other guides.

- **Rick Steves** (ricksteves.com). Rick Steves started his travel empire with the publication of *Europe Through the Back Door* in 1980 and has since published more than thirty guidebooks, covering mostly cities and countries in Europe. Rick takes a somewhat casual approach to travel, and his books are particularly popular among those visiting Europe for the first time. He tends to focus on the highlights of each country, leaving out less touristy cities and towns.

- **Rough Guides** (roughguides.com). Rough Guides generally appeal to the same travelers who like Lonely Planet but are written with more of a British sensibility and arguably more information about politics, history, and culture. The series was founded in 1982 by Mark Ellingham, who wrote his first book about his travels around Greece after college and now covers more than two hundred destinations worldwide. Although the name might suggest "roughing it," the company now aims for a broader demographic than its original backpacker focus.

- **Time Out** (timeout.com). Perhaps better known for its weekly magazines covering cities like New York and London, Time Out began publishing travel guidebooks in 1990 and now sells more than sixty guides to urban destinations all over the world. Its colorful books have lots of photos, a breezy writing style, and better coverage of where to eat, drink, shop, and find entertainment than in many other guides, albeit with mostly younger travelers in mind.

■ **Zagat Surveys** (zagat.com). New Yorkers Nina and Tim Zagat published
their first restaurant guide in 1979 and now have books covering more
than seventy cities and regions around the world. The guides are based on
surveys in each market of restaurant goers, who rate each establishment's
food, service, and décor. Zagat also publishes guides to hotels, resorts,
and spas and offers access to its restaurant reviews on line; a subscription costs $25 per year or $5 for one month.

On-line Travel Forums: Advice
from Fellow Travelers

When you're planning a trip, a strange phenomenon happens the
minute you start telling people you're thinking about going to Mexico or you just bought tickets to Hawaii. Suddenly, it seems that everyone you meet has already been there or knows someone who
just got back and can't wait to give you advice.

Often, this is a great way to learn about a destination or get answers to questions like where to find the best margaritas in Puerto
Vallarta or whether you should spend more time on the Big Island
or Kauai. But what happens if the person you just met doesn't drink
margaritas or didn't really care much for anything about Hawaii?
Or you're thinking about going somewhere your friends haven't
been?

Then you need to seek out some like-minded travelers on line.

With all the travel communities that have blossomed on the Web
— and for the most part, survived the dot-com bust — I'd venture
to guess that there's not a single travel question you can't find someone to answer in some on-line forum.

Many of these Web sites started as one person's personal passion
but have gradually become on-line gathering points for distinct
groups of travelers: FlyerTalk for frequent fliers, CruiseMates for
cruise aficionados, and BiddingForTravel for people trading advice
about getting a bid accepted at Priceline. There are also on-line
travel communities affiliated with guidebook publishers, sites
where you can read or submit hotel reviews, and places where you
can post a journal and photos from a recent trip — or read other

peoples' travel diaries, if you're so inclined (see the sidebar on page 16 for where to point your browser).

Ask a question, get answers

Most of these Web sites have message boards or forums where you can post a question that other visitors can read and answer, or you can browse through what's been posted and offer a response. Sometimes, you have to become a member to join the dialogue — which is usually free — but you can generally read what other people have written without signing up.

So what do people discuss in these forums? Pretty much anything related to travel: where to see orangutans in Borneo, which cruise lines have the most restrictive smoking policies, or whether insects are a problem in Alaska in July. Many of these message boards are organized geographically, so you can often post your question in a forum designated for discussions about a specific region or country, which increases the likelihood that someone else will post a response.

Pros and cons

One advantage of these on-line forums is that you can participate anonymously, so you can ask the types of questions you might be reluctant to raise in person, lest your cocktail party companions roll their eyes when you walk away. Plus, it's free advice, which can save you time, money, and the misery of having a bad experience when someone warns you away from a shady tour operator or a resort that nickels and dimes its guests.

Like any Internet community, these travel forums also have some drawbacks. The advice is sometimes contradictory (four people rave about a hotel five other people thought was horrible), the opinions can get obnoxious from time to time (though I'm generally impressed by the level of discourse at travel sites), and you may have to weed through a lot of irrelevant messages to find the information you want. That said, most of these forums offer some type of search function, which can help locate that needle in a haystack, and their search tools are getting better all the time.

TRAVEL COMMUNITIES: WHERE TO POST AND READ ADVICE

Here are some of the best on-line travel communities that I've found. Besides message boards, many of these sites offer articles with travel tips or reviews of hotels, cruise ships, or theme parks. But before you dive into any discussions, read the rules of engagement — often described in a FAQ (a list of frequently asked questions). And try the search feature before you post a question, since the topic you're interested in may have already been discussed.

AIRLINES AND FREQUENT FLIER PROGRAMS

- **FlyerTalk** (flyertalk.com). Although this site is meant primarily for frequent fliers, who trade advice on earning and using miles, its active message boards cover a broad range of travel topics. There are dedicated forums for discussions about the major airlines, hotel chains, and car rental companies, as well as forums about specific destinations and topics like dining out or using technology on the road. There's probably not a travel question the experts at FlyerTalk can't answer, but the site is populated mostly by business travelers, so it's a better source for advice on where to eat in Tokyo — or how to get there using miles — than tips on which beach to visit in Thailand.

- **Other options: FrequentFlier.com** (frequentflier.com) and **MoreMiles.org** (moremiles.org) also have message boards where frequent fliers swap strategies but on a much smaller scale than FlyerTalk.

GENERAL TRAVEL ADVICE

- **Lonely Planet's Thorn Tree Forum** (thorntree.lonelyplanet.com). The Thorn Tree message boards attract travelers who buy Lonely Planet guidebooks: independent types who like to wander to the far corners of the world. The forums are organized mostly by region, so this is a good source for advice about getting a visa to visit Libya or how to travel to Cuba despite the U.S. embargo. But you'll also find plenty of discussions about more popular tourist destinations, as well as general travel topics — like round-the-world travel, staying healthy, or taking the kids along.

- **Frommer's Travel Talk** (frommers.com/travel_talk). Frommer's well-organized message boards are another good source for general travel advice. Besides forums for specific destinations, you'll find discussions about various activities, like water sports, road trips, or adventure travel; what Frommer's calls "lifestyle boards," targeting honeymooners, families, seniors, and other demographic slices; and general travel tips, covering practical topics like packing, booking, and photography.

- **Other options: Fodor's** (fodors.com), **Let's Go** (letsgo.com/community), and **Rough Guides** (roughguides.com) all have message boards, which are generally populated by readers of their guidebooks.

CRUISING

- **CruiseMates** (cruisemates.com). This is one of the best on-line sources for advice about cruising, offering ship reviews, news about the cruise industry, message boards, and a wide range of articles for both experts and first-timers. Its message boards are sorted into four categories — destination, cruise line, type of cruiser, and practical advice — so you can easily navigate your way to topics like cruising in the Caribbean, the food on board Princess ships, singles cruising, or how to pack for a cruise with a more formal dress code.

- **CruiseCritic** (cruisecritic.com). CruiseCritic is another useful source for ship reviews, message boards, and help finding a cruise, although some of the articles are less critical than you'd expect from the site's name. But the ship reviews submitted by members are well organized and easy to browse. CruiseCritic also compiles average ratings based on the ones submitted, which gives a general consensus about each ship if you don't have the patience to read through them all.

HOTEL REVIEWS

- **TripAdvisor** (tripadvisor.com). Once the go-to source for on-line hotel reviews, TripAdvisor still offers a place to read or post opinions about hotels and resorts around the world. But after the site was acquired by the company that owns Expedia and Hotels.com, TripAdvisor's hotel reviews haven't been the centerpiece they once were — buried among advertisements for hotel deals and links to these other sites. But once you find the reviews, you can search for a specific hotel and see what others have to say about it or browse by destination and see which hotels in that area are the most popular.

- **HotelShark** (hotelshark.com). HotelShark is another source of hotel reviews from past guests; you can browse through other travelers' comments or submit your own opinion about a hotel. Although it has more of a singular focus and a cleaner design than TripAdvisor, HotelShark doesn't cover as many properties or have as many reviews of each hotel.

- **HotelChatter** (hotelchatter.com). HotelChatter is more of a blog about the hotel industry, tracking hotels that have recently opened, gotten a makeover, or for some reason are generating buzz. You can type in a destination and read what's been posted about hotels in that city, or become a member and submit your own reviews. But for the most part, HotelChatter focuses on boutique and high-end properties.

- **Other options:** Some hotel booking sites, like **Expedia** (expedia.com) and **Travelocity** (travelocity.com), also let members read or submit opinions about hotels.

BIDDING ON PRICELINE

- **BiddingForTravel** (biddingfortravel.com). This site is essentially a user's guide for bidding on Priceline, with advice on what to bid to get Priceline to accept your offer — and how to succeed the second time around if your first offer doesn't fly. These days, the emphasis is mostly on hotels and car rentals and, to a lesser degree, flights. But if you're thinking about giving Priceline a try, this should be your first stop. (For more about bidding on Priceline, see page 76.)

THEME PARKS

- **Theme Park Insider** (themeparkinsider.com). Proving that there's a Web site for all sorts of passions, Theme Park Insider is a gathering place for those who have logged lots of miles going up, down, and around amusement parks all over the world. This site offers reviews of dozens of theme parks in the United States and abroad, as well as visitor ratings for specific attractions (aka "rides") and restaurants and hotels in and around the parks. There's also practical advice on planning your visit and finding discounts, as well as previews of new rides.

TRAVEL JOURNALS

- **IGoUgo** (igougo.com). IGoUgo is one of several Web sites that provide a place for people to post journals and photos from their travels. Reading these on-line scrapbooks can be a hit-or-miss experience, but IgoUgo manages to harness its members' trip reports in a way that's useful for other travelers. You can search for a specific destination and get links to journals written by people who have been there or browse categories like "beaches" or "nightlife" to find journals that cover those topics.

- **VirtualTourist** (virtualtourist.com). VirtualTourist is another publishing portal for travelers, with advice organized in a way that makes it easy to browse. You can look up a destination and find links to tips submitted by other VirtualTourist members, like hotel and restaurant reviews, advice on what to do and how to get around while you're there, and tourist traps to avoid.

▪ **Other options: BootsnAll** (bootsnall.com) and **TrekShare** (trekshare.com) offer similar services but tend to attract a younger, backpacker crowd.

Visitor and Tourist Offices: On the Web, a .com for Every Destination

Another good source of travel information is one many people overlook: the tourist offices that serve as a destination's official liaison to the camera-toting crowd. Even if you've never explored what these agencies have to offer, you've probably seen their ads in travel magazines or on billboards — often showing an enticing beach scene just when the snow is starting to fall at home.

Although they go by various names, such as the Greek National Tourism Organization or the Italian Government Tourist Board, nearly every country in the world has one, except the United States, where each state has its own. Many cities and regions also have some type of tourism entity, which are often more useful than their national counterparts.

What they offer

Before the Internet, these agencies weren't all that accessible to travelers unless you hunted one down to request a visitors' brochure — which often arrived in the mail three weeks after your trip or not at all. But now that they have Web sites, usually in multiple languages, tourist offices can be much more useful when planning a trip, with advice on what to do, where to eat, where to stay, and how to get around.

These agencies are tasked with promoting tourism, so they're not the most critical sources you'll come across. In other words, a tourist office will never start a sentence with "Don't bother . . ." But they're still a good place to find practical information about local festivals and events, typical weather patterns, national parks and attractions, suggested itineraries, transportation options, and travel agents who specialize in the region — as well as the occasional odd find, like a downloadable screensaver to get you in the mood, recipes for local dishes, or advice on getting married locally.

Another advantage of these Web sites is that they're not limited by printing costs, so they sometimes offer more detailed information than you'd find in a guidebook, especially if you're researching a small city or town. For instance, when I was planning a trip to Búzios, a resort town north of Rio de Janeiro, I found that the city's Web site (buziosonline.com.br) had much more information about the area's nearly two dozen beaches than I got from any guidebook or magazine article. (No, I didn't get to all those beaches — but I tried.)

How to find them

The one catch is, it's not always easy to find these organizations on-line. It would be great if there were some consistent naming convention for these agencies or at least their Web sites. Instead, they live at Internet addresses ranging from the simple (spain.info or australia.com) to the more descriptive (incredibleindia.org or magicalkenya.com) to the downright commanding (visitmexico .com or discoverhongkong.com). Even U.S. states go their own way — there's virginia.org, traveltex.com, and arizonaguide.com — and cities are just as unpredictable: nycvisit.com, barcelonaturisme .com, and visitlondon.com.

So how can you find the tourist office for the place you're planning to visit? One source worth trying is the Tourism Offices Worldwide Directory (towd.com), which has a fairly comprehensive list of country, state, and some city tourist offices, with links to their Web sites — although at the city level, it's not nearly as thorough. For destinations within the United States, try SeeAmerica.org. This Web site, developed by the Travel Industry Association of America, includes basic travel information about each state and links to the state's official Web site.

Another option is to search the Internet for the name of your destination plus the word "visitor" or "tourist" or "tourism," which will usually lead you to the official tourism agency, if there is one. Within the United States, you can often find city agencies by searching for the name of the city and the phrase "convention and visitors bureau."

Beware imposters

Figuring out whether you've happened on the "official" agency is another challenge. Because anyone can register an Internet address that includes the name of a city or a country, you may come across a Web site that *looks* as though it's operated by an official tourism office but doesn't have any government ties. The site may still be useful for research purposes, but if it's primarily selling a tour package or soliciting hotel bookings, chances are it's not an official site.

The Local Perspective: When Going to Rome, Ask a Roman

Leafing through a guidebook or a magazine article is a great way to get an overview of a destination, but these sources also have some limitations. For one thing, they're written specifically for travelers — often, a wide range of travelers — which lends them something of a generic, outsider focus.

They're also usually written by people who are tourists themselves — which can be a good thing when it comes to choosing a hotel or learning about places locals don't visit, but it often means that the writer isn't connected to the city's real pulse. And books aren't as useful if you want to find out what's going on somewhere next week or next month.

So how do you get that up-to-date, insider perspective on a destination? From someone who lives there, of course. Reading local newspapers and magazines is a good place to start, and with the Internet, you don't have to wait until you arrive to hit a newsstand — most of these publications are available on line. (See the sidebar on page 23 for advice on getting tours from locals once you're in town.)

How to find local publications

Almost any newspaper Web site offers information useful to travelers, including restaurant reviews, event listings, and local coverage of arts and culture. Reading the news is helpful, too, so you'll know whether you're arriving in the middle of a festival or whether transit workers are contemplating a strike.

Two Web sites that list newspapers and magazines all over the world are World-newspapers.com and Newslink.org. You can search by country, state, or city to see what newspapers are published wherever you're traveling, and both sites link to the publications, if they're available on line.

Although the two sites are fairly similar, there are a couple of differences that make bookmarking both worthwhile. World-newspapers.com includes only English-language publications in its listings for foreign countries (most major cities have at least one), whereas Newslink lists foreign-language publications as well. Newslink also links to radio and TV stations throughout the United States, another source for local news and events.

Other ways to get the local scoop

Besides reading newspapers and magazines, you can get the local flavor of a city by searching out community-oriented Web sites. One of the pioneers of that genre is Craigslist.com, which began as an on-line classifieds service for San Francisco residents but now has versions for more than one hundred cities, mostly in the United States. Although Craigslist is meant primarily for local residents, its message boards are active and wide ranging, and each city has an events calendar, which is one way to connect with people in another town.

You can also try searching the Internet for more home-grown on-line communities, though if you're headed overseas, it helps if you understand the language, since these sites don't usually offer English translations. One that does is Inyourpocket.com, which offers several dozen downloadable guides to cities and countries in Eastern Europe — all written by locals.

Sports, hobbies, and clubs can also open doors when you're traveling or help you get beyond a destination's usual tourist haunts. So if you play soccer, love to knit, or belong to a sailing club at home, search for a soccer league, yarn store, or yacht club wherever you're going. That's often the best way to cross that invisible barrier be-

CITY GREETER PROGRAMS

If you really want to get the local flavor of a city, find out whether your destination has any kind of "city greeter" program: services that match visitors with local residents who have volunteered to act as tour guides for an afternoon. New York City's Big Apple Greeter program is probably the most well known (bigapplegreeter.org). Since 1992, the group has offered free tours to more than 50,000 travelers; call or e-mail at least three weeks before your trip to sign up. Other cities that have similar services are Chicago (chicagogreeter.com), Buenos Aires (cicerones.org.ar), and Melbourne (thatsmelbourne.com.au), with more cities likely to follow, based on the success of these programs.

tween travelers and local residents, who — let's be honest — normally avoid the areas where tourists hang out.

When to Go: Avoiding Hurricanes, Honeymooners, and Holidays — or Not

When planning a trip, travelers sometimes overlook a key question: When is the best time to go? Or alternatively, when might hordes of spring-break revelers, monsoons, or local festival goers ruin your vision of quiet sunset strolls?

Sometimes, these timing issues are fairly well known. For instance, most people thinking about heading to Rio de Janeiro in late winter are either planning their visit to join in the Carnival bacchanalia or know enough about Brazil's biggest party to steer clear of the crowds.

But other time-and-place considerations aren't always so obvious. My sister and I once celebrated her September birthday with a trip to a Mexican resort where we were the only guests who hadn't just tied the knot (though apparently, some of those honeymooners thought we were a couple, since several reacted to meeting us by saying to their spouses, "See, I *told* you they looked like sisters!").

On the plus side, we had perfect weather during our four-day stay — a lucky break in the torrential rain that had recently passed through the area. Turns out we were also there during hurricane season, another issue I had overlooked.

So before you put down a deposit on that beach bungalow in the Caribbean or buy four plane tickets to Rome for Easter, here are some factors you should consider as you weigh various dates on the calendar.

Weather

I'm a slow learner when it comes to looking up the weather before a trip — not the seven-day forecast but average highs and lows during the time I'm planning to be in town. But if you don't want to risk having your trip ruined by hurricanes, tropical rainstorms, extreme temperatures, or even pests that make regular visits to a particular area, these things all follow predictable patterns you can research before you book.

Guidebooks are often the best source of information about seasonal weather patterns and issues like when a black-fly invasion might keep you from venturing beyond the screened-in porch. You can also post a message at an on-line travel forum (see page 14), and a couple of weather sites let you look up average temperatures for a specific destination and month: Try Weather.com's travel feature or Wunderground.com's "trip planner" option.

Holidays and events

Holidays and events aren't necessarily a negative: Many people plan trips specifically to attend celebrations like the running of the bulls in Pamplona or New Year's Eve in Times Square. But if you don't know about a big festival or local holiday that draws huge crowds, it may not be a pleasant surprise.

I've been caught off guard in Italy when the trains were standing-room only due to the local Labor Day holiday, accidentally timed a visit to Amsterdam on Queen's Day — Holland's biggest party — and once drove into Las Vegas at the beginning of a three-day weekend with no hotel reservation, not realizing that the city would be sold out. Besides crowds, another drawback of traveling during a local holiday is that museums, restaurants, and other places you want to visit might be closed.

So whether you plan to join the party or want to avoid it, guide-books, on-line travel forums, and local tourist boards are all good sources of advice. You can also search the Internet for the name of the country you're visiting and the phrase "public holidays," which will often point you to a list posted somewhere on line.

There are also a few Web sites that track what's going on around the world. Festivals.com lists art fairs, music festivals, and other local and community events, mostly in the United States. Whats OnWhen.com offers a searchable database of events worldwide, in-cluding local celebrations; art fairs and exhibits; music, theater, and film festivals; and sports competitions. And some events have their own Web sites, such as Venice's Carnival (venice-carnival.com) or the U.S. Open (usopen.org), so another option is to search the Internet for the one you have in mind.

Other guests

It didn't occur to me to inquire about demographics when I booked the trip to that resort in Mexico, but when I asked the owner whether his September guests were typically honeymooners, he quickly rattled off the seasons that corresponded to his changing clientele: newlyweds in the summer, families during the holidays, and retirees throughout the winter months.

Getting the lowdown on your fellow travelers is more important if you're staying at a secluded resort or taking a cruise, since you'll all be stuck together in a confined area. As a general rule, you're more likely to find families vacationing during school holidays, and spring break often means a partying crowd. Sunny destinations tend to attract more older travelers between January and March — "snowbirds" escaping colder climates up north.

Regardless of the time of year, cruises sometimes host groups of travelers that tip the demographic balance on board, which can make you feel trapped at an event you didn't intend to join (such as a company retreat or a club outing). Before you book, ask your travel agent or the cruise line to check whether any big groups are signed up for the cruise. Your agent might not know who else is sailing, but it's worth trying to find out.

Seasonal prices

The time of year you travel also affects how much you'll pay for your trip, including your plane tickets, cruise, or hotel. Most destinations have "high," or "peak," seasons, which correspond to the months when the weather is best or when most people want to travel. Holidays usually fall within peak season, though "holiday" rates sometimes are even higher than peak prices.

If you're on a budget, try to book your trip during the off-peak, or low, season, though there's often a reason it's a less desirable time to visit, a factor you should investigate before you snap up a seasonal bargain. Another option is to travel during what's called "shoulder" season — typically, spring and fall — when prices are lower than you'll find during high season but not as low as the deep discounts offered to drum up business in off-peak months.

Government Travel Advisories: Reading Between the Lines

If you're planning a trip overseas, you might not think to pay the State Department a visit as you're making the rounds of travel Web sites — and if you're just going to Cancun for the weekend or crossing the Canadian border for a ski trip, it may be overly cautious to suggest that you see what the government has to say about your destination before you make any plans. Then again, the State Department has put some of your tax dollars to work compiling information about the travel situation in nearly every country in the world — why not see what you paid for? In fact, some of the information is rather eye opening, even for destinations you might not consider especially dangerous. And if you *are* planning a trip to a country where the political or military situation is precarious, best to know what you're getting into before you commit.

Country reports

Although you probably know that the State Department issues travel warnings from time to time (more on that later), it also publishes "consular information sheets" for about two hundred countries, territories, and regions, which you can find on line (see travel.state.gov). Don't expect a lively read — these are government documents, after all — but each report offers useful information about the country's overall security and crime rate (and penalties for crimes like drug possession), an assessment of local medical facilities and any health risks, an overview of traffic and road conditions, and whether the country's aviation system meets international safety standards. You'll also find contact information for the local U.S. embassy or consulate and notes about specific issues in each country, like scams that prey on tourists, problems with ATM machines, or places where consuming alcohol is illegal — all useful information to have before you land.

Incidentally, if you're ever accused of a crime in a foreign country, be aware that you're subject to the laws and penalties of that nation, which often don't include things we take for granted in the United States, like the right to a trial by jury or access to a lawyer. If you find yourself in trouble, you should certainly contact the closest embassy, but its ability to help you may be limited.

Travel warnings
Besides these country reports, the State Department issues a variety of advisories to inform travelers about potentially hazardous situations abroad. The most severe of these are "travel warnings," released when the U.S. government recommends that Americans avoid travel to a particular country, usually due to political instability, outright hostilities, or ongoing concerns about terrorism.

The State Department also issues "public announcements," generally for more short-term crises, like a coup, a specific terrorist threat, an outbreak of a contagious disease, or a natural disaster. These announcements typically have an expiration date and aren't necessarily limited to what most people would consider dangerous parts of the world: For instance, in March 2002, the State Department released a public announcement about a terrorist threat against several Italian cities during Easter. A third type of advisory, a "worldwide caution," advises Americans to be careful wherever they're traveling, which has basically been the case since 2001.

Not surprisingly, some travelers find these advisories frustratingly vague, and foreign governments frequently object when a warning is issued, because of the negative effect it has on tourism. One complaint is that travel warnings are generally issued for a whole country rather than a specific region, even though there may be a big difference between an area affected by military unrest or a natural disaster and the situation in cities hundreds of miles away.

But on the flip side, people also complain when the government doesn't release enough information about travel concerns. In fact, the current policy about issuing travel advisories was adopted after the bombing of a Pan Am flight over Lockerbie, Scotland, in 1988, when it was later revealed that the U.S. government had information about a terrorist threat against flights on that route, which it shared only with its own employees. After that, the government adopted regulations requiring that whenever a warning about overseas travel or threats was circulated internally, it had to be released to the public, too.

Ultimately, you should use your own judgment if you're planning to travel to a country where there are political, safety, or health risks — and do enough research about the situation so you know what you're getting into (see the sidebar on the facing page for other sources of advice).

Registering your travel plans

Another service that the State Department offers is the ability to register your itinerary and emergency-contact information before traveling abroad (you can fill out a form at travelregistration.state .gov). Although the government has long encouraged travelers and expatriates to contact the local embassy or consulate after arriving in a foreign country, the on-line form — a relatively new option — has made that task much easier.

You may not be comfortable sharing information about all your travel plans with the State Department, but if you're heading somewhere remote or to a place where security is dicey, the benefits of having a local embassy know your whereabouts and whom to contact if something happens to you probably outweigh any privacy concerns.

In any case, don't assume that the government knows where you

WHERE TO FIND TRAVEL ADVISORIES

If you want a second opinion about the travel climate in a particular country, one option is to find out how other governments are advising their citizens about travel abroad. Australia, Canada, and the United Kingdom all publish country reports and travel advisories similar to the ones issued by the U.S. State Department, though there may be heightened concerns for Americans traveling overseas that these other reports don't reflect. For information specifically about health issues, the best source to check is the Centers for Disease Control and Prevention (see page 219 for more about travel and health).

U.S. State Department (travel.state.gov)
C.D.C. Travel Health Information (cdc.gov/travel)
United Kingdom's Foreign & Commonwealth Office (fco.gov.uk)
Canada's Consular Affairs Bureau (voyage.gc.ca)
Australia's Consular Assistance Service (smartraveller.gov.au)

are just because you got on a plane and left the country. After the tsunami struck in 2004, many relatives and friends of people in affected areas were surprised to find out that the U.S. government doesn't keep tabs on every American traveling or living abroad. Believe it or not, there's still a wide technological gap between Uncle Sam and Big Brother, so if you want government officials to know where you are, register your travel plans — or at least share your itinerary with someone else on the home front.

2 Organized Trips

IF THE THOUGHT of planning a trip and then making dozens of decisions along the way leaves you feeling like it might be more relaxing to stay home, one way to have a vacation without all that responsibility is to leave the organizing and trailblazing to someone else.

That doesn't necessarily mean signing up for a traditional escorted tour — though there are plenty of those around. These days, lots of other travel options put someone else in charge of the itinerary, meaning that you can simply sign up, show up, and follow merrily along. Among the options: river-rafting excursions, bike trips, wilderness expeditions, and culinary tours, not to mention spa getaways, yoga retreats, and volunteer vacations — trips that combine service projects with opportunities to see the world.

This chapter explains how to find these and other types of outings, as well as more traditional guided tours. And even those trips have evolved beyond the stereotype of a whirlwind tour of Europe's capitals, with a growing number of companies leading groups to places like Alaska, the Amazon, Egypt, or Vietnam.

But before you join any kind of group, especially one that's going to occupy your precious vacation time, it's important to make sure that you won't be a square peg trying to fit into a round hole. So this chapter also offers advice on how to decide whether an organized trip is a good fit — and if you're traveling solo, how to find vacation options that aren't going to make you feel like an uninvited guest on Noah's ark.

Going with a Group: Tours Aren't Necessarily Just for Tourists

For many travelers, "tour" is a four-letter word, conjuring up images of travelers in comfortable footwear climbing on and off a big bus.

Although that stereotype is sometimes right on the mark, many companies organize trips offering totally different experiences, from trekking in Tibet or climbing in Colorado to visiting farmers' markets in Tuscany or learning about wildlife in the Galapagos.

Although some of these companies might shy away from the word *tour* — preferring *trip, vacation,* or *adventure* — they all basically operate on the same principle: organizing travel opportunities for small groups (about ten to forty people), led by a guide the company hires. The trip operator plans the itinerary and makes all the arrangements for lodging, meals, activities, ground transportation, and sometimes air travel, but beyond that, the differences can be enormous.

Types of trips

Among the many companies that offer escorted trips, some specialize in exotic destinations most people wouldn't travel to on their own, like Bhutan, Kenya, Mongolia, or Tasmania; some organize trips around athletic activities, like biking, hiking, or river rafting; and some cater to a specific demographic, like high school students, seniors, or women. And plenty of companies arrange more conventional sightseeing tours, sometimes focusing on a specific region or country.

The sidebar on page 34 lists some of the more well-known tour operators, as well as resources to help you find others. The rest of the sections in this chapter list companies with certain specialties, such as culinary tours, outdoor adventures, or trips that are a good fit for solo travelers.

Besides the options mentioned in this book, hundreds — if not thousands — of other organizations arrange travel opportunities for small groups, including college alumni associations, museums, nonprofits, churches, and clubs. So the companies you'll find here are just the tip of the iceberg, but the advice applies no matter who is doing the organizing.

Pros and cons

On the plus side, traveling under a trip leader's wing means that you don't have to make all the decisions, deal with logistics, or solve problems that come up, which can be a liberating way to travel. (In fact, the first time I did an organized trip — with Outward Bound — the main appeal was having someone else plan each day's agenda.) But that also means that you don't *get* to make all the decisions or call all the shots, which can be frustrating if a trip doesn't meet your expectations or you're used to more independent travel.

Organized trips also tend to have designated departure dates, which may not work with your vacation schedule, and traveling with strangers can be a crapshoot: You may make friends you keep in touch with the rest of your life or be annoyed by a constant complainer who drives everyone nuts. (In my experience with group travel, there's almost always a couple of people you click with — even if you'd never cross paths back home.)

Customized trips
If you like the idea of relying on a tour operator's expertise but don't feel comfortable traveling with people you don't know, most companies that offer group tours also plan trips for clients who prefer to travel on their own. In this sense, they function more like travel agents, typically putting together packages that include airline tickets, hotels, and perhaps a rental car and sometimes excursions or a private guide. These customized trips are generally more expensive than a scheduled tour, but it may be worth paying extra for the freedom to go where and when you want.

Choosing a group trip
Organized trips can cost thousands of dollars per person for a week-long getaway, so if you're on the fence about surrendering control of your vacation, test the waters with a shorter or less expensive trip first. You might also consider working with a travel agent to help you book a trip; since tour operators still pay commissions, this is one area where you can find an agent to help you out (see page 86 for advice on working with an agent). Either way, here are some tips on vetting a tour company before you send a deposit.

Find out who else is going. When you're invited to a dinner party, it's considered rude to ask, "Who else is coming?" but when you're spending precious money and vacation time to travel with people you don't know, it's not a faux pas. Most trip operators will share demographic information about other participants if you ask, but other clues about your potential companions include the destination, type of tour, category of hotels, and the trip's cost. As a general rule, the average age on escorted trips is above fifty, but if the main focus of a trip is mountain climbing or hiking through the jungle, you can expect a younger crowd. You should also ask about the person leading the tour — and if you're traveling abroad, find out whether local guides will be used as well. (Local guides often have more expertise or insights into their own history and culture but may not speak English as fluently as a nonnative guide.)

Ask what's included. Some companies are very specific about what's included in the price quoted for a trip, but in other cases, you'll have to ask for details. "Some meals" might mean dinner but not breakfast or lunch, and "sightseeing" may mean a guide and local transportation but not admission fees or tips. Another good topic to investigate is your accommodations. Some tour operators don't commit to specific hotels but simply promise three- or four-star properties, so if you're picky about lodging, ask where the group stayed on past trips. And if you and your traveling companion want two separate beds, confirm that up front.

Probe the itinerary. Almost any itinerary looks great when you're reading it on a computer screen in an office cubicle ("Day 3: Visit markets in Bangkok" — what's not to like?). But once you're in Thailand, you'll probably care a whole lot more whether you can breeze through the market on your own and walk back to the hotel for a nap or whether you have to stick with the group, patiently offering opinions on your companions' souvenir selections because the hotel is a half-hour away by bus. Oh, and about that bus — how much time are you going to spend on one? If that's not how you envision your vacation, think twice before you put down a deposit.

Check the tour operator's background. No license is required to be a tour operator in the United States — meaning that anyone can hang out a shingle and start leading trips around the world — so it's up to you to check out the company's background. If it's a member of the United States Tour Operators Association, that's one measure of credibility, because before joining, USTOA members

TOUR OPERATORS TO CONSIDER

FOR ACTIVE/ADVENTURE TRIPS

These companies offer a wide range of what are sometimes called "active" vacations, from bike trips through California's wine country to trekking in Patagonia to touring places like Oman, with varying degrees of exertion involved (and sometimes not much exertion at all). But even the trips to more remote destinations typically promise a certain level of comfort (for example, vans to transport your luggage on a bike trip, candlelight dinners in the desert, and staff to cook and clean up). Often, there's a price tag to match this level of service, but rates vary considerably, so poke around to find a trip that suits your budget. You can find other tour operators through the Adventure Collection (adventurecollection.com), an association of adventure travel companies that includes some of the ones that follow. (And if you're looking for a more rugged outdoor experience, see page 35.)

Abercrombie & Kent (abercrombiekent.com)
American Museum of Natural History — AMNH Expeditions
    (amnhexpeditions.org)
Backroads (backroads.com)
Butterfield & Robinson (butterfield.com)
Geographic Expeditions (geoex.com)
Lindblad Expeditions (expeditions.com)
Micato Safaris (micato.com)
Mountain Travel Sobek (mtsobek.com)
National Geographic Expeditions
    (nationalgeographicexpeditions.com)
Smithsonian Journeys (smithsonianjourneys.org)
Wilderness Safaris (wilderness-safaris.com)
Wilderness Travel (wildernesstravel.com)

FOR MORE TRADITIONAL TOURS

If you prefer a more traditional escorted tour — and there are certainly people who do — these companies offer a range of group trips to destinations all over the world. To find others, search the membership database of the United States Tour Operators Association (ustoa.com) or the National Tour Association (ntaonline.com). You can also find ads for tour companies in travel publications, which occasionally run articles about the best tour operators in various categories, or search the Internet for the word *tour* and the name of the place you want to go.

Collette Vacations (collettevacations.com)
Gate 1 Travel (gate1travel.com)

General Tours (generaltours.com)
Globus & Cosmos (globusandcosmos.com)
Mayflower Tours (mayflowertours.com)
Maupintour (maupintour.com)
Pleasant Holidays (pleasantholidays.com)
Tauck World Discovery (tauck.com)
Trafalgar Tours (trafalgartours.com)
Travcoa (travcoa.com)

have to post a $1 million bond, which is used to reimburse travelers who have paid for trips if the company folds. That doesn't guarantee that you'll get all your money back, but it's better than no safety net at all (see page 277 for more details). You should also ask how long the company has been in business, try to get references from past participants, and check any affiliations the company cites, such as membership in the American Society of Travel Agents, California's travel seller consumer protection program, or a local chamber of commerce. If a tour operator has won any awards or been included in any "best of" lists in travel publications, that's another indication that the company has a loyal following.

Ask whether the trip is definitely a go. Although tour operators typically have strict policies if customers cancel — usually keeping some portion of the deposit, which increases as the trip's departure date approaches — they often reserve the right to cancel the trip themselves if not enough people sign up. Make sure that you understand both sides of the cancellation policy before you commit, especially if you're buying plane tickets on your own. And if it's an expensive trip or you're going somewhere far from good medical care, you may want to buy travel insurance (see page 71 for more details).

Get Outdoors: Hiking, Biking, and Other Active Travels

One of the most difficult niches to pin down in the travel industry is what's often referred to as *active,* or *adventure,* travel. The problem is, no one seems to agree on what these terms mean, so what one company describes as an "active" vacation — a walking tour of the Irish countryside — you might find no more taxing than a stroll in the park. And some companies consider their trips "adventure" travel simply because the destination is exotic or remote. That's why this section skirts both of those terms and focuses on a different distinction: trips that involve some degree of physical activity outdoors.

Hiking, biking, kayaking, and river rafting tend to be the most common activities tour operators offer, but you can also find trips built around horseback riding, sailing, mountain climbing, fishing, and many other sports. And for those who have shorter attention spans or find the thought of spending six days in a kayak about four days too long, there are even "multisport" trips, which combine several activities into one outing.   :

Organized versus do-it-yourself trips

Although this section focuses on organized trips, most of these activities are things you can easily incorporate into your own itinerary — like renting a bike or a kayak for a day or booking a rafting excursion — and the resources mentioned in the sidebar on page 39 can help you make those plans, as well as find a group tour. But if you really want some type of athletic endeavor to be the focus of your vacation, an organized trip offers an experience most of us wouldn't have the resources to put together ourselves. These trips also tend to go places you can see only on foot, by bike, or by boat, with more of a payoff the farther you get from highways and hotels.

In other words, it's not that tough to plan a camping trip to a national park on your own, but if you want to go trekking in Bhutan or do a week-long rafting trip through the Grand Canyon, chances are you'll need some logistical help. But those trips are generally more expensive than the do-it-yourself route. Prices vary widely, depending on the type of trip you choose, but you can expect to spend at least $250 a day per person — and, sometimes, quite a bit more.

What to consider

Outdoor excursions come in many shapes and sizes, running the gamut from luxurious service, accommodations, and cuisine to more rugged expeditions that involve carrying your own backpack, pitching your own tent, and digging your own hole when the nearest bathroom is miles away. So here are some factors to consider as you research your options.

The level of difficulty. Most outfitters clearly describe each trip's level of difficulty, explaining how many hours a day you can expect to spend hiking, how many miles you'll cover on a bike, or what class of rapids you'll encounter. They can also give you advice on choosing a trip; after all, they don't want a dozen disgruntled clients complaining that one person slowed down everyone else.

That doesn't mean that you have to be in great shape to consider these types of trips; plenty of options are suitable for beginners or even someone who hasn't broken a sweat in months. But don't overestimate your abilities (or your traveling companion's). Some of these trips involve lots of hard work, and factors like a high altitude or rustic sleeping conditions can make the experience much more challenging than your usual gym workout.

Your comfort zone. Even if you're up for a physical challenge, you may not relish the idea of spending your vacation sleeping in a tent with only a thin pad between the ground and your spine. Not to worry: Lots of trips let you get a good workout during the day, then enjoy a gourmet meal and a comfortable bed at night. The accommodations can range from tent camping to staying at a hotel or a lodge, although some of those tents can be pretty luxurious (it's amazing what money can buy in the desert).

If you're not in the mood to rough it, other issues you should explore are the bathroom facilities and what you'll be eating for breakfast, lunch, and dinner (you may even eat some meals in restaurants). Another variable is whether you'll be expected to carry your own gear or help out with cooking, cleaning, and other chores. Usually, support staff handle the heavy lifting — your pack is transported in a van or on a four-legged animal, not on your back or your bike — but there are certainly exceptions if you don't want to be quite so pampered.

The schedule. If you're not a morning person — and I definitely am not — one drawback of many outdoor trips is that they often involve rising, if not necessarily shining, at an hour that may actually be earlier than when you'd normally wake up at home. That's something you should take into account as you ponder the itinerary, as well as how much free time you'll have to shop for trinkets at a local market or poke around a nearby town. If you don't want to be on a bike every day for a week, pick a trip that includes other options or, if you're more of a free bird, one that doesn't have every minute scheduled.

The itinerary's flexibility. It's not always possible to get sixteen people with the same skill level to sign up for a trip that leaves on a designated date, so many companies design their itineraries with varying abilities in mind: You can opt for a twenty-mile bike ride one day instead of the thirty-mile route or get picked up in a van whenever you tire. For river trips, there's often a boat standing by when your arms can paddle no more. So whether you think you'll be ahead of the pack or straggling behind, seek out a trip that lets you go at your own pace.

The company's philosophy. A lot of the outfitters that organize group outings have a pretty clear philosophy about how they travel. Often, you can get a sense of this approach by reading the company's mission statement or history on its Web site, and it's something you should definitely investigate before you sign up. It's not that you have to be a die-hard environmentalist to join a trip organized by the Sierra Club, but if you think that recycling is a waste of time, you'll probably find yourself traveling among a hostile crowd.

That said, one of the more rewarding aspects of engaging in a physically challenging experience with a bunch of strangers is that unlikely friendships form, and certain organizations do more to foster these bonds. A few years ago, I went on an Outward Bound trip that included a day of rock climbing, fully intending to opt out of any activity that involved heights above the top bunk. But Outward Bound is all about conquering such fears — with a little help from your new friends — and lo and behold, I ended up scrambling up a sixty-foot rock wall. (OK, maybe it was only forty feet high. But my feet never would have left the ground without everyone in my group cheering me on.)

WHERE TO FIND OUTDOOR ADVENTURES

Here some Web sites that can help you find a wide range of outdoor trips, along with a few of the more well-known companies that offer these outings. Most of these sites have some type of "trip finder" feature — you can search by destination, departure date, or activity — and some have information that can help you make your own plans if a group trip doesn't float your boat. This list includes mostly outfitters that lead trips all over the world, some of which charge premium prices; companies that specialize in a particular region or activity may offer more economical options.

DIRECTORIES AND ASSOCIATIONS

- **Gordon's Guide** (gordonsguide.com). Originally a book, Gordon's Guide is now a Web site with a database of hundreds of adventure travel companies, which you can search by activity or destination. Categories include river rafting, canoeing, biking, fishing, horseback riding, and hiking and a few more niche sports, such as heliskiing or dog sledding.

- **GORP: Great Outdoor Recreation Pages** (gorp.com). Owned by the same company that publishes *Outside* magazine, GORP is a useful resource if you're researching outdoor destinations and national or state parks, but if you hunt around, you can also find information about group trips.

- **Specialty Travel** (specialtytravel.com). This is another directory that offers a database of tour operators, searchable by interest or destination. Besides categories for most athletic activities, there are also dozens of more eclectic options, such as garden tours, northern lights viewing, truffle hunting, and whale watching.

- **Other options: AllAboutRivers** (allaboutrivers.com), **American Hiking Society** (americanhiking.org), **TheBackpacker.com** (thebackpacker.com), **BicyclingWorld.com** (bicyclingworld.com), **National Bicycle Tour Directors Association** (nbtda.com), **Professional Association of Diving Instructors** (padi.com), and **Ranchweb** (ranchweb.com).

MAGAZINES

- ***National Geographic Adventure*** (nationalgeographic.com/adventure). Part of the National Geographic family of magazines, which also includes *National Geographic Traveler* (nationalgeographic.com/traveler), the more adventurous member of the family caters to an active, outdoorsy crowd. Search the archives to find articles about a particular destination or sport.

- ***Outside*** (outsidemag.com). *Outside* magazine's Web site is part of the Away network (away.com), which also operates the GORP site mentioned earlier. *Outside* is a great source when you're planning any type of outdoor trip, with articles on topics like the best ecolodges in the world or the best guided trips for various sports.

- **Other options:** *Backpacker* (backpacker.com), *Outdoor Life* (outdoor life.com), *Field and Stream* (fieldandstream.com), *Paddler* (paddler magazine.com), *Scuba Diving* (scubadiving.com), *Ski* (skimag.com), *Skiing* (skiingmag.com), and *Surfer* (surfermag.com).

WILDERNESS COURSES

- **NOLS: National Outdoor Leadership School** (nols.edu). Although similar to Outward Bound, NOLS is more focused on training people who want to lead outdoor expeditions, and its courses last longer than most Outward Bound trips — from two weeks to twelve. Adult education courses cover climbing, backpacking, sea kayaking, fly fishing, rafting, sailing, and "horsepacking," which teaches how to travel with horses.

- **Outward Bound** (outwardbound.org). Outward Bound is best known for its outdoor education trips for high school and college students, but it also offers a wide range of adult courses, many lasting seven to ten days instead of a month. Because it's a nonprofit organization dedicated to wilderness education, its trips take more of a "roughing it" approach than do most for-profit companies, with a focus on promoting personal growth. Options include backpacking, sea kayaking, climbing, hiking, rafting, skiing, and sailing, and trips that combine several sports.

TRIP OPERATORS

- **Backroads** (backroads.com). Backroads specializes in biking, walking, and multisport trips, some of which involve camping, whereas others opt for a more comfortable inn or hotel. Most trips take place in Europe or North America, but there are also excursions to Australia, New Zealand, and various countries in Asia. Backroads organizes a handful of trips each year for solo travelers, as well as options designed for families.

- **Equitours** (equitours.com). Equitours organizes riding vacations all over the world. Domestic trips take place mostly in the western United States; the international offerings include riding excursions in Africa, Asia, Europe, South America, and the South Pacific.

- **Geographic Expeditions** (geoex.com). Best known for its trips to out-of-the-way destinations, Geographic Expeditions specializes in taking mostly wealthy clients to places like Antarctica, Mongolia, Tibet, and Tunisia, in a generally comfortable style of travel. Some trips involve trekking, horseback riding, or kayaking, but others approach adventure from the vantage point of an SUV or a boat.

- **Mountain Travel Sobek** (mtsobek.com). Mountain Travel Sobek leads small groups of travelers with a particular yen for visiting places like Cambodia, Kilimanjaro, Libya, or Myanmar. Some of these adventures involve biking, trekking, rafting, kayaking, or other activities, but there are also options for those who prefer to explore on the back of a camel or by boat.

- **OARS: Outdoor Adventure River Specialists** (oars.com). One of the largest outfitters operating in the western United States, OARS offers rafting, sea kayaking, and multisport trips in Alaska, California, Idaho, Oregon, Utah, Wyoming, and the Grand Canyon, as well as a few trips abroad. Some of its excursions are designed specifically for families; others, for solo travelers.

- **REI Adventures** (reiadventures.com). The outdoor-goods retailer REI is also in the travel business, offering climbing, cycling, hiking, paddling, rafting, and multisport trips to destinations in the United States and abroad. Most trips last from a weekend to two weeks, with levels of activity ranging from "easy" — one to two hours of activity daily — to "strenuous" — a full day of climbing at high altitudes.

- **Other options: The Adventure Collection** (adventurecollection.com) is an association of adventure-travel companies that specialize in active travel, including some of the tour operators listed earlier.

Relax, Already: Spa Vacations and Yoga Retreats

Theoretically, a vacation should offer plenty of opportunity for what used to be called R&R. That's rest and relaxation, folks — remember when that used to be the point of a week off? But somehow, vacations started taking on the activity level of a military boot camp ("Breakfast at 0800 hours, reconvene in hotel lobby at 0900 . . ."), and technology pretty much dashed any hope of getting away from it all.

Cue the ambient music, fire up the aromatherapy candles, and dim the lights to a soft glow. The spa vacation has arrived to save us from ourselves. Of course, strictly speaking, some version of the spa experience has been around since the Romans dropped their togas for a soak, but in recent years, the idea of planning a trip around the pleasures of mineral baths, massages, and mud masks has become a travel category of its own. And for those who want to relax their minds along with their muscles, yoga and meditation are becoming a standard part of the spa experience, as well as the focus of vacation retreats themselves.

The spa spectrum

At the high end of this trend are *destination spas* — typically, located in bucolic locations where you can start your day with a healthy smoothie and proceed through a regimen of treatments and activities that promise to clear your mind, release your tension, and make your skin glow. Hikes, detoxifying meals, and yoga and Pilates classes are optional, though the food is generally of the healthy sort. That doesn't mean that you'll eat only granola and tofu, but you probably won't find a vending machine selling potato chips and chocolate bars in the hall. But if you *are* looking to lose weight, there are certainly places that will help you work on any dietary concerns.

Among the more famous of these destination spas are Canyon Ranch (canyonranch.com) or Miraval (miravalresort.com) in Arizona or the Golden Door (goldendoor.com) in California. For the most part, these palaces of rejuvenation cater to a well-heeled crowd, with expensive room rates and prices that start above $100 for treatments. Meals, some activities, and a credit toward spa treatments are usually included in package prices for weekend or week-long stays, which can cost several thousand dollars.

For those who don't want their vacations to be quite so spa-centric, equally attractive spa facilities can be found at a growing number of high-end hotels and resorts. Cruise ships and more midrange hotels and resorts are also jumping on the spa bandwagon, but even at less luxurious locations, expect to pay $100 to $200 (or more) for a body wrap, scrub, or massage.

Although not all spas are priced beyond the reach of the typical traveler, a spa getaway tends to be on the expensive end of the vacation spectrum. Still, you can sometimes find more moderately priced options near hot springs in Arizona or California or resorts in foreign countries where the exchange rate makes luxuries more affordable. You can also find deals on off-season or midweek stays (see the sidebar on the facing page for help finding a spa that suits your agenda and budget).

PLANNING A SPA VACATION

Here are some resources that can help you plan a spa getaway, whether you're looking for a week-long package or an overnight trip somewhere close to home. You can also find spa reviews at some of the Web sites that collect customer feedback about hotels (see page 17 for details).

- **International SPA Association** (experienceispa.com). Although this membership organization is primarily for the spa industry, the group's Web site offers useful resources for consumers, too. You can search for spas in a particular state or country and even specify what type of facility you're looking for — like one that has mineral springs or a destination spa. The site also offers a glossary of spa terms, advice on spa etiquette, and a list of travel agents who specialize in spa getaways.

- **Spa Finder** (spafinder.com). As the name implies, Spa Finder's main goal is to help the stressed-out or muscle-cramped find a place to relax, rejuvenate, and unwind. Spa Finder offers a tool to search for a spa by zip code or browse through special-interest categories, like spas appropriate for families, solo travelers, or mothers bonding with their daughters. The site also offers a glossary of spa terms and advice on spa protocol.

- *Spa Magazine* (spamagazine.com). *Spa Magazine*'s Web site offers a selection of articles from the print publication, as well as a search tool to find a spa. The magazine typically covers the latest spa trends, new destinations, and topics like how to bring the spa experience home.

- **Zagat Surveys** (zagat.com). Zagat publishes two guidebooks that include reviews and ratings of hotel and destination spas: *Top U.S. Hotels, Resorts & Spas* and *Top International Hotels, Resorts, & Spas.*

- *100 Best Spas of the World,* by **Bernard Burt and Pamela Price** (Globe Pequot). This guidebook for spa goers has color photos, descriptions, and contact information for spas in more than thirty countries.

Spa treatments 101

If you're new to the spa experience, make sure to research the "spa menu" before you leave home. Spas are increasingly venturing beyond the familiar, offering treatments like watsu (a type of shiatsu administered in a pool) or craniosacral therapy (a massage that focuses on the skull and spinal column), as well as incorporating local ingredients into the experience, like a chocolate massage in Hershey, Pennsylvania, or a coconut rub in the Caribbean.

These offerings sometimes turn out to be more of a gimmick than a breakthrough in bodywork, so think twice before you're swayed by an exotic description in a glossy brochure. (One friend who tried an aromatherapy massage reported, "There was no *massage* — they were just waving stuff around in the air!") When in doubt, ask lots of questions or go with what you know, but you'll probably be less intimidated if you research your options before you arrive. In fact, at many spas, you'll actually need to book your appointments ahead of time.

But one drawback of getting spa treatments on vacation is that when you're not a regular customer, you don't know which therapists are going to leave you feeling like a million bucks or like you just wasted a couple hundred dollars. You can try asking other guests for feedback or cozy up to a staff member at the resort and try to get a recommendation (then tip well). But before you commit to a half day of pampering, try a shorter, less expensive treatment, which can help you gauge whether it's worthwhile to splurge.

Yoga and meditation retreats

With the growing popularity of yoga, another way more travelers are choosing to unwind is by signing up for yoga retreats, usually weekend or week-long getaways held in destinations away from the frenzy of urban life. These retreats often take place at institutions that host other wellness or spiritual workshops, such as the Omega Institute (eomega.com) in Rhinebeck, New York, the Kripalu Center for Yoga and Health (kripalu.com) in Lenox, Massachusetts, and the Pura Vida Retreat and Spa (puravidaspa.com) in Alajuela, Costa Rica.

You can generally find information about these types of getaways through a yoga studio in your hometown. Another good source is *Yoga Journal* (yogajournal.com). The magazine's Web site has a travel section that lists yoga retreats around the world, as well as a directory of yoga teachers and studios you can search by location — useful if you simply want to take a class wherever you're going.

Yoga retreats vary in intensity and the number of other activities you can participate in during your stay, like meditation workshops, hikes, or massages. So if you don't want to spend a week taking yoga classes all day, find out what else there is to do and whether you'll be able to do any exploring nearby. You should also make sure that your ability level matches the classes you'll be taking, since your idea of an "intermediate" workshop may get a quick reality check if everyone else is doing handstands away from the wall.

Culinary Adventures: When Food Is the Focus

For many people, food ends up being a major part of any trip, since finding a place to eat and then actually eating several times a day can easily take up most of your waking hours. But for those who truly want to let their stomachs lead the way, a growing number of organized trips combine travel with a passion for food: cooking it, eating it, seeing where it's grown, and learning how various delicacies are made.

Sometimes referred to as culinary travel, other times marketed as a gastronomic tour or a cooking vacation, this travel niche encompasses a wide range of experiences — from a ten-day tour of a region known for its cuisine or wine, with stops at local farms, markets, or restaurants, to a week-long session at a cooking school, where students don aprons and wield knives most of the day. In between, you can find trips that mix cooking, eating, and drinking with sightseeing and other activities — say, a hike to work off all the cheese and olive oil you sampled. (See the sidebar on page 47 for where to find these tours.)

The food travel landscape

Many culinary escapes are trips organized by someone with a professional connection to food or cooking — a food writer, cookbook author, restaurant owner, or chef — but some tour operators specialize in culinary travel or offer these trips as part of a broader mix, often partnering with a well-known restaurateur or chef.

You can also find cooking vacations — cooking classes aimed at tourists — offered by local culinary schools in regions or countries with a rich gastronomic tradition, exporting the secret to making a perfect Bolognese sauce or a mouth-watering mole. These classes typically range in length from half a day to a week — so you don't have to spend your entire trip hovered over a chopping block if you simply want to learn a couple of dishes to show off at a dinner party back home.

Popular destinations for culinary adventures reflect contemporary eating habits and cooking trends: Italy and France tend to dominate the food travel scene, but China, Greece, India, Japan, Mexico, Spain, and Thailand also offer lots of ways to incorporate their culinary traditions into a vacation, as do various regions in the United States. A few cruise lines are also starting to jump on the culinary bandwagon, offering cooking classes on board or a themed cruise in partnership with a chef or a food magazine.

Choosing a culinary escape

Because culinary travel options offer such a wide range of experiences, choosing one that's a good fit can be a challenge. Here are some things to consider as you mull over descriptions of winery tours, visits with cheese artisans, and sushi-making classes.

- *Do you want to eat or do you want to cook?* Even if you love to cook, you may not find it much of a vacation to be in a cooking class all day, every day, for a week. Be realistic about how much time you want to spend in the kitchen — one day may be plenty. And if you've never taken a cooking class, try one closer to home before you spend a lot of money on a week-long course halfway around the world.
- *Who's the teacher (or trip leader)?* If you're a huge fan of a particular chef or cookbook author, it may be worth paying a premium for that person's expertise; but sometimes, these celebrity participants aren't as hands-on as you might expect. Find out how much your food guru is involved before you commit to the trip — and if you don't know anything about the person teaching the class or leading the tour, do some research before you sign up.

FOOD-RELATED TRAVEL

FINDING COOKING VACATIONS AND CULINARY TRIPS

Although culinary travel has become somewhat trendy in recent years, it's still a rather fragmented segment of the travel industry, so you may have to do some digging to find a cooking class or tour that suits your interests. Many tour organizers rely on word-of-mouth referrals or a celebrity connection to drum up business, but if you're starting from scratch, here are some ways to research your options.

- **ShawGuides** (cookforfun.shawguides.com). This site offers a directory of several thousand cooking and wine vacation programs worldwide: You can search by date, destination, or cuisine. Its *Guide to Cooking Schools* is a print directory of recreational and professional cooking programs.

- **Cooking magazines** *Gourmet* (gourmet.com), *Food & Wine* (foodandwine .com), and *Bon Apetit* (bonappetit.com) frequently publish articles about culinary travel or ads for companies that offer these trips. Some publications even organize their own cooking-themed cruises or tours, often in conjunction with a food writer or a celebrity chef.

- **Chefs, cookbook authors, and restaurants** Search the Internet to see whether your favorite food guru has a Web site listing any cooking classes or culinary trips he or she is teaching or participating in. Among those who do: Emeril Lagasse (emerils.com), Patricia Wells (patriciawells.com), and Faith Willinger (faithwillinger.com).

- **Cooking schools** Well-known cooking schools like Le Cordon Bleu (cordon bleu.com), the French Culinary Institute (frenchculinary.com), and the Institute of Culinary Education (iceculinary.com) offer classes for both recreational and professional chefs.

- **Visitor and tourist bureaus** Countries known for their food or wine often have information on their Web sites for gastronomically minded visitors, like guides to wine-producing regions or local farmers' markets. Don't overlook regional sites, such as champagne.fr or napavalley.com. (For tips on finding official tourism sites, see page 19.)

FINDING FOOD FESTIVALS

If you'd rather plan your itinerary to overlap with a food festival, FoodRefer ence.com and WhatsOnWhen.com are two sites that list food festivals around the world. Many of these events have their own Web sites, so if you have a festival in mind, an Internet search will usually point you to the right spot. As a general rule, food festivals take place during summer and fall.

- *Do you want to stay in one place or move around?* Trips that focus on cooking tend to spend a lot of time in one location, whereas culinary tours are more likely to visit various regions. If you're flying to a distant destination, you may regret seeing only one town (one solution is to add a few days of touring on your own). But if you prefer to stay put, choose a trip that doesn't involve unpacking several times.
- *What are the accommodations?* Most culinary tours include accommodations, but the options can vary from a villa with a shared bathroom to a five-star hotel. If you're taking a cooking course, you may have to make your own arrangements for lodging, or you might have the option of staying in housing affiliated with the school.
- *How much free time will you have?* Cooking vacations, and even culinary trips, tend to have fairly organized itineraries, so if you're more of a free spirit, look for options that set aside time for guests to explore on their own — or take a nap after a big lunch.

Volunteer Vacations: Trips That Make a Difference

Vacations tend to be primarily about self-indulgence: sleeping late, eating foods that aren't on your diet, and spending money more freely than you would at home. (Who hasn't justified a travel extravagance by saying, "Hey, we're on vacation — why not?")

But if you're looking for a way to use your time off more altruistically, many organizations match volunteers with short-term service projects all over the world. Loosely referred to as *volunteer vacations,* these trips offer opportunities ranging from teaching, assisting refugees, or building houses to restoring hiking trails, participating in an archeological dig, or working with animals. You can find a project to fit just about any interest either in the United States or abroad.

Although you don't need any particular qualifications to participate in most programs, if you have specialized skills — in medicine or construction, for example — there are certainly opportunities to use them. And you usually don't have to speak the local language, but if you do, that's always a plus — in terms of what you'll get out of the experience and what you can offer.

Fees, trip length, and logistics

But just because you're volunteering your time doesn't mean that you'll get a free trip in return. Most organizations that place volunteers charge a fee to participate, which generally covers program expenses and room and board. These fees vary, depending on where you're going, the accommodations, and the cost of running the program, but you can expect to pay about $500 to $1,000 per week, plus airfare; if the organization you choose is a nonprofit, at least some of these costs are tax deductible.

Most trips have scheduled departure dates and last from one to three weeks, but you may be able to find a weekend project if you can't get away for more time. Some programs place volunteers with local families, but you could also find yourself sleeping in a tent, bunking in a dorm room, or staying in a hotel. In most cases, you'll be traveling with between five and twenty other volunteers and, sometimes, a team leader, and some of your fellow volunteers will probably be from other countries, especially if you're headed abroad.

People who do longer volunteer vacations tend to be on the younger side — college students and recent graduates in their twenties — but on shorter trips, the age range is generally more diverse, and a few organizations encourage families to sign up. Because most of these programs are designed for people traveling on their own, volunteer vacations are a good way to visit a place you might not feel comfortable going to by yourself — though your free time may be limited, so if you want to do any sightseeing, plan on adding a few days to your itinerary before or after the project.

Choosing a program

Most programs have some type of application process, though that's more of a formality than a competition to get accepted. Still, you need to plan ahead, since many trips fill up months before their scheduled departures and you'll get a better deal on any plane tickets you have to buy.

Two types of organizations offer volunteer vacations: (1) nonprofits that coordinate these trips in addition to other outreach or advocacy work they do, like the Sierra Club or Habitat for Humanity, and (2) groups whose main mission is to arrange service projects for people interested in volunteering abroad. (See the sidebar on the facing page for where to find various options.)

Most of these organizations are nonprofits, but a few for-profit companies place volunteers too, so if you want to take a tax deduction for the cost of your trip — or simply prefer to support a not-for-profit agency — make sure to ask about the group's status. Some groups also have religious or political affiliations, which they generally disclose up front, but if you get a sense from the organization's Web site that there's a more subtle agenda at work, ask for more details, lest you find yourself in a foreign country representing a cause you don't necessarily espouse.

What to expect

Some agencies outline in great detail the type of work you'll be doing, whereas others are a bit vague on specifics. So if you don't want to be surprised by a task like chicken-coop clean-up, try to find out as much as you can about the project, including the day-to-day itinerary, how much interaction you'll have with locals, and whether a trip leader or support staff will be at your location.

But volunteer programs generally don't follow a strict itinerary like some other group trips, so be prepared to go with the flow. And if you're traveling to a less developed country, keep in mind that things like indoor plumbing and electricity are luxuries you may have to do without.

Other topics to ask about: whether travel insurance is included in the trip's cost — important if you're going somewhere remote (see page 71 for details) — whether any of the program fees go to the local community, and whether you'll receive training for projects that require specific skills. In most cases, that isn't necessary, but some programs do offer crash courses in things like the dos and don'ts of an archeological dig.

WHERE TO FIND VOLUNTEER VACATIONS

Following are a couple of directories that list volunteer opportunities offered by a wide range of organizations, as well as a few nonprofits that either organize their own volunteer trips or coordinate projects on behalf of other groups. The options listed here are just the tip of the iceberg; for more ideas, check out the book *Volunteer Vacations,* by Bill McMillon, Doug Cutchins, and Anne Geissinger, which lists more than two hundred programs in the United States and abroad that accept volunteers.

DIRECTORIES LISTING MULTIPLE PROGRAMS

- **International Volunteer Programs Association** (volunteerinternational .org). IVPA is an alliance of nonprofit, nongovernmental organizations that send volunteers and interns to do work in other countries. You can search IVPA's database by destination, type of work, or trip length to find opportunities offered by the group's members. The "type of work" choices are impressive: more than a hundred options, including veterinary work, wildlife surveying, organic farming, and literacy.

- **Volunteer Abroad** (volunteerabroad.com). This site is part of a larger database, GoAbroad.com, that lists international education and alternative travel opportunities. Within the volunteer section, you can search for service projects by destination, trip length, or type of work to find programs offered by various organizations.

ORGANIZATIONS THAT OFFER VOLUNTEER TRIPS

- **American Hiking Society** (americanhiking.org). If you want to get a workout outdoors, the American Hiking Society organizes volunteer vacations that involve constructing or rebuilding trails, cabins, or shelters in backcountry locations all over the United States. You can search for a trip by date or by state; these projects generally require roughing it, but the cost is quite a bit lower than other volunteer options.

- **Cross-Cultural Solutions** (crossculturalsolutions.org). Founded in 1995, Cross-Cultural Solutions organizes volunteer trips to ten countries: Brazil, China, Costa Rica, Ghana, Guatemala, India, Peru, Russia, Tanzania, and Thailand. Trips last between two and twelve weeks and generally involve working with people in local communities — teaching, helping out in a clinic, or caring for infants or seniors.

- **Earthwatch Institute** (earthwatch.org). Earthwatch is an international organization that coordinates volunteers to work alongside scientists and researchers in the field; programs typically last one to three weeks. Since its founding in 1971, Earthwatch has sent volunteers to more than a hundred countries and many U.S. states to work on projects ranging from archaeology and zoology to biodiversity and international health.

- **Global Citizens Network** (globalcitizens.org). GCN sends teams of volunteers to work on projects determined by local needs in rural communities around the world; past projects include building a health clinic, renovating a youth center, and planting trees. Each group of six to ten volunteers is accompanied by a team leader, and families are welcome to participate.

- **Global Service Corps** (globalservicecorps.org). A project of the Earth Island Institute in San Francisco, Global Service Corps sends volunteers to Tanzania and Thailand to work on health, education, and agriculture initiatives. Trips generally last two weeks and are open to families or other groups traveling together.

- **Global Volunteers** (globalvolunteers.org). Global Volunteers arranges one to three-week service projects in nearly twenty countries, including the United States. Most of the projects involve community development work, such as construction, working at an orphanage, or teaching English and other subjects.

- **Habitat for Humanity** (habitat.org). Best known for its housing projects within the United States, Habitat for Humanity also organizes "work trips" to build houses in other countries. Trips generally last two weeks and include some time for sightseeing in nearby areas.

- **Oceanic Society** (oceanic-society.org). The Oceanic Society is a San Francisco–based marine conservation organization that accepts volunteers to assist researchers studying marine animals in places like Africa, Belize, the Baja Peninsula, and the Galapagos Islands. These outings are described as "expeditions" and tend to be more expensive than other volunteer programs.

- **Sierra Club** (sierraclub.org/outings). Besides offering other travel programs, the Sierra Club organizes nearly one hundred service trips each year, primarily restoring wilderness areas, maintaining trails, and cleaning up campsites in state and national parks. You have to become a Sierra Club member to participate (the lowest level of membership costs $25 per year), and most projects involve at least a moderate level of physical work.

- **Volunteers for Peace** (vfp.org). VFP is a Vermont-based nonprofit organization that has been coordinating international service projects since 1982. Its "workcamps" tend to be less expensive than other volunteer opportunities, which means that accommodations are more rustic and volunteers cook their own meals. VFP offers two-to-three-week trips in many foreign countries; projects vary, depending on the needs of the local community.

Options for Solo Travelers: Resources, Trips, and Travel Companions

People seem to have one of two equally strong reactions to the idea of traveling alone: horror ("Eat in a restaurant by myself? I'd rather starve!") or adventure ("You meet so many interesting people when you're on your own!").

Of course, business travelers frequently find themselves at a table for one, and plenty of people embark on solo adventures to destinations all over the world. But when it comes to a typical vacation, it's safe to say that most people prefer not to go it alone.

For those who don't have built-in travel companions based on marriage, blood, or some other bond, lots of travel options offer company on the road — and with the Internet, more ways than ever to seek them out.

Group trips: Single versus solo

Many of the group trips listed in other sections in this chapter are well suited to solo travelers: The key is to ask *before* you sign up whether everyone else will be traveling in couples. In general, volunteer vacations, yoga retreats, and outdoor adventures attract more people traveling on their own. Overseas language programs are another good option — the National Registration Center for Study Abroad (nrcsa.com), GoAbroad (goabroad.com), and GoNomad (gonomad.com) all list language courses you can take in various foreign countries.

Some tour operators that cater primarily to customers traveling in twos also offer trips for people traveling on their own. For instance, Backroads (backroads.com) offers more than a dozen hiking, biking, and multisport trips for adults traveling solo or with friends — these trips are listed as "Singles and Solos Trips."

There are also lots of trips organized specifically for the solo travel market (see the sidebar on page 56 for ways to find them). Although some of these trips are geared toward "singles" — in the wink-wink lingo of the travel industry, those who have romance on their agenda — there are also plenty of companies that don't aim to double as a dating service, welcoming people who have left their spouses, kids, or boyfriends at home.

Single supplements and how to avoid them

The only catch is, some tour operators — and most cruise lines — charge solo travelers what's known as a single supplement, a surcharge that can double the cost of the advertised price, so the trick is finding a way to either avoid or minimize this charge.

Although it's easy to interpret these supplements as a penalty for being single — as if driving while reading a map weren't punishment enough — it really comes down to simple math and how travel companies promote their products. Most trips that include accommodations are priced "per person, based on double occupancy," because it looks cheaper, which means that anyone traveling alone has to make up the difference in the room's cost. That's why you may face a single supplement for vacation packages, cruises, or tours — basically, any trip that includes lodging.

Where it gets a bit galling is when companies factor into their single supplements not just the difference in lodging but also what they consider lost revenue from the missing traveler — for instance, what that person would have spent during a cruise for drinks, shore excursions, or spa services. In general, prices that include a single supplement range from 125 percent to 200 percent of the cost "per person, based on double occupancy." So if the trip you're considering is at the upper end of that range, you're paying double the per person price.

The best way to avoid paying a single supplement is to travel à la carte — that is, book your flight and hotel separately rather than doing a group trip or a cruise — but if you have your heart set on a vacation at sea or a package tour, here are some tips on how to minimize the supplemental burden.

- *Offer to share.* Some tour operators or cruise lines will offer to find a roommate for anyone willing to share a room with a stranger (typically, of the same sex, and you can usually opt for a smoker or a nonsmoker). Some companies even offer what's called a guaranteed share: If they can't match you with a roommate, you don't have to pay a single supplement. Bunking with someone you don't know has its risks — you may end up sharing a small space with a hypochondriac, an insomniac, or someone whose personal habits drive you nuts — but some people find the savings worth the gamble.

- *Seek out a single cabin.* On some of their ships, a few cruise lines have single cabins that cost less than booking a regular cabin and paying a single supplement. Costa, Cruise West, Cunard, Norwegian, and Princess are among the companies that have a limited number of single cabins — but book early to be sure you get one. And don't expect a room with a view: Single cabins are usually on older ships in less desirable locations than double staterooms.

- *Travel at an off-peak time, or look for a last-minute deal.* Companies sometimes waive or reduce their single supplements when business is down, at off-peak times, or just before a cruise or a trip is scheduled to depart. Ask the cruise line or tour operator you're considering whether it ever offers this type of promotion — and when you're likely to catch it — or work with a travel agent who keeps track of these specials.

- *Find a company that charges a lower supplement.* How much companies charge as a single supplement varies quite a bit, so shop around. The travel agencies and tour operators listed in this section tend to reach out to the solo-travel market, so they can help you find trips that are more affordable for someone traveling alone.

- *Find your own travel companion.* If you're not comfortable sharing your vacation with any random stranger — travel companies don't make much effort to pair people who are both early risers or who like to party — another option is to find your own roommate. Before the Internet, a few membership services published directories listing people interested in finding travel companions, but now, most of this networking takes place on line. Besides the services listed in this section, the on-line travel communities described on page 14 can also help you find potential travel partners or people who live wherever you're going who might show you around town.

TIPS AND TRIPS FOR SOLO TRAVELERS

Here are some Web sites, tour operators, and travel agencies that offer trips or advice for solo travelers. For a more comprehensive guide, the book *Traveling Solo,* by Eleanor Berman (Globe Pequot), lists more than 250 vacation options for those traveling on their own.

- **Connecting: Solo Travel Network** (cstn.org). This organization publishes a bimonthly newsletter and the *Single-Friendly Travel Directory,* listing travel companies that offer room shares or single rooms without a surcharge. Membership costs $30 a year, which includes both publications and access to an on-line calendar listing tours and cruises for singles.

- **CruiseMates** (cruisemates.com). An on-line gathering place for cruise enthusiasts, CruiseMates has a dedicated forum with advice, booking tips, and networking opportunities for single passengers. There's also a regular columnist who covers these topics and a calendar listing upcoming singles cruises.

- **Elderhostel** (elderhostel.org). A nonprofit group that organizes trips for people fifty-five and older, with a focus on educational travel opportunities and a welcoming attitude toward single travelers.

- **O Solo Mio** (osolomio.com). A travel agency that specializes in what it calls "group trips for individuals," with a tag line noting, "We are not a dating service." The trips are operated by other tour companies or cruise lines and tend to go to popular destinations, such as Greece, Hawaii, and Italy.

- **SinglesCruise** (singlescruise.com). This travel agency organizes singles' cruises, booking blocks of rooms on the major cruise lines and hosting special events on board. The agency also arranges room shares so clients can avoid paying a single supplement. If you're not sharing a cabin, prices may be higher than if you booked the same cruise on your own, but by booking through SinglesCruise, you get to dine and socialize with other single passengers — and there are likely to be more singles than you'd find on a typical cruise.

- **Singles Travel International** (singlestravelintl.com). A travel agency that organizes trips that cater to a younger, more active single crowd. Options include cruises aboard major cruise lines and customized tours to destinations in the United States and abroad.

- **SoloDining.com** (solodining.com). This Web site lists restaurants, mostly in U.S. cities, that have a counter, bar, or shared-table seating, giving solo diners an alternative to a "table for one" when eating out. The SoloDining newsletter has been on hiatus, but you can still access its restaurant recommendations on the Web.

- **TravelChums** (travelchums.com). This site is essentially a matchmaking service for travelers, though romance isn't necessarily the goal. You can search the site's database to find people matching the gender, age range, location, and any keywords you specify — say, to find someone else interested in going to Australia. But you have to become a member (which is free) to contact people who have posted a profile or to use the site's message boards.

- **Windjammer Barefoot Cruises** (windjammer.com). A company that specializes in tall-ship cruises in the Caribbean, offering several singles-only cruises annually. Cupid is very much invited on board.

- **The Women's Travel Club** (womenstravelclub.com). An organization that arranges group trips for women, including married women whose spouses don't share their travel bug. Some trips go to far-flung destinations, such as Tunisia and Bali, whereas others involve shorter weekend jaunts to a U.S. city or a spa.

PART II

BOOKING

3 General Advice

SPENDING TIME RESEARCHING travel destinations is a great way to while away a rainy Sunday or a slow day at the office, but let's face it: The main thing everyone wants to know about booking travel is, Where can I find the best prices? And the answer is the same, and similarly unsatisfying, whether you're buying a plane ticket, booking a hotel, shopping for a cruise, or reserving a rental car: There isn't a single best place to book your trip — or even to compare prices.

Of course, every company that sells travel would have you believe otherwise, each claiming that its Web site is the best place to shop. But just like buying shoes, sunglasses, or a sofa, where you should spend your money or research your options depends on a lot of factors — in this case, where you're going, how soon you're traveling, what restrictions you're willing to accept, and how much you can afford to spend, not to mention who's having a sale at the time.

That doesn't mean that there aren't ways to find the best deal; the next few chapters outline specific strategies for booking everything from plane tickets to rental cars. It's just that there aren't Six Secrets to Saving Money on Travel or Ten Tips for Vacationing on a Budget or any other shortcut that makes for a great magazine headline. (Believe me, I wish there were; this book would have been a lot easier to write.)

Chapters 4 through 7 go into detail about booking airline tickets, lodging, cruises, and rental cars, but first, this chapter outlines some general shopping advice. Among the topics covered: whether buying a package is a good idea, how to figure out whether you need travel insurance, and why using a discount code won't necessarily get you a deal.

This chapter also explains where to look if you're booking a last-minute trip, how to use discount sites, like Priceline and Hotwire, and when you should consider working with a travel agent. Because even though we've all become our own in-house travel planners — or at least *someone* in the household has taken on that chore — there are times when it's better to leave the planning to a professional.

The Travel Marketplace: Everybody Wants Your Business, but Where Should You Buy?

One of the biggest challenges of do-it-yourself travel planning is figuring out when you're getting a good deal, which is complicated by the fact that travel sellers aren't always honest when they say they've got the lowest prices around. And with so many companies competing for your business, spending lots of money on advertising to sway your credit card their way, there are literally hundreds of places you could book your trip once you decide where you want to go.

The next few chapters will guide you through the thicket of making specific types of travel reservations. But no matter what you're booking, keep in mind some general shopping guidelines.

- *No Web site displays all your options.* Many companies claim to be a one-stop shop for booking travel, but the truth is, no Web site displays every flight, hotel room, rental car, or cruise available or even all your options in one of those categories. If you want to find the best deal, you have to shop around.
- *More choice isn't necessarily better shopping.* Even if one Web site *could* display all your options, you wouldn't necessarily be a more satisfied shopper. Some travel sites display hundreds of flight combinations when you search for a simple round-trip ticket, leaving you with the daunting task of weeding through all those results. Sometimes, it's better to choose a more selective site so you don't have to do all the selecting yourself.
- *The cheapest deal isn't always the best deal.* With so many resources

at our fingertips to research prices, it's easy to get caught up in the thrill of the hunt. But if the lowest price for a round-trip plane ticket means two stopovers each way, an early-morning departure, and a long layover in the middle of the night, it's probably not worth all that hassle — and the dark circles under your eyes — to save $50.

- *Price guarantees don't guarantee much at all.* Many travel sellers advertise some type of "lowest-price guarantee," promising to match a competitor's price and give some additional discount if you find a better deal elsewhere. The problem is, with all their caveats, these guarantees don't guarantee much at all. For starters, you generally have to find a better price on the exact same flight with the same fare code in order to collect — not any flight that day on any airline — or the exact same hotel room, not one with a king-size bed if your reservation was for two doubles. Oh, and you usually have to find a better deal within twenty-four hours after booking your original reservation. Once you've decided on a flight or a hotel, a price guarantee may give you some assurance that you're getting the lowest price for that specific purchase, but otherwise, these guarantees are rarely a reason to shop at a particular site.

- *The Web isn't always better than the phone.* In this self-service era, more and more companies are pushing their customers to turn to the Web for help, and some actually charge an extra fee if you call. But even if you have to pay a bit more, it's sometimes worth a few bucks to deal with a person rather than struggle with a confusing Web site to make a purchase or fix a problem. Of course, you'll probably have to work your way through a phone menu or wait on hold before you get to speak with an agent; even when you're paying for the call, the automated attendant is difficult to dodge.

- *Often, you get what you pay for.* Some travel companies swear it ain't so, but others will admit (at least, privately) what most customers have already figured out: If you book a discount air fare or a cheap hotel room, you generally won't get the same service as someone who booked direct or paid full price. The differences

TIPS: DECIDING WHERE TO BUY

No matter how many Web sites you check or companies you call, you may find that prices don't vary much — or at all. If that's the case, here are some other factors to consider when you're deciding where to take your business, some of which may trump the bottom line.

- *Is there a service charge?* Many travel sellers charge a service fee to handle your reservation, but they don't always disclose this amount until late in the booking process. Before you hand over a credit card number, make sure that you know whether you're paying any extra fees that will show up in the final total.

- *Can you get any kind of bonus by booking direct?* Some reward programs will give you extra frequent flier miles if you book your flight at an airline's Web site or similar bonus points if you book your hotel direct. If you belong to these types of loyalty programs, that may be a reason to redirect your mouse.

- *Do you have a coupon?* If you have a coupon or a discount code from an airline, hotel chain, or car rental company (say, from a newspaper ad or a travel voucher), you may have to book direct in order to take advantage of that discount.

- *What's the policy on changes or cancellations?* These policies can vary quite a bit, depending on where you book, even for the same flight, hotel room, cruise, or car rental. That's because some travel agencies assess their own penalties on top of whatever the supplier dictates — or don't let you make changes at all.

- *Is there a toll-free number you can call?* When you're booking on line, you may not even notice whether the Web site lists a phone number. If it doesn't, that's a good reason to buy from a company that gives you the option of calling.

- *Do you get any member benefits?* If you've already filled out a profile or become a member at half a dozen travel Web sites, booking through one of those companies may get you extra perks — or at least save you typing time.

may be subtle: Your window will look out on an air shaft instead of the city skyline, or you won't get rebooked quite so quickly if your flight is canceled, but accepting such trade-offs may be worth saving a few hundred dollars.

Evaluating Vacation Packages: When They're a Bargain and When They're Not

These days, it seems that everywhere you click, someone is trying to sell you a vacation package — basically, travel deals that include some combination of flights, hotel, and car rental all in one price. Expedia, Orbitz, Travelocity, most airlines, many hotels, and even clubs like AAA or Costco are all pushing packages, promising that these deals offer substantial savings over making all your reservations à la carte. But the truth is, vacation packages aren't always a great buy. Here's how to tell whether you're getting a good deal by purchasing a package and whether what's inside that package fits your style of travel.

How packages work

Packages used to be a one-size-fits-all proposition — for instance, a deal at a certain hotel in the Bahamas, available for specific dates, often involving charter flights. But in recent years, the build-your-own approach has really taken off. The idea is that you create your own customized vacation from a set of choices, often using tools available on line.

Typically, you first choose a destination, your travel dates, and the number of people traveling; then you select a hotel and a flight from the options displayed. You can't necessarily create a package for any destination — they're available mostly for major cities and popular vacation spots, like the Caribbean, Florida, Hawaii, or Mexico — but the package trend is definitely starting to spread far and wide.

You'll also find that the accommodations offered as part of a package tend to be larger hotels or resorts (that's because big hotels have more unsold rooms to fill, which is how packagers get their inventory). And packages are generally priced based on two people traveling together, so if you're taking the kids or going solo, booking a package deal may not be an option.

Usually, the price of the package changes as you make your se-

ALL-INCLUSIVE RESORTS

Some resorts, typically in beach destinations, offer all-inclusive vacation packages covering meals, drinks, tips, entertainment, and activities, like tennis or windsurfing in the price of your stay. Club Med (clubmed.com), Sandals (sandals.com), Beaches (beaches.com), and Couples Resorts (couples.com) are a few of the companies that specialize in all-inclusive vacations, but lots of other resorts offer these packages in addition to their standard à la carte rates. You can book these options direct or through a travel agency; search the Internet for "all-inclusive," "vacation," and a destination, and you'll find plenty of options to choose from.

For some travelers, knowing how much they're going to spend on a trip — and minimizing the risk of going over budget — has some appeal. But be sure that you understand exactly what's included (and what isn't) before you commit. Also, these resorts tend to be isolated from the local culture, so guests mingle mostly with other pale tourists looking for a place to relax and escape colder temperatures at home. So if you're a light drinker on a diet who likes to explore different places, an all-inclusive resort vacation probably isn't the best fit.

lections, depending on your hotel choice, the dates you want, and whether you choose a direct or a connecting flight. In other words, the initial low price you see advertised will be for a more modest hotel and an early-morning flight with a stopover, but once better digs and a nonstop flight catch your eye, the price ends up being a lot higher.

Clicking back and forth to view your options can get frustrating: The hotel you want may not be available for the dates you've chosen, so you either have to change your travel dates or pick a different hotel, and if you're comparing packages for various destinations or multiple travel dates, the research process can last longer than your actual vacation. But if you know exactly what you want, you may find the booking process less taxing.

Adding up the extras

With many packages, you can also opt for an all-inclusive deal, which means that all or most of your meals, and sometimes drinks, are included in the price. Think hard before you go for this option, especially if you don't drink much alcohol or are picky about what you eat. The one time I purchased a package, the resort's cuisine was pretty mediocre, so I was glad we didn't opt for the all-inclusive deal — the food was much better (and cheaper) in town. (For more about all-inclusive resorts, see sidebar on the facing page.)

Most companies that sell packages also offer other add-ons: airport transfers, excursions, event tickets, or tours. These options are often marked up from what you'd pay if you booked on your own, so compare prices before you throw in any scuba lessons or sightseeing around town. Prepaying for these extras also gives you less flexibility to make plans as you go and may lock you into an arrangement that turns out to be more of a hassle than other options you find when you arrive.

For instance, I did opt for airport transfers for the package I bought, but there was no one to meet us at the airport, so we waited twenty minutes for the shuttle company to show up and then had to pay an extra $5 for an air-conditioned ride. It would have been much quicker, and a little cheaper, to simply grab a cab once we landed.

Do you need protection?
Another option most packagers offer is some type of vacation protection plan, which allows you to cancel and get most of your money back — usually, what you paid for the package minus the cost of the plan and perhaps a $100 fee. This option is worth considering, since most vacation packages don't allow you to cancel your trip and get a refund or make any changes to your travel dates, whereas if you book all your travel reservations separately, you usually have more flexibility. But make sure that you're buying a plan that allows you to cancel for any reason, as opposed to more conventional travel insurance, which allows you to cancel only under certain circumstances (for more about travel insurance, see page 71).

The bottom line
So is it ever a good idea to buy a package? Sometimes, you can find a good deal, especially if you're not traveling on a holiday and plan

WHERE TO FIND VACATION PACKAGES

Travel agencies and airlines are the biggest sellers of vacation packages, but you can also find these deals through hotels, car rental agencies, last-minute discounters, and other companies that sell travel. Airlines tend to offer packages on the routes they fly the most, so you're more likely to find a deal on carriers that serve your home airport or the destination you have in mind — and don't overlook foreign airlines if you're thinking about a trip overseas. Although many companies offer on-line tools to help you create a package, pick up the phone when you're ready to book. It's often difficult to make changes once you book a package, so best to get some personal help before you commit.

TRAVEL AGENCIES THAT SELL PACKAGES

Expedia (expediavacations.com)
Hotwire (hotwire.com)
Orbitz (packages.orbitz.com)
Priceline (priceline.com)
LastMinute (lastminute.com)
Travelocity (travelocity.com)

AIRLINE PACKAGE SITES

Alaska (alaskaair.com)
American (aavacations.com)
Continental Airlines (covacations.com)
Delta (deltavacations.com)
Jet Blue (jetblue.com/getaways)
Northwest (nwaworldvacations.com)
Southwest (swavacations.com)
United (unitedvacations.com)
US Airways (usairwaysvacations.com)
Virgin Atlantic (virginvacations.com)

to spend your vacation in a major destination, like Cancun, Las Vegas, New York City, or Orlando. (See the sidebar above for more on finding vacation packages.)

But if you prefer small boutique hotels in less touristy destinations or are picky about what room you get or what airline you fly, you're probably better off booking everything à la carte.

Member Benefits: When a Discount Isn't a Deal

Everybody loves getting a discount — after all, a penny saved is a penny you can put toward another trip down the road — and the travel industry is a hotbed of these offers, dangling discounts to seniors, students, companies that have negotiated special rates, or members of clubs like AAA or Costco. In theory, these affiliations can save you money on a range of travel purchases — flights, hotel rooms, cruises, and car rentals — or even get you reduced admission fees at museums and national parks. But in practice, these types of discounts don't necessarily give you a better deal than the lowest price available, so if you're inclined to discount shop, here are a few things you should keep in mind.

Opportunities to use a discount may not be obvious

Travel sellers don't always go out of their way to ask whether you're eligible for any discounts, so it's up to you to figure out whether you qualify for a special rate. When booking over the phone, sometimes an agent will ask whether you have a corporate rate or AAA number — say, if you're booking a car rental or hotel — but don't count on getting this prompt. On the Web, it's not always clear where you should enter a discount code as you're shopping for rates, so if you can't find a place to enter one, call.

Discounts usually apply only to certain types of reservations

Just because you're sixty-seven years old, a student, or a AAA member doesn't mean that you'll get a discount on every travel purchase you make. Discounts are usually valid for only specific types of reservations, such as a midsize car rented for a week or a hotel room at a particular chain booked for a weekend. You may also have to make your reservation through a designated outlet in order to use some discounts — for example, by calling a special reservations number or booking with a student travel agency (see the sidebar on page 70 for discounts worth investigating).

DISCOUNTS WORTH INVESTIGATING

SENIOR AIR FARES

Although U.S. airlines have stopped selling the senior coupon books they used to offer, many carriers — including American, Continental, Northwest, Southwest, United, and US Airways — do have special senior fares for passengers sixty-five and older. A few of these airlines, and some travel agencies, offer a place on their Web sites where you can indicate that you're a senior when you search for fares (sometimes you have to choose "advanced search" or "more search options"); in other cases, you have to call. Senior fares are generally available only on certain routes or for flights booked at least fourteen days in advance, and carriers don't necessarily reveal which routes qualify or how much you can save. So compare the senior fare to the airline's lowest price; you may find that regular prices are cheaper.

AARP DISCOUNTS

Members of AARP — open to anyone age fifty or older — can get discounts on car rentals, cruises, hotels, and vacation packages, with varying levels of savings, depending on the company offering the deal. AARP's Web site (aarp.org) lists details and participating travel partners and recommends that members compare AARP discounts with other promotional rates.

AAA RATES

The Automobile Association of America (aaa.com) offers its members discounts on a range of travel purchases, including hotel reservations, cruises, and car rentals. These discounts are limited to specific travel companies that have partnered with AAA, and each regional club may offer its members different deals. Although these discounts aren't always better than current promotions or sales, AAA membership sometimes gets you other benefits, such as booking a hotel's nonrefundable rate without any restrictions on canceling or changing your reservation. You may also get a better room or a newer rental car by booking a AAA rate.

STUDENT DEALS

By booking through a student travel agency, such as STA Travel (statravel.com) or Student Universe (studentuniverse.com), backpackers and back-to-schoolers can take advantage of special fares these agencies have negotiated with various airlines. Who qualifies for these fares depends on what each airline stipulates: Some deals are available to all high school, college, and graduate students; others are more limited or have age requirements. (Teachers can even qualify for some educational discounts.) Student fares are available for domestic and international flights and often allow longer stays and have lower change fees, which means that you can fly to campus in September and come home for a visit in December on one ticket, without running into any maximum-stay requirements. Some agencies also offer student deals on one-way flights. The main drawback of student tickets is that they often don't earn frequent flier miles, and these special prices aren't available for all flights.

Discount prices aren't always the lowest price available

Internet travel booking has revealed a dirty little secret that wasn't so obvious when we were all making travel plans over the phone: Discount prices may be *higher* than the lowest price available to any customer booking that day. It's not so much that travel companies try to hide this fact as they don't always let you know about a cheaper price. So if you're booking over the phone, ask whether the discount price is the lowest price available; if you're shopping on line, do two searches: one with the discount code and one without. Discounts often can't be used in conjunction with a sale, so when you're reading the fine print of an offer, phrases like "not combinable with any other promotion" are a clue that you should compare the "discount" price to other promotions or sales.

Travel Insurance: What It Does and Doesn't Cover

One of the most confusing purchases travelers face is deciding whether to buy travel insurance, which basically reimburses you for some expenses if certain worst-case scenarios come to pass. Like a homeowner's policy or automobile insurance, travel policies tend to be written in small type with a lot of complex provisions that no one ever manages to slog through, leaving you with the nagging feeling that you don't really know what's covered. The difference is, auto and homeowner's insurance are often required by law or the bank that gave you a loan — so you generally just write the check and hope for the best — whereas travel insurance is optional, and the benefits aren't quite so obvious. Here's how to tell whether it's worth the investment.

Why get insurance?

People buy travel insurance mainly to protect their investment if they have to cancel a trip or to get medical coverage when they're traveling abroad. Once you're outside U.S. borders, most private health insurance companies and Medicare don't provide any coverage, even in an emergency — a fact travelers tend to learn about only after their claims from foreign hospitals are rejected (see page 219).

You can purchase three main types of policies: (1) package travel policies that offer multiple benefits, including coverage for trip cancellation, lost baggage, and emergency medical expenses; (2) policies that cover only emergency medical care, either for a single trip or multiple trips within a year; and (3) medical evacuation policies, which cover primarily the cost of transportation to a decent hospital if you're injured or get sick.

If you're considering buying travel insurance, it's important to understand that it covers only certain precisely defined circumstances or events — and there are a lot of exceptions lurking in the fine print. For instance, you can't simply decide that you don't feel like traveling and cancel a trip; you have to cancel for an approved reason in order to submit a claim. And you can't buy travel insurance in order to get a cheaper root canal overseas — these policies cover only emergency medical care.

Travelers often complain that insurance companies deny claims for reasons that weren't clear when they bought the policy, so be sure that you understand all the details before you sign on the dotted line. (See the sidebar on page 74 for an overview of what's generally covered.)

What it costs

Travel insurance is typically priced based on a combination of factors: your age, the amount of coverage you want, and the cost or

TRAVEL INSURANCE SELLERS

Here are some of the main travel insurance providers in the United States. All sell insurance direct, but you can also purchase their policies through third parties, such as InsureMyTrip.com.

Access America (accessamerica.com)
CSA Travel Protection (csatravelprotection.com)
International Medical Group (imglobal.com)
Medjet Assist (medjetassist.com)
Travel Guard (travelguard.com)
Travelex (travelex-insurance.com)

length of your trip. A general guideline is that package travel policies cost 4 percent to 7 percent of the trip's price (so about $200 to $350 to insure a $5,000 trip), whereas a travel medical policy for a single trip costs roughly $20 to $50 for $50,000 to $100,000 worth of coverage. You can also buy a standard medical evacuation policy for less than $50 per trip.

Where and when to buy

One of the best places to compare the benefits of various travel insurance policies is InsureMyTrip.com. If you enter your age, the cost of your trip, and your travel dates, you'll get quotes from more than a dozen providers, presented in a chart that describes what each policy covers, what's excluded, and the monetary limits on each benefit. You can buy a policy through InsureMyTrip.com or directly from the insurance company; either way, the price is the same. (See the sidebar above for a list of travel insurance providers.)

It's best to buy travel insurance within two or three weeks of paying for your trip, since some insurance companies will waive their exclusions for preexisting medical conditions if you buy within that time frame. Purchasing insurance before this deadline also protects you if your airline, cruise line, or tour operator goes out of business; otherwise, you don't get coverage for financial default.

TRAVEL INSURANCE, DEMYSTIFIED

Here's a breakdown of the coverage provided by most travel insurance policies. These are general guidelines, so read your policy's fine print to make sure that you understand its benefits. The details may vary from what's described here, as not all policies are alike, and insurers change their benefits from time to time.

PACKAGE TRAVEL POLICIES

Package travel policies generally cover a single trip and offer a number of benefits, primarily the ones described here. A package policy may also include some type of car rental coverage, flight insurance, or an accidental-death benefit, but those provisions are more likely to vary, depending on which policy you buy.

Trip cancellation: Allows you to cancel a trip and get most of your money back, up to whatever limit is outlined in the policy you purchased, but you can cancel only for reasons defined in the policy, which typically include

- Unforeseeable illness or injury, except those related to preexisting conditions, which are usually excluded

- Death of a family member (who counts as a family member is precisely defined)

- Strikes, natural disasters, or weather that disrupts services (for example, the airport at your destination is closed)

- You're called for jury duty or you lose your job

- Your airline, tour operator, or cruise line goes out of business (though most insurers have a list of companies they won't cover, such as any airline operating under bankruptcy protection, and often you have to buy the travel policy within a week or two of booking your trip in order to qualify for this coverage)

- Some acts of terrorism, as defined by the insurance company (acts of war generally aren't covered)

Trip interruption: Allows you to interrupt your trip and get some of your money back (depending on how many days you missed and how much insurance you purchased); also covers some additional expenses to return home early, such as fees to change your plane ticket. But you can interrupt your trip only for certain reasons — usually, the same ones defined in the trip cancellation coverage.

Baggage loss or delay: Reimburses you if your airline loses your luggage but only up to a defined limit (usually $1,000), and you have to try to collect from the airline first. Also offers some coverage for expenses like clothes and a new toothbrush if your bags are delayed but usually only $200 or $300.

Travel delay: Covers some expenses if you're delayed during a trip but only for specified reasons — for instance, if your flight is canceled because of a snowstorm or you lose your passport and have to delay your return until you get a replacement. Usually covers only defined expenses, such as meals and extra hotel nights but only up to the limit specified in the policy (typically, $500 to $1,000).

Travel-emergency assistance: Most insurance providers have round-the-clock hotlines that you can call if you need help finding a doctor, getting a lost passport replaced, or need other aid in a pinch.

Medical expenses: Covers emergency medical care and sometimes dental care up to whatever limit is defined in the policy (usually up to $1 million for medical and a few hundred dollars for dental). You often have to pay a deductible.

Emergency medical evacuation: Covers transportation and other expenses if you need to be evacuated to a medical facility for treatment, which is usually the nearest "appropriate" facility, not the hospital of your choice (check the fine print). Also typically covers the cost of getting you back home and a medical escort, if necessary, and repatriating your remains in the event of your death. Together, all these benefits have a maximum, which varies considerably, depending on the policy ($100,000 to $250,000 is a typical range).

TRAVEL MEDICAL POLICIES

If you want coverage only for emergency medical care overseas, you can buy a travel medical policy. This provides coverage for either a single trip (up to a year in length) or multiple trips within a year (the length of each trip can't exceed a defined maximum number of days). Most travel medical policies include evacuation coverage, too.

MEDICAL EVACUATION POLICIES

A medical evacuation policy covers your transportation costs to either the nearest appropriate facility or the hospital of your choice (policies that let you pick are generally more expensive). Some policies will pay for this benefit only if the evacuation is deemed "medically necessary" — and who makes that decision is clearly stipulated (it may not be up to you). Some evacuation policies are sold only as an annual plan, and many exclude injuries that result from high-risk activities like skydiving.

Bidding and Booking Blind: How You Can Save with Priceline or Hotwire

For those willing to trade certainty for savings, two companies have turned the booking process into something of a game. Both Priceline and Hotwire offer travelers the opportunity to save money by selling what's become known as "opaque" inventory. You don't find out exactly what you're buying until you've committed to the deal — but once you commit, you can't cancel or change your reservation.

For travel companies, working with Priceline and Hotwire is a way to fill up unsold hotel rooms, rental cars, and airplane seats without publishing rock-bottom prices that might train customers to wait for a sale. So these discounters tend to have better deals in a slow travel market — when companies have empty seats and beds.

Are these sites worth a gamble? If you're somewhat flexible with your itinerary (for flights, think early-morning departure and stopovers along the way), you can sometimes save a lot of money by booking through Priceline or Hotwire, especially on hotels. But using these sites can be a bit daunting for first-timers, so here's a cheat sheet if you're just getting into the game. (For tips on bidding, see the sidebar on page 78.)

Priceline: Name your own price

Priceline (priceline.com) pioneered "name your own price" bidding in 1998, and the process is still much the same: Travelers submit a bid indicating how much they're willing to pay to fly a certain route on specified dates (or rent a car or get a hotel room); Priceline then queries its partners to see if there are any takers at that price. If not, you can increase your bid, subject to certain rules; for example, you may have to wait a few days before bidding again.

For bidders, the gamble is that you don't find out which airline you'll be flying — or your flight times or how many connections you have to make — until *after* you submit a credit card number and commit to the deal. When bidding on hotels, you can specify your preferred neighborhood and the star rating that's acceptable (*Note:* Priceline's idea of a four-star hotel may not match yours —

see page 138), but the name of the hotel that accepted your offer is revealed only at the end. The same goes for car rentals.

Over time, it's become apparent that travelers aren't always willing to take a gamble on their vacation plans, so Priceline has added more traditional booking options for flights, car rentals, and hotels. The company also sells cruises and vacation packages in a conventional way, but "bidding blind" still gets you the cheapest prices.

Priceline's "name your own price" option is best for hotels, especially if you're not picky about where you stay, since the savings can be substantial compared to booking a published rate. You generally won't save as much by bidding on a car rental; with plane tickets, the savings really depend on the route you choose and whether a discount carrier offers a cheap fare for that flight.

Hotwire: Blind but no bids

Hotwire is another site that specializes in blind, or "opaque," booking, but it works somewhat differently from Priceline. For its most deeply discounted air fares, Hotwire lets users enter their travel dates, departure airport, and destination. It then displays the lowest price it has available for that route — without displaying exact flight times, the number of stopovers involved, or the name of the carrier (though in some cases, you get to see approximately when the flight departs: for example, between 6:00 A.M. and 11:00 A.M.).

You can book a hotel room or a car rental through Hotwire more or less the same way: You enter details about your travel itinerary, and Hotwire displays a price, but you don't find out the name of the hotel or the car rental company until after you book.

Because Hotwire doesn't involve a complicated bidding process, it's often worth a quick stop during your research to see whether the site offers an enticing price (mostly for domestic travel). Its deepest discounts are for hotels, and the best deals are available outside peak travel times, which is when hotels, car rental companies, and airlines give Hotwire more inventory to sell.

But read all the terms of your reservation before you book, and compare prices to those you can find elsewhere. The savings at these sites aren't always worth the sacrifices you have to make, and if the travel industry is booming, really good deals are scarce.

TRAVEL BIDDING TIPS

If you're looking to improve your bidding skills, check out BiddingFor
Travel.com, an on-line community that's become an unofficial Priceline
users' guide. Through the site's message boards, regular bidders trade advice and strategies, including posting successful bids to tip off other travelers about how much it takes to get an offer accepted. Here are some basic
bidding tips if you're thinking about rolling the dice.

- *Like bets at the blackjack table, all bids are final.* One of the main drawbacks
  of booking through Priceline or Hotwire is that you can't change or cancel
  your reservation once you hand over your credit card. So if you're saving
  only $30 on a car rental or $50 on a hotel, it's probably not worth giving up
  the flexibility to change your mind. If your flight is canceled and/or your
  meeting time changes, you won't get a refund if you pick up your car or
  check in to your hotel a day late.

- *Start by checking the going rate.* To figure out what to bid, first check other
  travel sites to get the going rate for the hotel, car rental, or flight you want;
  then bid some percentage of that price. Try starting at 50 percent to 75
  percent of the market rate, but if it's a peak travel time or the industry is
  booming, don't expect a low-ball offer to fly.

- *You can't always get what you want.* One disadvantage of booking on an
  opaque site is that you can't specify all your preferences; so for instance,
  there's no guarantee that you'll get two double beds instead of one king.
  As soon as you know which hotel accepted your offer, you can always call
  and request a change, but there are no guarantees that it will accommodate your request, so don't book through Priceline if you're traveling with
  someone you don't want to snuggle up against. Also, anytime you book
  through a third party, it's a good idea to confirm that the hotel has a record of your reservation, since hotel reservation systems often rely on an-
  tiquated technology: the fax machine.

- *Past performance is no guarantee of future results.* Just because someone
  posted a successful bid on BiddingForTravel.com or you got a great deal
  yourself a year ago, you cannot count on Priceline to accept that bid today.
  When occupancy rates are high, hotels are less likely to sell rooms at a
  deep discount. Hotels are also less likely to accept bids with a Saturday
  check-in, holding out for a guest who wants to stay the whole weekend.

- *Make a backup reservation you can cancel.* If you're bidding on a car rental
  or a hotel room, it's a good idea to make a backup reservation somewhere
  else that you can cancel without paying a penalty. That way, if you don't

have any luck with Priceline (some people keep bidding down to the wire), you'll have an option you can fall back on.

- *Don't expect first-class service for discount prices.* One complaint about booking through discounters like Priceline or Hotwire is that some hotels, airlines, or car rental companies treat the discounters' customers less favorably than travelers who pay the market rate. Some travel companies write this off as an urban legend, but I've heard too many stories about travelers getting the "Priceline treatment" to dismiss them entirely. And really, if you ran a hotel, which guest would you give the room with the best view: someone who booked a heavily discounted rate or someone who paid full price? You shouldn't have to sleep in a wing of the hotel that's under construction just because you paid a lower rate, but don't expect any special favors.

Help for Last-Minute Planners:
Options at the Eleventh Hour

Back when travel was more of a rare indulgence, planning a trip generally involved at least one luxury: time. Travelers spent weeks if not months poring over colorful travel brochures, and some people claimed that looking forward to a vacation was half the fun. But these days, it's not unusual to jet off to a distant destination weeks or even days after getting the urge to flee, leaving little time to dream about the trip in advance.

Travel sellers have responded to the increase in last-minute bookings with special deals crafted for customers willing to pack a bag at a moment's notice, and there are even companies that specialize in this market. With names like Go-Today.com and Last MinuteTravel.com, these companies make it clear that they're not marketing to early birds, though some do also book travel further ahead of time.

To get the best deals on a last-minute getaway, it helps to be flexible about where you're going. Travel companies offer special prices based on where they have empty hotel rooms or unsold seats on planes, which may not coincide with your destination of choice. But if you have an open mind, you can often find a bargain, even booking down to the wire.

Here's how to find packages, flights, cruises, and hotel rooms if you're making plans at the last minute, whether you're taking a spur-of-the-moment vacation or suddenly have to hop on a plane.

Packages

Last-minute specialists, like LastMinute.com, 11thhourvacations.com, Go-Today.com, and LastMinuteTravel.com, offer packages mostly for travel within the next two weeks — usually, some combination of a flight, hotel, and car rental. A few of these companies also sell cruises or airline tickets on an à la carte basis, but some variation on a package is more the norm — often, priced based on two people traveling, but you can still find good deals if you're going solo.

Typically, last-minute packages are for travel to major cities in the United States: Boston, Las Vegas, New York, San Francisco, or Washington, D.C. Options for travel abroad tend to be to nearby destinations in Canada, the Caribbean, Europe, or Mexico, though sometimes you can find late-breaking deals farther away, should you suddenly have a hankering to visit Shanghai. But before you book a last-minute trip abroad, make sure that your passport isn't about to expire and that you can get any visas or vaccinations you need on short notice (see chapter 8 for advice).

Even if you need only a flight or a hotel, it's worth checking prices for a package, which may be cheaper than a flight or a hotel room alone. That's because when you buy a package, you see only the total cost, which allows travel companies to discount their products below the lowest published price. So if you suddenly have to fly to Chicago to visit your parents, you may find it cheaper to buy a package that includes a car rental rather than to purchase a plane ticket at the lowest published fare — and you won't have to ask to borrow your dad's car.

Flights

One way to find out about last-minute deals on flights is to sign up for the weekly e-mail newsletters most airlines offer. These e-mails, usually sent out midweek, typically list special fares for travel the following weekend or within the next two weeks — generally for

WHAT ABOUT BEREAVEMENT FARES?

Although many airlines still offer bereavement fares — special prices for travelers who need to fly somewhere for a funeral or to visit a seriously ill relative — often you can get a cheaper last-minute ticket by shopping around. That's because prices have dropped quite a bit for walk-up fares, and the carriers that do offer bereavement tickets don't necessarily price them below their lowest published fares.

It's still worth calling a few airlines to see what price they quote for a bereavement fare (you have to book these tickets over the phone, but Delta and most low-fare carriers don't offer them). One advantage of bereavement fares is that you can usually change the return date without penalty and sometimes even leave the return date open when you book your outbound flight.

Airlines that offer bereavement fares typically list which relatives qualify as "immediate family members" on their Web sites, but most cast a pretty wide net, including aunts, uncles, nieces, nephews, in-laws, step-parents, stepchildren, and domestic partners, in addition to a child, spouse, sibling, parent, or grandparent. You'll need to provide contact information for a funeral home or a hospital to purchase one of these fares — and yes, the airlines do call to check.

flights departing Friday or Saturday and returning Sunday, Monday, or Tuesday. The discounted fares are for specific destinations, both domestic and international, and there are usually more options departing from an airline's hub airports — for instance, from Dallas on American or Detroit on Northwest.

If you don't want to be inundated with half a dozen airline e-mails each week, you can also look for these deals on the airlines' Web sites when a weekend getaway is on your mind. And don't overlook foreign carriers, which sometimes offer special deals from U.S. gateways to their home countries (so if London is calling your name, check British Airways and Virgin Atlantic for specials).

Another option is to sign up for a weekly e-mail from Smarter Travel (smartertravel.com), a service that tracks all the specials most airlines announce each week and sends them in one message to subscribers. You can even designate which airports you live near, so you'll get only deals that depart from those hubs. If you don't want to get an e-mail every week, you can look for these specials on SmarterTravel's Web site, where you'll also find advice on airfare sales, frequent flier programs, and senior travel.

Another service, Travelzoo, offers a weekly e-mail you can subscribe to that lists twenty top deals on vacation packages, cruises, flights, car rentals, and hotels. Although these aren't all last-minute specials, they're often for travel within the next couple of months. Travel companies pay a fee to be included in this newsletter, so it's really a collection of advertisements, but if you don't mind getting another e-mail every week, one of these specials may catch your eye. Travelzoo also lists last-minute deals on their Web site, travelzoo .com. (For information on bereavement fares, see the sidebar on page 81.)

Hotels

If you're looking for a hotel at the last minute, discounters like Hotwire and Priceline are good sources to try (see the sidebar on page 78 for advice on using these sites). But one thing to keep in mind when you're booking really late — two or three days before your trip — is that some hotels stop taking reservations through other channels the closer it gets to your arrival date, so you should definitely call direct if you have a particular hotel in mind. And when it seems that there's no room at *any* inn you call, check with the local chamber of commerce or visitor's bureau; these agencies often know which hotels or inns still have rooms available when "no vacancy" signs are all over town.

Cruises

If you live within driving distance of a major port, cruises are an attractive last-minute vacation option, since cruise lines typically offer deep discounts a few weeks before departure to make sure that the ship doesn't sail with any empty cabins. The downside of booking at the last minute is that you may not get a cabin with an ocean view or a balcony, and if you don't live near a port, flying to get there on short notice can wipe out any savings you're getting on the cruise itself. Most agencies that sell cruises offer some last-minute bargains (see page 177 for a list of cruise discounters). You can also check SoldOutShips.com, a site that lists cabins travel agents have for sale on ships a cruise line considers "sold out." (These agencies still have space to sell because they purchased blocks of cabins themselves.)

Using a Travel Agent: What an Agent Can Do for You — And Where to Find One

OK, so the whole idea of this book is to help you navigate the do-it-yourself era of travel. And for most trips, when you're simply buying plane tickets, booking a hotel room, and reserving a rental car, there's really no reason not to make your plans on your own. In fact, travel agents no longer earn commissions on those types of reservations, so unless you've been a client for a long time, you'd probably have a tough time finding an agent willing to help you.

But travel agents haven't gone the way of T-Rex and the pterodactyls. Although their ranks have thinned in recent years, lots of agents are still booking leisure travel, and sometimes it's worth at least investigating what an agent can do for you.

The new *specialized* agent
Ever since the airlines stopped paying commissions to travel agents, the most resourceful ones have survived by shifting their focus to bookings that still pay a commission, such as cruises or tours, or by specializing in planning trips that travelers can't easily arrange on their own, like a honeymoon in an exotic destination, a family reunion for thirty people, or a postretirement trip around the world.

Many agents have reinvented themselves as "travel specialists," developing expertise in a particular region, activity, or even demographic (say, families or those honeymooners), and the best ones have cultivated contacts throughout the industry, so they can tell you which safari operator in Botswana has the best guides or where to rent a sailboat in the Caribbean — with or without a captain. Sometimes these agents can even pull strings to get you a room with a view, a private winery tour, or a reservation at a hotel that's supposedly booked solid.

So if you're planning a trip to celebrate a special occasion, spending a lot of money, or going to a place where the travel infrastructure isn't quite so developed, you may find that it's worth paying an agent for the benefit of his or her expertise and connections, which may save you from spending thousands of dollars on a trip that turns out to be a disappointment.

Talking money
Of course, travel agents don't offer their services for free, so you should expect to pay some kind of fee for an agent's help. How much varies pretty widely, depending on the trip you're planning and whether the agent earns a commission on the services you decide to book.

For instance, if you're booking a cruise, the agent typically earns a commission from the cruise line, so you may not have to pay anything extra or only a small fee (less than $40). If you manage to find a travel agent willing to make a flight reservation for you, expect to pay about $35 per ticket, maybe more if you're booking a complicated ticket with three stopovers.

For help planning an entirely customized trip, the going rate is anywhere from $100 to $400, though some top agents who cater to wealthy clients may charge quite a bit more. Negotiate this fee up front, so you aren't surprised by the final bill (see the sidebar on page 86 for advice on working with an agent).

Where did all those agents go?
With so many travel agents closing shop in recent years, you'd think that the ones still doing business would be clamoring for clients. But actually, it's not that easy to find a good agent when you decide that you could use some help.

There's been a lot of consolidation in the industry, so some agents work for large companies that have bought up struggling mom-and-pop shops, like Liberty Travel, which operates mainly on the East coast, whereas others work for agencies that are part of a consortium, like Virtuoso, a network of more than 250 travel agencies that focus on the luxury leisure market. Some agencies still have storefront locations, but others do business only on line or over the phone; in fact, a growing trend is for agents to work at home.

One way to find an agent is through associations like the American Society of Travel Agents (astanet.com) or the Association of Retail Travel Agents (artaonline.com). On its Web site, ASTA offers a tool that lets you search for an agent by specialty or zip code, but with more than 20,000 members in its database, many listing dozens of specialties, that's not necessarily the best way to find a true specialist — kind of like choosing a doctor at random from your health insurer's network. But you may get lucky and find someone you like.

Other sources for referrals

Asking for recommendations from friends and colleagues is always a good bet, but if that's a dead end, you can also check with the tourist office of the country you're visiting (see page 19). Many of these organizations keep lists of travel agents who specialize in the region, but their knowledge about the country may vary quite a bit. In other words, one agent might have visited the country a dozen times and knows all the hole-in-the-wall restaurants and the managers of the best hotels, whereas another agent may have been there once and still has all the brochures the tourist board handed out.

To find the real pros in the business, another strategy is to check out the lists of top travel specialists published annually in magazines like *Condé Nast Traveler* (which usually publishes its list in August) and *Travel + Leisure* (which generally publishes its list in September). Although many of the agents on these lists focus on the high-end market, they're a good resource to turn to when you're planning a real blow-out trip or have some extra money to spend. Some of these agents openly admit that they don't accept clients working below a certain budget, so don't bother calling a Tiffany agent if you're traveling on a Target bank account.

TIPS: WORKING WITH A TRAVEL AGENT

If you haven't used a travel agent in a while, you may feel like you're reentering the dating pool after a long hiatus. The agent/client relationship has changed while most of us were hunched over our computers making our own travel plans, so here are some tips on what to ask — and expect — if you're considering reaching out for help.

- *Be clear about your budget and plans.* Be prepared to tell your agent in some detail where you want to go, what you'd like to do, and how much you can afford to spend. That way, the agent won't waste time checking availability at five-star hotels if that's not in your budget or researching a camel trek if you can't stand the desert. And make sure that you and your traveling companions agree on an itinerary before you ask an agent to find you those camels.

- *Discuss what — and how — the agent charges.* If an agent isn't forthcoming about fees, don't be shy about asking. Since agents earn commissions from travel suppliers on some bookings, the fee you pay may depend on what reservations you ultimately book; for some trips, an agent may not charge you a fee at all. Also, ask whether the agent plans to give you an itemized list of costs for your trip or simply a total bill. If the total-price approach doesn't sit well with you, say so.

- *Ask about the agent's background.* You're paying your travel agent for help planning your trip, so you should know what value you're getting in return. Some agencies have "preferred" relationships with certain travel companies, which means that their clients may get free upgrades or first shot at special deals, but it can also mean that an agent steers you toward cruise lines or tour operators that pay a higher commission. If you feel like you're getting a hard sell, ask why the agent is recommending a particular company. As for some of the affiliations travel agents tout — like a Certified Travel Counselor (CTC) designation or some kind of "destination specialist" credential — take those with a grain of salt. Sometimes, those certificates don't beat the real expertise someone can get simply by visiting a place over and over. Follow your instincts: If you seem to know more about a destination than your travel agent does, you probably don't need to work with one.

- *Don't expect special favors the first time you call.* One of the advantages of working with an agent is benefiting from his or her connections, but don't expect an agent to work miracles the first time you call. If you call on December 1 hoping to get a reservation for the holidays at a hotel that's booked solid, you'd better have been referred by one of the agent's best clients.

- *Find out whom you can reach after hours.* Another reason to work with a travel agent is having someone to turn to if something goes wrong. But if the agency is open only 9 A.M. to 5 P.M. on weekdays and doesn't answer calls after hours, you'll be left high and dry if the hotel you thought you had booked has no record of your reservation or if you get stuck at the airport on a Sunday night. Make sure that you can reach someone after hours in case you have a real emergency, but don't call simply to complain about the scratchy towels at your hotel.

4 Plane Tickets

IT'S NO SURPRISE that most of us approach buying a plane ticket with an attitude that's the flip side of the saying "You get what you pay for." We know what kind of service we're going to get, so that's all we're willing to pay.

Although prices for airline tickets have fallen quite a bit in recent years — partly because the Internet has made comparison shopping so much easier — do-it-yourself booking isn't without its own headaches. With dozens of travel companies all promising the best deals, it's difficult to know where to search or what to do differently to find the best fare — or when to simply click the buy button and call it a day. And if you have to purchase a more complicated ticket, solve a problem, or change your plans, travel Web sites don't always offer much support.

This chapter aims to help fill the void, with tips on how and where to search for fares and advice on booking specific types of tickets: one-way trips, international flights, and frequent flier awards. (Yes, there are ways to use all those miles you've earned.) This chapter also explains what to watch out for when you're buying a plane ticket, namely, expensive change penalties, service fees, and other rules the airlines don't make particularly clear — that is, until you break them.

But even armed with all the tricks of the trade, keep in mind that there are times when you're just not going to find a rock-bottom fare or be able to book the sale price you saw advertised (chalk that up to bait-and-switch tactics, rampant in an industry that advertises prices *"from* $29" or *"starting at* $59"). In other words, it's not you or where you're shopping or how you're searching; sometimes, it's simply not out there for you to find.

Where to Research Fares: No One
Web Site Displays Them All

On the one hand, searching for airfares is remarkably easy these days: Launch your browser and type a couple of airport codes and your travel dates, and within minutes, you can see your options on multiple airlines. But spend a little more time clicking around, and inevitably, the search process gets more frustrating.

Trying to find a sale fare you saw advertised is like a game of Where's Waldo — only it's not clear that the low price you saw is anywhere to be found. If you walk away from your computer or jump to another Web page midsearch, you get weird error messages saying things like "your results have expired." And even if you're willing to be flexible — say, flying from *any* airport near New York City to *any* airport near Los Angeles during *any* weekend in August — some sites can't handle such an open-ended search.

But the biggest limitation of fare-comparison sites is that *no single Web site shows you all your options*. Sure, some travel sites display dozens of flights for whatever itinerary you choose but still don't include every airline that flies that route or every flight combination you could buy. So to find the best fares or the most convenient flight times, you have to repeat your search at multiple Web sites and know how to take advantage of the various features each site offers.

Of course, you may not want to go to all that trouble if you find a decent fare at the first site you search, but if you want to cover your bases, here's an overview of your main options. Keep in mind that the best place to search for fares may not be where you end up buying your ticket — a thorny topic covered later in this chapter.

On-line travel agencies

Expedia, Orbitz, and Travelocity are the pioneers of Internet travel booking, and they're often the first stop for travelers searching for fares. All three agencies keep adding features to their Web sites to make searching easier, including options that let you input a range of travel dates, include more than one airport in your search, or choose your outbound and return flights separately (rather than selecting from the combinations offered). For the most part, the big-three agencies offer similar tools — when one site introduces a new feature, the others tend to follow. But the agencies don't always turn up the same fares for the same search, so if you've got time to kill at your keyboard, try more than one.

There are also a few agencies that specialize in discount tickets. CheapTickets, Hotwire, and Priceline sell a mix of published and unpublished fares, and the latter may be lower than the prices you'll find at other sites. But with unpublished fares, you often don't find out which airline you're flying or your flight times until after you hand over your credit card — and you may end up with flights that are at inconvenient times or that require extra stopovers. But if you're willing to accept these trade-offs, you may find a bargain. (For more about booking with Priceline or Hotwire, see page 76.)

Best bets: The big-three on-line travel agencies: Expedia (expedia .com), Orbitz (orbitz.com), and Travelocity (travelocity.com).

Other options: Discount agencies, such as CheapTickets (cheap tickets.com), Hotwire (hotwire.com), and Priceline (priceline.com).

Best for: When you have no idea which airlines serve your destination or you want to get a quick price comparison. With the discounters, it helps if you're flexible about which airline you fly — and what time you have to wake up to get to the airport.

Drawbacks: On-line travel agencies lead you to believe that you're seeing all the available options but don't show prices from every airline — like JetBlue or Southwest — or even all the flights offered by the carriers they do have permission to include. The agencies have also gotten very aggressive about marketing add-ons like a hotel, car rental, airport transfers, or a city tour. For some people, this "You want fries with that?" approach can be a turn-off.

Airline Web sites

For a long time, the airlines were playing catch-up with the big-three on-line agencies, but the race to build a better Web site has started to even out. Now, many carriers offer tools that rival or even surpass what the agencies offer, like the ability to view aircraft seat maps, search for various fare types — for example, a business-class fare without restrictions — or use a travel credit or voucher when you buy your ticket. And because some airlines don't work with the on-line travel agencies, you'll have to visit the airlines' Web sites if you want to see their fares.

Best bets: Among domestic carriers, the ones with the most robust Web sites are Alaska (alaskaair.com), American (aa.com), Continental (continental.com), Delta (delta.com), JetBlue (jetblue .com), Northwest (nwa.com), Southwest (southwest.com), United (united.com), and US Airways (usairways.com).

Other options: Other domestic airlines, mostly discounters, include AirTran (airtran.com), ATA (ata.com), Frontier (frontier airlines.com), Midwest (midwest airlines.com), Spirit (spiritair .com), and Virgin America (virginamerica.com); visit their Web sites to see where they fly. To find foreign carriers, try airlinecontact.info; if you choose a country, you get a list of national carriers and links to their Web sites.

Best for: When you know which airline you're likely to fly, either because service to your destination is limited or you're loyal to a particular airline. It's also your best option if you want to find flights on JetBlue or Southwest, whose fares generally don't show up on all the other travel sites. (See the sidebar on page 92 for more details about these two carriers.) And an airline's Web site may show more of its own flight combinations for the route you choose than you'll see at an agency site.

Drawbacks: It could take hours to search every airline's Web site, reentering your travel dates each time. So if you want to compare fares, start your search with a site that displays prices from multiple airlines.

Travel search engines

More recently, a new category of travel Web sites has entered the fray: sites that let you compare prices for flights (and in some cases, hotels or car rentals) but don't handle booking — you have to buy your ticket from a travel agency or the airline. Some of these companies offer more powerful search tools than you'll find at other travel sites, especially when it comes to sorting and filtering a long list of results.

The most comprehensive search engine — and my favorite — is

WHAT ABOUT JETBLUE AND SOUTHWEST?

With so many options showing up at fare-comparison sites, you may not even notice what's missing from the list — flights on Southwest. The airline doesn't share its fares with Expedia, Orbitz, or Travelocity, so if those are the only sites you search, you may be missing out on a much cheaper flight.

If you're not already a fan of the low-fare airline that turned the industry on its head, Southwest isn't just about the south or the west anymore; its planes fly all over the United States. To see exactly where, go to south west.com and click on the route map link. If you roll your mouse over a city, up pops a spiderweb of lines indicating where Southwest flies from that airport; you can even choose to see only nonstop flights.

JetBlue, the other success story of the low-fare landscape, does let some of the travel search engines display its fares (though executives say that's an experiment subject to change). But to see exactly where you can fly on JetBlue — and have your own TV screen at your seat — go to jetblue.com and click "our cities." That will take you to a graphic route map with a similar web of lines linking the cities JetBlue serves, including destinations in the Bahamas, the Dominican Republic, and Puerto Rico.

Besides lower fares, JetBlue and Southwest offer more flexible change policies and sell all their tickets based on one-way fares, so they're especially worth checking if your plans are likely to change or you need a one-way flight.

ITA Software (itasoftware.com), a technology company that makes the software used by many other travel agencies and airlines. It's not trying to build a consumer brand, so you have to hunt around its home page for the link to its flight-search tool, and some of the fares it turns up involve flights on multiple airlines. That means you have to find a travel agent to sell you the ticket or pick a fare you can buy directly from the carrier.

Although travel search engines sometimes offer hundreds of options, they still don't include prices from every airline or travel agency (which may not give permission to show their fares). So don't expect the "one-stop shopping experience" many of these sites advertise.

Best bets: ITA Software (itasoftware.com), Kayak (kayak.com), SideStep (sidestep.com), and Yahoo! FareChase (farechase.yahoo .com) display more options than most travel agencies and generally offer better tools to filter your results. You can narrow down a long list of results by eliminating certain airports or airlines, flights with too many connections, or options that are out of your price range.

Other options: Sites such as Cheapflights (cheapflights.com), Mobissimo (mobissimo.com), and Qixo (qixo.com) aren't nearly as comprehensive or easy to use but may get better over time.

Best for: Seeing most of the flight combinations available for the route you choose. These sites are particularly useful when you're searching for a one-way or multicity ticket or want to see a wide range of flight times.

Drawbacks: The number of flights these sites display can be overwhelming, and some of the itineraries they offer are difficult to recreate when you go to buy your ticket from an agency or an airline. These sites also don't show prices from every carrier that flies the route you search, since some airlines — like Southwest — don't share their fares with the search engines.

Search Tips for Plane Tickets: It's Not Just Where You Look, but How

You can go to great lengths to check air fares at a dozen Web sites, taxing your clicking finger and making your head spin with flight times and prices, but an exhaustive search isn't all it takes to find the best deal. Sometimes, when and how you search for prices is just as important as where you look.

When to buy

In most cases, the earlier you buy your plane ticket, the less you're going to pay. A basic rule of thumb is that it's best to buy your airfare at least three weeks before your flight, since the lowest fares often have a twenty-one-day advance-purchase requirement. Of course, that still may not be early enough to snap up the cheapest fares, which can sell out much sooner — especially on flights to a popular destination, on a route with limited service, or at peak travel times (for example, if your boss won't let you leave until after 5 P.M. on the Wednesday before Thanksgiving).

What about booking *really* far in advance: six months or more?

The main risk is that your plans could change and you'd be stuck paying hefty penalties to rebook. Another drawback is that you may miss a sale that comes up later. For holiday travel, some people take that chance (most airlines let you book up to 335 days in advance). But for off-peak travel, you might as well wait.

Catching a sale

Typically, fares go on sale after peak travel times: early fall, the beginning of the year, and after spring break — basically, when everyone is back home again and the airlines want to stimulate travel. Most airlines aren't shy about advertising sales, buying full-page ads in major newspapers and promos on the radio and TV. But if your iPod and TiVo have taken you out of the media mainstream, sign up for some of the e-mail newsletters that track these deals. Most airlines, and many travel agencies, send out weekly e-mail newsletters that include news about last-minute fares and other sales. And if you're thinking about a trip abroad, don't overlook the foreign carriers that serve whatever destination you have in mind.

If you don't want to get several messages from multiple airlines every week, SmarterTravel.com publishes an e-mail newsletter that tracks deals on most domestic and some international carriers (you can even opt to get news only about sale fares departing from nearby airports). Other options are the Orbitz DealDetector service, which watches a particular route for you and lets you know if it goes on sale, or Travelocity's FareWatcher feature, which tracks prices on up to five routes that you select. And Southwest lets you download an application called DING! that will alert you about special sales.

With all these promotional fares, there's one caveat you've probably noticed if you've ever tried to take advantage of a sale: Airlines typically advertise an incredibly low price that applies only to a couple of less-traveled routes or a limited number of travel days, but prices are often much higher for more popular flights. For instance, I recently clicked a link in an e-mail newsletter advertising "one-way flights from $34 . . . coast-to-coast bargains." Well, that $34 price was to fly from Louisville to Washington, D.C. (not exactly coast to coast), and nearly all the other sale fares on the list were $84 to $104 each way — not including taxes and fees. So be prepared for some slippery advertising tactics from the airlines and the travel agencies that promote these sales.

Tweaking your search

Knowing certain search tricks can also increase your chances of finding a low fare, so if the prices you first turn up don't exactly make you lunge for your wallet, here are some strategies you can try to find a better deal. And remember: Most travel sites show only a fraction of the flight combinations available for any route, so each time you change the parameters of your search, you're likely to produce a whole different list of results.

- *Check nearby airports.* You can often save money by flying into an alternate airport near your destination: Oakland instead of San Francisco, Long Beach instead of Los Angeles, or Chicago Midway instead of O'Hare. The reason is that many low-fare carriers built their businesses flying to these alternate airports, and their older competitors tend to match the lower fares on these routes. But this secret has been out of the bag for a while, so the price differences aren't as big as they once were. Also, some sites don't offer a way to search multiple airports at once, so you may have to try a different site or do several searches, using different airport codes each time.
- *Look for flights on off-peak days.* You're more likely to find low fares if you can fly on a Tuesday or a Wednesday (and sometimes Thursday or Saturday), since these tend to be lighter travel days. It's generally more expensive to fly on a Monday, Friday, or Sunday, because that's when business travelers typically take to the skies.
- *Try different departure and return dates.* You may find a much lower fare simply by shifting your departure or return date by a day or two — or more, if you have that flexibility. Some travel sites let you specify a range of dates when you search or even look for the best-available fare during upcoming months, so try moving around the calendar until you find a lower price.
- *Don't be picky about flight times.* If you limit your search to a certain time of day — say, a morning departure — you may miss

seeing a lower fare for a flight that leaves in the afternoon. Generally, the cheapest tickets are available at times most people don't want to fly: the first or last flights of the day. So if a travel site gives you the option to select a time-of-day preference when you enter your search, skip it or pick "anytime."

- *Consider a connection.* If you search for only nonstop flights, you may end up paying more than if you consider flights that require a change of planes. The savings may not be worth the hassle of making (or possibly missing) a connection, but if you're on a budget, keep an open mind.

Choosing a Flight: Why Price Shouldn't Be Your Only Concern

Once you've compared airfares at a few Web sites and have an overview of what's available, you'll probably find that several airlines charge roughly the same price for the ticket you want — say, within a $50 price range. And even if you have only a couple of carriers to choose from, you'll at least have a selection of flights.

Chances are, you're not automatically going to pick the least expensive one, especially if it leaves at 6:00 A.M. or means traveling overnight. Besides departure and arrival times, here are some other factors to consider as you weigh your options.

Connection times — and places

If you have to make a connection — or are willing to accept a stopover to save money — you may have a few choices about where you change planes. Try to avoid cities that are plagued by bad weather and airports that are prone to delays (on both counts, Chicago's O'Hare Airport is one to pass up). But if you can't avoid a congested airport or you're traveling at a three-year-old's pace, try to book a longer layover. You can't always find options on line that give you more than forty-five minutes between planes (my pet peeve), so if not, call the airline and ask the agent to book a connection that gives you more time. I do this often, though sometimes you have to stand your ground when an agent insists that forty-three minutes is *plenty* of time to change planes.

Some international carriers close the door to the plane as early as an hour before it pulls away from the gate, so build in extra time if you're connecting to a foreign airline, in the United States or overseas. And anytime you have to change planes, try to avoid booking the last flight of the day. If you miss your connection, chances are you'll be spending the night at the airport or paying for a hotel yourself, since the airlines rarely give out hotel vouchers (see page 263 for more about flight delays).

On-time performance

Like the friend who always arrives late, some flights are notorious for departing behind schedule. The Department of Transportation requires airlines to tell you a flight's on-time record if you ask, and some carriers include this percentage with the flight details when you search for fares on line. Only about 75 percent of flights arrive on time, but certain flights have a far worse track record, so if you can't avoid booking a real laggard, don't plan anything important after you land — unless you're meeting that tardy friend.

Airport transportation

Many cities have multiple airports nearby, one of which may be closer, more convenient, or easier to get to using public transportation. So factor transit costs into your math when you compare ticket prices; there's no point saving $30 on airfare if it means spending twice that amount on a taxi — each way. Airport Web sites usually list transportation options, including schedules and prices. (For a list of airports that are well connected to nearby cities via subway or train, see page 239.)

Type of aircraft

With more airlines relying on smaller planes these days, you can't assume that you'll be flying on a large aircraft, even for longer flights. The smaller the plane, the more you'll feel every dip, turn, bump, and gust of wind, so if you're a nervous flyer, opt for a ride in a bigger plane. Most airline sites (and many travel agencies) list the aircraft type when you search for flights, but if you don't know a 747 from a DC-9, visit Seatguru.com. This helpful Web site not only shows layouts for most of the planes the major carriers fly but also offers insider tips about each aircraft's seating arrangements. Move your mouse over a graphic that shows the aircraft's layout, and you'll see notes explaining which seats have more legroom, are close to power outlets, or are farthest from noisy engines — as well as which ones have smaller armrests, no overhead storage, don't recline at all, or convert to comfy beds. Flatseats.com is another source for feedback about the sleeping amenities on various airlines.

On-board services

Lately, it's not so much a matter of which amenities an airline offers as which ones it hasn't taken away. Meals, magazines, movies, and even blankets and pillows have gone the way of the dinosaurs on many carriers, leaving not much left to compare besides the few on-board entertainment services that still exist. On that note, JetBlue sets the standard among domestic carriers, with individual TV screens at every seat and several dozen channels to choose from (Virgin America and Frontier also offer live TV). These and other carriers are also experimenting with movies on demand, audio programming, and games — though except for a few foreign carriers, there hasn't been much progress on offering Internet access in the air. If you're flying an airline that still serves food and want a preview of your meal, check out Airlinemeals.net, which posts photos and reviews of airline food, submitted by passengers who snapped a shot of their breakfast, lunch, or dinner tray and sent it in.

Penalties and perks

If collecting frequent flier miles is still a priority for you, keep in mind that airline alliances have made it possible to buy a ticket on one carrier — say, Continental — and earn miles for the flight from one of its partners — in Continental's case, Delta or Northwest. So if you're buying a ticket on a carrier you don't usually fly, check its partners; you may be able to earn miles on a carrier you do fly instead (see page 117 for more about airline alliances). Other factors to consider are the airline's policies about making ticket changes, flying standby, or upgrading — all discussed in other sections of this book. Sometimes, it's worth paying a little more for a ticket on a carrier that gives you more flexibility or better perks.

Where to Buy: Agencies versus Airlines; the Web versus the Phone

The Web site you like best to search for fares isn't necessarily the best place to purchase your ticket, which is why a growing number of travelers compare prices at an on-line travel agency, then click over to the airline's Web site when they're ready to buy.

This is potentially a problem for the travel industry — not to mention travelers — because Expedia, Orbitz, and Travelocity aren't going to be around much longer if customers continue to abandon them before clicking the buy button, and then where would we all go to compare fares? (Travel search engines may not fill the void.)

Yet on-line travel agencies aren't really doing much to make a compelling case for customers to stick around — in fact, they're adding penalties and service fees that make it difficult to recommend buying from them, while the airlines are making it more attractive to shop direct.

That doesn't mean that you should never buy a ticket from a travel agency. You might like the convenience of booking your entire trip through one agency, or you may find a good deal you can't get if you book direct. But here are some factors you should consider as you decide where to buy your ticket and why sometimes, it's worth paying extra fees to book by phone.

Prices and service fees

Travel agencies usually charge the same price as the airlines for a plane ticket — assuming the itinerary is identical — but typically add service fees that bump up the total price. If you buy from Expedia, Orbitz, Travelocity or CheapTickets, Hotwire, or Priceline, these fees range from $5 to $16 per ticket, whereas traditional travel agencies charge an average of $35 per ticket (though this fee varies, depending on what else you're booking).

That said, many airlines charge service fees of their own — that is, if you need human help. American, Continental, Delta, Northwest, United, and US Airways all charge up to $10 per ticket if you book through an airline representative over the phone and up to $15 per ticket if you buy from an agent at the airport. Southwest takes a different approach, offering special discounted fares if you book using its Web site — basically dangling a carrot rather than using a stick to keep you from picking up the phone.

But there is one good reason to opt for the phone rather than your mouse: Some carriers will hold a reservation made by phone for twenty-four hours, guaranteeing the price for that time period. On line, you can sometimes put a reservation on hold, but the price usually isn't guaranteed (though some airlines plan to offer this option down the road).

Change penalties
Another downside of booking your ticket through an on-line agency is that many charge their own fees to change or cancel your itinerary, in addition to the $100 fee most airlines charge. Expedia, Orbitz, and Travelocity charge $30 per ticket if you need to make a change, bringing the total penalty up to a whopping $130 for tickets on some airlines. Cheaptickets charges an even higher change fee, $50 (along with the airline's penalty), which makes its tickets not so cheap if your plans happen to change. You can try calling the airline directly to avoid paying the additional change penalty, but some carriers will send you back to the agency if that's where you bought your ticket. It's possible that the agencies will drop these change fees if more customers protest; in the meantime, this is a good reason to book direct. (In most cases, you can change your mind and get a ticket refund without penalty within twenty-four hours of making your purchase; see the sidebar on page 102 for details.)

Bonuses
When they were first trying to entice customers to buy tickets using their Web sites, many airlines offered frequent flier miles as a bo-

nus for booking direct. These promotions aren't as common as they once were, but some carriers still offer them. The best way to find out is to check the airline's Web site; it will usually advertise any on-line booking bonuses on its home page.

Service

One of the problems with on-line travel agencies is that they're operating as middlemen without providing the added service that middlemen — that is, travel agents — once offered to travelers. In fact, some people claim that they get *worse* service from the airline if they buy their ticket through an agency — say, if your flight is canceled and you need to rebook. Although that opinion is difficult to prove (after all, most airlines don't have a reputation for treating any of their customers particularly well), it makes sense that an airline would be more helpful to passengers who book direct.

The airlines also offer other features on their Web sites that the agencies can't or don't consistently match, such as the ability to use a travel credit or voucher when you purchase your ticket, enter your frequent flier number with your reservation, choose your seat as you make your purchase, or sign up for flight-status alerts (see page 242 for details). Some on-line agencies offer a few of these options, but you're more likely to find all of them at the airline's Web site — and you don't have to rely on an agency to pass along your frequent flier number or seat request.

Understanding Ticket Rules: Change Fees, Cancellation Policies, and Refunds

One of the most maddening things about air travel is that airlines reserve the right to leave late, cancel a flight, or sell more tickets than there are seats on the plane — also known as overbooking — but woe unto you if you get stuck in a traffic jam on the way to the airport or have to cancel your trip because you got the flu. If your plans change, you'll probably have to pay.

Even more aggravating is the fact that most airlines, and many travel agencies, are rather secretive about disclosing their change

TWENTY-FOUR HOURS TO CHANGE YOUR MIND

Here's a secret most travelers don't know: When you purchase a plane ticket, you usually have twenty-four hours to change your mind and get a full refund. That grace period was originally established by the Airlines Reporting Corporation, which handles ticketing services behind the scenes for more than 130 airlines. It was adopted long ago to give customers a chance to address any second thoughts or for a travel agency to review a ticket and correct any problems — say, the agent accidentally booked you a flight to Rome instead of to Milan.

Most airlines and travel agencies still offer customers twenty-four hours to cancel a ticket and get a full refund, but many companies don't go out of their way to tell customers about this policy. So if you get your ticket receipt via e-mail and notice that you inadvertently booked a redeye when you thought you chose a morning flight, or a ticket to Long Beach airport instead of to Los Angeles, you may be able to get a full refund if you call within twenty-four hours after buying your ticket.

But if you want to buy a different ticket after canceling the one you bought by mistake, keep in mind that you can book only currently available fares. So a cheaper price you saw a day earlier may have already disappeared.

or cancellation policies, often leaving it up to passengers to wade through pages of fine print. Some airlines are more lenient than others when it comes to a change in plans, so here's what you should look into if you value that flexibility.

How to find fare rules

If you buy your ticket over the phone, the agent will usually tell you whether the fare you're purchasing is refundable or nonrefundable and how much it will cost to make a change. But if you buy your ticket on the Web, get out a magnifying glass — this information can be nearly impossible to find.

Most airlines and many travel agencies do offer a link to a ticket's "fare rules" at some point during the booking process. The problem is, these links often lead to documents that are dozens of pages long, written in capital letters, and full of cryptic acronyms that were originally meant for travel agents to decipher. (Yet some Web sites make you check a box saying that you've read and understand the fare rules before you can complete your purchase!) If you scroll through a lengthy list of fare rules and you still don't understand the change policy, pick up the phone — it's often quicker to simply call the airline and ask.

Typical cancellation penalties

Most discounted airline tickets are technically "nonrefundable" — meaning that you can't cancel your trip and get all your money back. Generally, only the most expensive tickets are refundable and can cost hundreds or thousands of dollars more than the nonrefundable price. But even when you buy a nonrefundable ticket, you don't lose your whole investment if you have to cancel. Most airlines let you apply the value of your ticket toward a future flight — minus a change fee. That fee is typically $100, though some carriers charge less.

The only catch is, many airlines stipulate that in order to get that credit, you have to call and cancel *before the plane takes off* or at least by midnight on your scheduled departure day. There may also be a limit on how long you have to use that credit — usually, a year, though some carriers don't give you that much time to rebook. So if you're going to miss the plane, take the time to call and cancel your reservation and find out how soon you have to use the credit (which, by the way, is generally nontransferable).

Making changes

If you simply want to change your travel dates, most tickets — even the cheapest ones — can be changed for a fee, plus any difference between the fare you purchased and the lowest fare available for the new flight. But there are exceptions: If you buy an unpublished fare from a consolidator or a discounter, like CheapTickets, Hotwire, or Priceline, those tickets usually don't allow any changes.

Change fees can vary quite a bit: Most airlines charge $100 (sometimes $200 for international tickets), though Delta charges $75 (plus an extra fee for tickets not booked through Delta), JetBlue charges $35, and Southwest doesn't charge any fee. But remember: All these fees are in addition to any difference between the price you paid and the fare for the new flight. If you bought a sale fare months earlier and have to change your plans at the last minute, the new ticket will probably cost a lot more.

Some on-line travel agencies charge an additional fee to make ticket changes, on top of what the airline charges. For instance, Expedia, Orbitz, and Travelocity all charge a $30 fee for ticket changes, in addition to the airline's penalty, whereas CheapTickets charges $50 — so if you think your plans might change, buy your ticket directly from the airline.

Bending the rules

Occasionally, airlines will waive their change penalties, either because of an event that affects many passengers (like a snowstorm or a hurricane), or for one customer on a case-by-case basis (like a serious illness or a death in the family). Don't count on much sympathy simply because you have a sore throat, but if your plans change because of extraordinary circumstances, the airline may agree to waive its penalty. It's worth calling and asking, but if your pleas seem to be falling on deaf ears, hang up and try again.

International Flights: Where to Shop for Fares When Traveling Abroad

In some sense, buying a ticket for international travel isn't all that different from a trip closer to home: All the sites listed in the first section of this chapter are still good sources to compare prices, and the earlier you make your plans, the better your chances of finding a good deal.

But if you're traveling overseas, a few other strategies are worth considering before you hand over your credit card. Yes, that means more legwork — and for some people, it's not worth hours of research to save enough money to cover the cost of one night on the town. Then again, international tickets are expensive, sometimes *really* expensive, so the savings may be well worth the headache of shopping around.

When to go and when to buy

With international travel, when you go and when you shop tend to have a bigger effect on the price of your ticket. For instance, you can often find winter fares from the United States to Europe for $500 or $600, but if you're traveling when the cobblestones are warm, that same fare is likely to cost $800 or more. In the fall, prices drop again — not quite as low as the winter specials, but still a bargain compared to summer fares.

That means you can save a lot of money by traveling during your destination's low season or "shoulder season," which is a month or two just before and after peak travel times. What time of year is considered low season varies; it's summer in the southern hemisphere in January and February, so that's when fares will be higher. But weather patterns can also affect the price of travel (not to mention your tan line), so for some destinations, heat waves or monsoon season can cause prices to drop.

If you can't avoid traveling during high season, the best way to save money is to buy your tickets as far in advance as possible. For off-season travel, that's not necessarily the best strategy, since you might miss a winter or fall sale. But for peak travel, try to buy your ticket at least six months before your trip. Once the cheap seats sell out, you have to pay a higher price; the airlines don't lower fares when they expect their planes to be full.

Foreign travel sites

Although you'll often find the lowest price for travel from the United States to another country on an American site, that's not always the case, and foreign sites are especially worth checking if you need a ticket that originates abroad or if you're traveling from one foreign country to another. For instance, a British site called Opodo (opodo.co.uk) — dubbed "the Orbitz of Europe" because it also was created by a group of airlines — compares fares from hundreds of airlines flying to and around Europe.

To find prices on European discount carriers — which generally don't show up on U.S. travel sites — try Openjet.com, Applefares .com, or Skyscanner.net. Although there's some overlap among these three sites, each works with a different set of airlines, though Skyscanner.net doesn't sell tickets, so you have to click over to the airline or a travel agency to buy. Another option is Europebyair.com, an agency that sells $99 "flight passes" you can use on participating carriers to fly between cities all over Europe (you need one pass for each flight); the site's route map shows which city pairs qualify. (For more about European low-fare carriers, see the sidebar on the facing page .)

To find discount carriers in other countries, WhichBudget.com is your best bet. Plug in two cities to see which airlines fly between them, but you have to go to the carrier's Web site to look up fares and buy a ticket.

International carriers

It's also worth checking fares from foreign carriers that operate in the country or region you're visiting. Although some of these airlines show up when you search sites like Expedia or Orbitz, that's not always the case, and you can sometimes get a better fare by booking direct.

Flying with a foreign carrier isn't always the cheapest way to go, but you may be willing to pay extra for the superior service offered by carriers like Cathay Pacific or Singapore Airlines (particularly in first or business class, where cloth napkins, lie-flat beds, and fine cuisine are still the norm). And if you're looking for a bargain, Aer Lingus and Icelandair have developed reputations as low-fare carriers across the Atlantic, so even if you're not headed to Ireland or Iceland, both airlines offer service to other cities in Europe.

Of course, purchasing a ticket from a foreign carrier or travel agency can involve a few challenges. Although most international airlines have English-language versions of their Web sites, prices aren't always listed in dollars, so you may have to do the currency conversion yourself (there's an on-line tool at www.xe.com), and international sites don't always include taxes and fees in their initial display of prices. You should also check the ticket rules carefully and make sure that the site will either issue an e-ticket or ship a paper ticket to the United States; sometimes, this last wrinkle is a deal breaker.

EUROPEAN LOW-COST CARRIERS: PROS AND CONS

Europe has experienced a boom in low-cost carriers, led by the British airline easyJet (easyjet.com) and Dublin-based Ryanair (ryanair.com). These and other discounters occasionally sell flights between European cities for a few dollars each way, somewhat gimmicky promotions valid for limited flights and days, but you can often find one-way tickets for less than $50. So flying within Europe may be cheaper than taking the train.

But these fares aren't always as attractive as they seem at first glance. First, prices generally don't include taxes and fees, which can be expensive in Europe. And most low-fare carriers fly into or out of secondary airports, such as Stansted, Gatwick, or Luton outside London or Beauvais near Paris. Sometimes, these alternate airports are much farther from the city center or don't have convenient transportation options, so that's a factor you should look into before you book. The discounters also tend to be less flexible about ticket changes.

And you get what you pay for in terms of service. These are mostly bare-bones operations, which generally encourage on-line booking, often don't have assigned seating, and usually enforce stricter limits on the amount of baggage you can bring on board or check. Also, some of these airlines have been criticized for excessive flight delays, so if you're on a tight schedule, check the carrier's on-time record before you book.

Consolidator tickets

Another option worth investigating for a trip overseas is buying your ticket from a consolidator — sometimes called a "bucket shop." These companies negotiate contracts with major carriers to sell a certain number of tickets below published prices, but these tickets come with a few strings attached.

On the plus side, tickets sold by consolidators (or a travel agency that works with consolidators) usually don't have minimum or maximum stay restrictions or advance-purchase requirements, and you generally know which airline you're flying and your itinerary before you make your purchase. But these tickets tend to have higher change fees and don't always qualify for frequent flier miles. Consolidators offer the best deals on international routes during peak travel times, but you should shop early because these fares sometimes sell out months ahead of time.

Although some consolidators still advertise in newspapers and travel magazines — look for the small ads usually toward the back of the publication — these days, you can also find them by searching on line. Search for *consolidator* and *airline* (or *tickets*); Yahoo and Google also list consolidators in their directories of travel Web sites.

Another way to find a consolidator is through U.S. immigrant communities, where you'll often find travel agencies that book a lot of tickets for expats to fly home. Publications, restaurants, even stores in these neighborhoods are all sources that may connect you to a consolidator or a travel agency that specializes in a certain region, though it's a strategy that works best in big cities and doesn't always pan out. (I once suggested that a friend stop by a few Indian restaurants in New York City to look for flyers advertising cheap flights to India; during dinner at an Ethiopian restaurant shortly afterward, he complained that my idea was a bust. But on our way out of the restaurant — lo and behold, a stack of flyers advertising discount fares to Africa!)

That said, some agencies that sell consolidator tickets operate on the margins of legitimacy, so before you buy a ticket from a company you don't know, especially one you found on line, make sure that the company checks out. For instance, verify that the agency exists in the real world (via a street address and a phone number), and check any affiliations it claims, like membership in a travel association or a local chamber of commerce. And pay with a credit card, which gives you some protection if you have any problems. If anything about the transaction seems fishy, buy your ticket somewhere else.

One-Way or Multicity Tickets: Tricks to Keep Costs Down

For some reason, most airlines prefer that their customers travel in a predictable path: from point A to point B and back again (ideally, with a Saturday-night stay in between). But sometimes, our lives involve more complicated journeys — say, from point A to point B to point C and then back to A (in other words, a trip that stops in two cities) or from point A to point B with no return (your basic one-way ticket).

For many years, airlines charged a hefty premium for such unconventional itineraries, mostly taking advantage of business travelers whose employers paid the bills. But with the growth of competition from low-cost carriers — which sell all their tickets based on one-way travel — the old guard has been forced to rethink some of these rules.

On some routes or with some carriers, you may still pay top dollar for a one-way or multicity itinerary, but in general, these ticket prices have come down to earth. Here are some tips on booking flights that don't involve standard round-trip travel, along with a word of caution about some carriers' byzantine ticketing rules.

Going one way

You can search for one-way fares at just about any airline or agency Web site, but for one-way tickets, your best bet is ITASoftware.com or Kayak.com, which tend to turn up more flight options than travel agencies or the airlines do. (For more about these sites, see pages 91 to 93.)

You should also check whether Southwest or JetBlue flies the route you need, since they sell all their tickets as one-way flights. (Even when you buy a round-trip ticket, it's priced based on adding up the fares for each one-way flight.) Their fares don't necessarily show up on other travel sites, so you have to search their sites directly, but you may have to be flexible about your airport choices. Both carriers tend to fly to alternate airports, but driving a little farther may be worth it to get a reasonable one-way fare.

You should also check round-trip prices, since it may be cheaper to use half of a round-trip ticket instead of buying an expensive one-way fare. Although some carriers technically prohibit this practice in their contract of carriage — a lengthy document drawn up by each airline outlining the terms of every ticket sale — they generally have no way of enforcing this rule, and it's not clear that it's even legal. Just be sure that the first half of the ticket is the one you're going to use. (See the sidebar on page 110 for more about these rules.)

WHAT'S IN THAT CONTRACT OF CARRIAGE?

When you buy an airline ticket, you probably don't realize that the terms of the sale are outlined in a detailed document called a *contract of carriage* (also known as *tariff rules*). That may be because you don't get a copy of this document when you purchase a ticket; you have to ask for it or find it on the airline's Web site — look for a link that says *contract of carriage* or something more oblique, like *customer commitment*.

The policies outlined in this contract, which can run more than one hundred pages, range from practical matters, like the fees charged for excess baggage and children flying alone, to more quirky topics, like how much it costs to transport a pole vault or the airline's right to deny boarding to anyone who smells bad. (I haven't seen that one enforced, but a few flight attendants I asked said that it does happen.)

Some older carriers, like American, Continental, Delta, Northwest, United, and US Airways, also include in these contracts rules that prohibit certain ticketing practices. Although a couple of court cases are challenging these policies — and one Supreme Court justice publicly admitted that he broke one of them (the rule against buying a round-trip ticket and using it for one-way travel) — they're worth knowing about even if you plan to flout them.

Among the practices that are forbidden, at least by the carriers named earlier:

- *Throwaway ticketing:* buying a round-trip ticket for one-way travel (and throwing half of the ticket away).

- *Back-to-back ticketing:* buying two round-trip tickets in order to circumvent minimum-stay requirements (for example, using half of one ticket for your outbound flight and half of the other ticket for your return, which can be cheaper than buying one round-trip ticket that doesn't include a Saturday-night stay).

- *Point-beyond/hidden-city ticketing:* buying a ticket to a city beyond your actual destination, then getting off at a stopover (a tactic some might try when the fare to the farther city is cheaper).

Although the first two ticketing policies aren't easy for the airlines to enforce (point-beyond ticketing is riskier), the carriers all outline various actions they may take if they catch anyone breaking the rules. Among the options: invalidating the rest of your ticket, forcing you to pay the difference between the fare you purchased and the price of a ticket on the route you actually flew, or deleting frequent flier miles from your account. You're least likely to get caught (or punished) for throwaway ticketing — as long as the return portion of your ticket is the one you throw away — but at least now you know what might happen if you do.

One trip but multiple cities

Another itinerary that gets more complicated to book is a trip that includes visits to more than one city. For instance, say you have to fly from Boston to Los Angeles for a wedding, but while you're all the way across the country, you want to stop and see friends in San Francisco. You have a couple of options: Buy a ticket from one airline that flies from Boston to Los Angeles, then on to San Francisco and back to Boston (in airline lingo, a "circle trip"), or buy what's called an "open jaw" ticket — an outbound flight from Boston to Los Angeles, returning to Boston from San Francisco. Then you can either buy a one-way ticket from Los Angeles to San Francisco on a low-cost carrier, like Southwest, or rent a car and drive up the coast.

The point is, whenever your trip involves multiple stopovers, it's worth comparing prices to stick with one airline or fly different carriers. Most travel Web sites let you search for either multicity or open-jaw trips, but ITASoftware.com has one of the best search tools for trips that involve multiple stops (for more about using this site, see page 92).

Frequent Flier Awards: What It Takes to Get the Flights You Want

Frequent flier programs were designed to reward passengers for their loyalty by giving travelers a free ticket once they flew a certain number of miles. But with companies handing out miles for every dollar you spend with the right credit card — not to mention car rentals, hotel stays, or shopping at an airline mall — it's gotten much easier to earn those tickets without being a particularly frequent (or loyal) flier.

Which may be why it's gotten so much more difficult to actually *use* these awards: Everyone knows that they're not really about loyalty anymore.

Although the airlines don't reveal how many seats they allocate for award travel — the number is different for every flight — it's safe to say that they're reluctant to let passengers travel for free in seats they think they can sell. That's why it's so difficult to use an award to fly to Hawaii during winter or Europe when it's warm enough to melt your gelato. In fact, many passengers would argue that it's nearly impossible to use an award to fly *anywhere* they want to go.

Tips for booking awards

So how do you manage to use frequent flier miles to get the seats you want? The truth is, sometimes it *is* impossible — there may not be any seats on a particular flight designated for award travel, or the two that were available have been claimed by someone who called months before you thought about cashing in your miles. But if you've got miles to burn, here are some strategies you can try to increase your odds of getting a free ride. (For tips on managing your miles, see the sidebar on page 115.)

Book early — really early. Savvy frequent fliers make a point of discovering exactly how far in advance you're allowed to book award seats. Then they call just after the stroke of midnight on the day those seats are released — even figuring out what time zone to follow — calling back if they get a busy signal or the seats haven't been released yet. This may seem like trying to win concert tickets over the radio, but that's often what it takes to use your miles on a popular route. The sidebar on pages 116 and 117 lists how far ahead you can book award tickets with various airlines — typically, almost a year before your trip, but some airlines wait longer to release award seats on certain routes.

Or book late. Often, airlines designate more seats for award travel as it gets closer to the flight's departure date, so sometimes you have a better chance of booking an award ticket a few weeks before your trip. It's not a good strategy to rely on for your only vacation of the year, but if you have to travel at the last minute (say, to visit a sick relative) or you get the urge to plan a spur-of-the-moment getaway, there may be seats on the route you want. And if you're not picky about your vacation destination, consider going wherever your miles will take you (well, maybe not *anywhere,* but if you're flexible, you may find some decent choices).

Use more miles. Although most airlines have eliminated blackout dates from their frequent flier programs (dates when they don't let passengers use awards, usually around the holidays), they still use what they call capacity controls — meaning that only a limited number of seats (if any) on each flight are designated for award travel. Most airlines will let you override these capacity controls if you're willing to part with more of your miles — typically, 50,000 miles instead of 25,000 for a free domestic ticket or 100,000 instead of 50,000 miles to fly to Europe. By using more miles, you can usually book any open seat on the plane, not only the ones allocated for award travel. Although it's maddening to give up double the number of miles for the flight you want, in some cases, it's better than not being able to use your miles at all.

Use the phone and the Web. It's sort of a toss-up which is more frustrating: trying to coax an agent into helping you find an available award seat or using the airline's on-line booking tool, which keeps flashing some variation on the message, "Sorry, no award seats are available for the dates you selected." It's always a good idea to try the Web before you pick up the phone, just so you know whether the pickings are really slim. And some carriers are developing better on-line tools to help you figure out when you can use your miles. For instance, Continental, Northwest, and US Airways all display a color-coded calendar to indicate which days have award seats available on the route you search, so you don't have to search each day of the month, one by one. But depending on the airline — and the personality of the agent you speak with — you may find it easier to get help over the phone. One advantage of booking by phone is that some airlines will hold your award reservation for up to two weeks before you have to ticket it — an option that's not necessarily available on line. But you may have to pay an extra fee ($10 to $15) to book an award by phone.

Try a partner. With so many carriers forming alliances these days, you have more options when it comes to earning and using miles. Not only can you earn, say, Delta miles for a Northwest flight, you can also use miles from one airline to book award seats on any of its partners. Of course, those seats are also subject to capacity controls and program rules, but you may find more availability on a partner carrier for the route you want, so it's worth calling to find out (you generally can't book partner awards on line). Most airlines have both domestic and international partners, which are usually listed on the carrier's Web site. (For more about airline alliances, see page 117.)

Don't follow the crowd. Not surprisingly, everybody wants to use miles to fly to Hawaii for spring break or London when school's out (two of the most sought-after destinations for award travel). You can increase your chances of finding a free seat by choosing a less popular destination or traveling at off-peak times. That doesn't mean you have to vacation in North Dakota when it's twenty below, but you can probably use your miles for an off-season visit to grandma's house (well, unless grandma lives in Maui). Or if you can't find a seat to Orlando, try Tampa — or if London is a no-go, try another city in the United Kingdom and then take a train or a low-cost carrier to London. Another option is to take the kids out of school for a few days and go when planes aren't so full. (Hey, I missed school for my first trip to Florida and suffered no long-term harm.)

Where to get frequent flier advice

If you're ready for the advanced course in frequent flier programs, a couple of Web sites can tell you everything you ever wanted to know about the ins and outs of travel awards. Although they focus mostly on frequent flier issues, these sites also cover hotel and car rental loyalty programs, not to mention a range of other travel topics.

Flyertalk.com. Flyertalk is one of the most useful travel communities on the Web, with active (and eclectic) message boards where you can find answers to pretty much any travel-related question you have. The forums are organized by topic, so you can easily find discussions about each airline's frequent flier program or read, post, and answer questions about other travel issues, like which shoes don't set off airport metal detectors or where to rent a cell phone for a trip to Tokyo. Flyertalk was started by Randy Petersen, who has made a business out of monitoring frequent flier programs. He also publishes a newsletter and another Web site, Webflyer.com, with news about program changes, awards, and bonuses.

Frequentflier.com. Although it doesn't have as large a community

TIPS: MANAGING YOUR FREQUENT FLIER MILES

Frequent flier miles are like any other investment: You have to manage your accounts if you want to protect their value. Some travelers spend a shocking amount of time on this task — trading advice about bonus opportunities, signing up for various promotions, even flying out of their way just for the chance to earn extra miles. Not everyone has the time or passion for such devotion, but at a minimum, here are two things you should pay attention to if you're going to bother with these programs at all.

- *Make sure you get credit for the flights you take.* I'm always amazed at how many times an airline doesn't credit my account with the miles I'm due, even when my frequent flier number was entered with my reservation. Often, this happens when I've missed a connection, a flight is canceled, or I've flown on a partner airline. So be sure to give the airline your frequent flier number when you buy your ticket or check in; then check your account to see whether you got credit for your trip. Most airlines now let you access your account on line, and you can even submit a request electronically to get credit for missing miles. (This is one of the most useful features the airlines have added to their sites.) You can also download an application — called MilePort from mileport.com — that automatically tracks your mileage activity in multiple frequent flier programs, saving you the trouble of manually checking all your accounts.

- *Don't let your miles expire.* With most frequent flier programs, your account must have some activity — by either earning or redeeming miles — at least once every thirty-six months to keep your miles from expiring. Some airlines are better than others about warning you when this is about to happen, but I've heard from lots of travelers who found out their account balances were zero as a very unpleasant surprise. With so many opportunities to earn miles besides flying, you can usually find some way to collect a few miles in a pinch: signing up for some type of promotion, getting (or using) a credit card affiliated with the airline, shopping with one of the carrier's partners. Check the airline's Web site for mileage offers if you find yourself with an expiration date coming up, or visit one of the Web sites described here for news about frequent flier promotions.

as Flyertalk, this site also has message boards that discuss travel loyalty programs. It's run by Tim Winship, who also writes about frequent flier issues and has posted various articles about earning and maximizing your miles.

COMPARING FREQUENT FLIER PROGRAMS

Everybody wants to know which airline has the best frequent flier program, but there's no one-size-fits-all answer to that question — it depends on which airlines you fly, where you travel, and how you plan to use your miles. Here are some general guidelines about award-booking rules and fees that may influence where you focus your loyalty. Most programs have similar rules and award levels, except for JetBlue and Southwest, which award points instead of miles.

Besides fees to make changes or book a ticket at the last minute, you usually have to pay taxes and security fees when you travel on an award ticket and sometimes a surcharge of $10 to $30 if you book over the phone instead of on line. Got status? Some of the fees listed in the chart are reduced or waived for "elite" members of the airline's frequent flier program. You can find more program rules and award charts on the airlines' Web sites.

Program name	Cost to change award tickets	Fee to redeposit miles	Surcharge for last-minute award tickets	Days in advance you can book award tickets[1]	How soon award reservations must be ticketed[2]
Alaska Airlines MileagePlan, 1-800-252-7522, alaskaair.com	$75, but no charge if change is made within 3 days of booking	$75	$60 if trip booked within 3 weeks of departure (no charge if booked on line)	330	Immediately
American AAdvantage, 1-800-882-8880, aa.com	$100 (no charge to change date or time, or to change AAnytime Awards)	$100	$50 for travel within 7–20 days; $100 for travel within 6 days	331	Within 14 days (immediately if no other award seats available)
Continental OnePass, 1-800-621-7467, continental.com	$50	$50	$50 for travel within 4–14 days; $75 for travel within 3 days	330	Within 5 days
Delta SkyMiles, 1-800-323-2323, delta.com	$50	$75	$75 for tickets booked within 20 days of travel	331	Within 14 days
JetBlue TrueBlue,[3] 1-800-JET-BLUE, jetblue.com	$45	n/a	n/a	n/a	Immediately
Northwest WorldPerks, 1-800-447-3757, nwa.com	$50 ($25 if change made online)	$50	None for account holder; $50 if ticket booked within 10 days of trip for someone else	352	Immediately

Program name	Cost to change award tickets	Fee to redeposit miles	Surcharge for last-minute award tickets	Days in advance you can book award tickets[1]	How soon award reservations must be ticketed[2]
Southwest Rapid Rewards,[3] 1-800-248-4377, southwest.com	None	n/a	n/a	About 90	Immediately
United Mileage Plus, 1-888-467-0507, united.com	$100 (no charge to change date or time)	$100	$50 for travel within 7–13 days; $75 for travel within 6 days	330	Within 72 hours
US Airways Dividend Miles, 1-800-428-4322, usairways.com	$100 (no charge to change date or time)	$100	$75 if ticket booked by phone within 14 days of trip (no charge if booked on line)	330	Within 24 hours

1. The earliest you can book award tickets, but seats aren't necessarily released for award travel this far in advance.
2. These time periods refer to reservations made by phone. Many airlines do not offer a way to "hold" an award reservation made on line, so you have to ticket it right away.
3. JetBlue and Southwest offer award programs different from those of the other airlines. You earn a free ticket if you collect a certain number of points in a year (JetBlue) or two years (Southwest); then you have a year (JetBlue) or two years (Southwest) to use the award.

Unraveling Airline Alliances: What's in It for You When Airlines Partner Up

At first glance, it may seem like understanding the ins and outs of airline alliances is about as important as knowing who makes your aircraft's engine or which company catered the beverage service.

But there are a few good reasons to pay attention to the various partnerships the airlines have formed. One is that because of these alliances, you may find yourself flying on a carrier different from the one you thought you'd booked, and that isn't always the "seamless" experience the airlines promise. But on the plus side, these partnerships create more ways to earn and redeem frequent flier miles, so it's worth knowing how you can take advantage of these opportunities — and what the potential pitfalls are.

How alliances work

You're most likely to encounter airline alliances when you're booking a ticket and discover that one of the flights is operated by a partner carrier. Airlines are required to tell passengers when a partner will be flying the plane, but on the Web, these notices don't always jump off the page. So even though you're buying a ticket from, say, Continental, you'll be flying on a different airline for at least one leg of the trip. That airline may be a small regional carrier, another big U.S. airline (Continental is in an alliance with Northwest and Delta), or one of Continental's international partners if you're flying overseas.

When an airline sells a ticket on a flight operated by another carrier, it's called a *code share*. Each airline assigns its own code to the flight, which is why you might see a flight number like COo225/ NW6525 on your computer screen or a monitor at the airport — two numbers, but it's the same plane.

How alliances affect you

One of the reasons airlines form these alliances is so they can sell tickets to places they don't fly themselves or offer more flight times on the routes they do fly. In some cases, this gives you more options when you're shopping for a ticket and, possibly, more competitive prices, since each partner can charge different fares for the same code share flight. So if you're thinking about booking a code share flight, it's worth checking prices with both partners, since one may have a lower fare available for that flight. (See the sidebar on page 120 for a list of some of the main alliances.)

Another benefit to passengers is that you can choose to earn frequent flier miles from either carrier — the one that sold you the ticket or the one that's flying the plane. You can also use frequent flier miles earned on one airline for a free ticket on one of its partners (if award seats are available), but you can't move miles between accounts. For instance, you can't take 10,000 miles from your Northwest WorldPerks account and add them to the 15,000 miles you have in your Continental OnePass account to get the 25,000 you need for a free domestic ticket; you have to book an award ticket with miles from one airline.

The airlines promise that passengers flying a portion of their trip on a partner carrier will barely notice the difference, but I've experienced a few glitches with these flights. Some of these problems are more likely to occur when an alliance is new and the airlines are still ironing out the kinks of coaviation, but they're worth knowing about if you're considering a code share flight or if one leg of your trip is on a partner carrier.

- *It's not always clear where you check in.* Airlines usually advise passengers to check in with the carrier operating the flight, but that isn't necessarily the case if you're checking in on line (you may not be able to use Web check-in at all). Before your trip, confirm where you should check in, and allow extra time at the airport in case you're shuffled between ticket counters.
- *If you have to make a connection from one airline to another, the partner's gates may be farther away.* This is often the case when your itinerary involves a small regional airline, typically relegated to a distant corner of the terminal, or you're changing from a domestic airline to an international carrier. If you can't book a longer layover, try to get your gate information in advance, and be prepared for a hike — or a sprint — to your connecting gate.
- *Frequent flier miles can take longer to show up in your account — or not show up at all.* Theoretically, frequent flier miles you earn for a code share flight should be credited to your account, if you provided that number when you made your reservation or checked in. But in the real world, miles earned on a partner flight can take longer to post or never appear — which is why you should always check your account after your trip. You can submit a request for missing frequent flier miles at most airlines' Web sites, and usually have up to a year after your flight to do so.
- *You may not get all the frequent flier miles — or other benefits — you expected.* Some international carriers don't award frequent flier miles for deeply discounted tickets or give the same upgrade privileges as their U.S. partners. For instance, if you book an inexpensive fare on one of American's foreign partners, like Qantas or British Airways, you may only earn half the miles you actually fly. So if you're considering flying with a foreign carrier and these benefits matter to you, double-check the airline's policy.

WHO'S ALLIED

Here are some of the main domestic and international airline alliances. Besides these alliances, which you might think of as marriages, most airlines also have other partners, which are more like friends. For instance, Alaska Airlines isn't in any of the big alliances, but it has partnerships with American, Continental, Delta, and Northwest. Most airlines list their partners on their Web site in the section describing their frequent flier programs. But these relationships are as fickle as romances — and equally subject to change.

U.S. AIRLINE ALLIANCES

- Northwest/Delta/Continental
- United/US Airways
- Southwest/ATA

INTERNATIONAL ALLIANCES

- oneworld (oneworld.com)
  American, British Airways, Cathay Pacific, Finnair, Iberia, Japan Airlines, LAN, Qantas

- Star Alliance (staralliance.com)
  United, US Airways, Air Canada, Air New Zealand, ANA, Asiana, Austrian, bmi, LOT Polish Airlines, Lufthansa, SAS Scandinavian Airlines, Singapore Airlines, Spanair, Swiss, South African Airways, TAP Portugal, Thai Airways

- SkyTeam (skyteam.com)
  Continental, Delta, Northwest, AeroMexico, Air France, Alitalia, CSA Czech Airlines, KLM, Korean Air

Foreign Carrier Air Passes: One Pass, Several Flights, Sometimes a Bargain

When you're looking at a map of the world, it's easy to underestimate the distance between one country and its neighbor — which somehow loses any scale when you can connect them with a forefinger and a thumb. Even within the same country, maps play time-warping tricks, making it *seem* like you can easily visit several cities during a two-week trip abroad.

Although our itineraries are often more ambitious than realistic, naively miscalculating the logistics of international travel, there is a way to make a multicity trip abroad more feasible. Many carriers sell special air passes to foreigners, designed to make a whirlwind tour of that country or region more economical than buying multiple plane tickets, not to mention more comfortable than traveling long distances on the ground.

I've purchased these air passes for visits to two rather large countries — Argentina and Brazil — and got to see more of both places because of the convenience of air travel. But these air passes aren't always a bargain, especially if you don't end up using all the flight segments you paid for, so map out your plans carefully before you commit to a schedule only a rock star could endure. (See the sidebar on page 122 for a list of carriers that sell air passes.)

Foreign air passes are generally sold by a particular airline and often must be purchased through a travel agent in your home country — mostly because they tend to have complicated rules, and carriers prefer to have travel agents handle the booking. These rules vary, depending on the airline, but how air passes work is pretty straightforward. You generally pay a set price for a designated number of flight segments, which you typically have to fly within a certain time period (often, a month or twenty-one days). The passes are usually for economy-class travel, but on some carriers, you can pay extra to upgrade. If you're considering buying an air pass, here are some other restrictions you're likely to face.

- *Purchase rules.* You generally have to purchase these passes in the United States, or outside the country you're visiting, before you start your trip. In some cases, you also have to fly to your destination on the airline that issues the pass (or one of its partners).
- *Routing quirks.* Some airlines make you book all your flights when you buy the pass, and there are often rules about how you can craft your itinerary; for example, you may have to start your trip in a certain city, or you can't fly through the same airport

AIRLINES THAT SELL AIR PASSES

Here are some of the carriers that sell air passes. Although these promotions can change at any time, most of these passes have been around for a while, and you may find similar deals from other airlines.

ASIA

Air Fiji (airfiji.com.fj): Discover Fiji Pass
Cathay Pacific (cathay-usa.com): All Asia Pass
Japan Airlines (japanair.com): Yokoso (Welcome) Japan Air Pass
Thai Air (thaiair.com): Discover Thailand/ASEAN Hip Hop Air Pass

AUSTRALIA

Qantas (qantasusa.com): Aussie Air Pass or Boomerang Pass

EUROPE

Scandinavian Airlines (scandinavian.net): Visit Scandinavia/Europe Air Pass

SOUTH AMERICA

Aerolineas Argentinas (aerolineas.com.ar): Visit Argentina or South America Pass
Varig (varigbrasil.com): Brazil Airpass or Mercosur Airpass

twice, and some passes allow travel only during specified seasons or on certain days of the week.

- *Extra fees.* The prices quoted for these passes don't always include taxes and fees, which can add up if you have to pay departure taxes at several airports. So before deciding whether a pass is a good deal, make sure that you factor in these surcharges.
- *Change policies and refunds.* Air passes are usually nonrefundable, and you may not be able to change the routing once you pick your itinerary (policies vary). But you generally can change your travel dates — for a fee.

5 Lodging

FINDING A PLACE TO STAY is probably the most difficult part of planning a trip and where the do-it-yourself approach has a tendency to backfire. The hotel you thought was on the beach? Turns out it's on an inland lagoon; you have to take a taxi to get to the ocean. The ski cabin the owner said sleeps eight? Depends on what you consider a bed. And the inn that looked so perfect in the photos? Well, how were you supposed to know that the walls were so thin?

Given the importance of finding the right hotel — or inn or bungalow or lodge — it's sort of surprising that there aren't more (or better) resources to help travelers answer the question, "I'm traveling to [fill-in-the-blank]: Where should I stay?"

Ideally, most people rely on recommendations from friends or acquaintances. But that strategy doesn't always work out: You may not know anyone who's been wherever you're headed, or your boss stayed somewhere you can't afford, or your friend was there five years ago, and a dozen new hotels have opened since then.

This chapter offers advice on where to look when your personal network comes up short or you want to make sure that the resort your cousin recommended isn't known for the bar band you can hear from every room in the hotel. This chapter also covers practical issues like how to get the best rate, decipher cancellation policies, and put hotel ratings into context (if you're seeing lots of stars on the Internet, it helps to know who's handing them out). And if a hotel isn't really right for your trip, there are tips on finding a bed and breakfast, renting a house or condo, or even arranging a home exchange if you're game to try a swap.

But the underlying theme is all about minimizing the risk of being disappointed when you show up, because nothing has the potential to ruin a trip quite like a lodging decision that turns out to be a dud. Except maybe a travel companion who keeps reminding you that you're the one who chose it.

Finding a Place to Stay: Where to Research Your Options

These days, many people turn to the Internet when they're looking for a hotel, but once you fire up your browser, it's easy to get overwhelmed. Type "Miami" and "hotel" into a search engine, and your bathing suit might not fit by the time you get through the results. Doing that same search at an on-line travel agency narrows the field considerably, but it's still a bit draining to weed through choices that range from the Ramada Inn to the Ritz-Carlton.

Travel companies are adding tools to their Web sites to make it easier to narrow down your options, with features that let you limit your search to a particular neighborhood, star rating, or price. But most of these sites are trying to sell you a room — any room — so their top priority isn't making sure that you find the *right* hotel. That means you need to look to other sources for more objective advice.

Here's an overview of various resources you can turn to when you're researching your options. All these strategies have pros and cons, and none is best for every trip or every budget, so your best bet is to check multiple sources and see where their recommendations overlap — and keep asking around. Word of mouth is often the best source for a referral.

Destination guidebooks
Guidebooks used to be the first place travelers turned to when they were looking for a hotel — and for some people, they still are. And with good reason: The author has presumably visited many hotels in each city and chosen only a few to recommend. Most guidebooks list hotels in various price ranges, though each series skews toward a particular budget. A few publishers, including Fodor's and Frommer's, post some of their hotel picks on their Web sites, so you can even do some of this research on line. (See the sidebar on page 11 for a list of other guides.)

Pros: Good writers call it like they see it — if the hotel is a landmark but is showing its age, they'll let you know. And most books include only hotels the author recommends in each price range, whereas agencies that book hotels are much less discerning about whose rooms they sell.

Cons: Because guidebooks don't usually list a lot of hotels, the places they recommend sometimes fill up with tourists all toting the same book. Guidebooks are also not the most up-to-date source of advice — a hotel may have changed owners and service is now suffering, or new options may have opened that the book doesn't cover.

Hotel guidebooks

A few guidebooks focus specifically on hotels, although they tend to skew toward the upper end of the market. Mobil publishes *America's Best Hotels & Restaurants,* which lists hotels that earned four or five stars in its annual review, and Zagat — best known for its restaurant guides — publishes two books based on similar customer surveys of hotels. Zagat's *Top U.S. Hotels, Resorts & Spas* and *Top International Hotels, Resorts & Spas* each rate about nine hundred properties, which you can browse by location or by lists like "best for romance," "best for families," or "top service." Zagat also publishes the *U.S. Family Travel Guide,* which lists family-friendly lodging.

Another publisher, Globe Pequot, publishes several books in its "100 Best . . ." series that cover places to stay, such as *100 Best All-Inclusive Resorts of the World.* (Go to globepequot.com and search for "100 Best" to see a current list of titles.) And if you stop by a bookstore or search for "hotels" at an on-line bookseller, you're bound to find other options.

Pros: Hotel guides tend to zero in on a specific niche, so if you find a book that covers your particular interest — such as pet-friendly hotels — you're in luck.

Cons: There isn't a hotel guide for everyone's special interest — say, unique hotels with great service that cost less than $200 a night — and books tend to get outdated more quickly than other sources.

Newspapers and magazines

Newspapers and magazines can be a gold mine for travelers looking for hotel recommendations, but the challenge is finding articles about your destination when you're ready to go — as opposed to when the editor decides to cover, say, the best places to stay in Prague. Many publishers have addressed this dilemma by making it easier to search their archives on line, but it can take some digital digging to find information specifically about hotels.

Condé Nast Traveler and *Travel + Leisure* both publish annual lists of top hotels around the world, based on reader surveys, and these lists are fairly easy to find on their Web sites (though their picks include mainly luxury hotels and resorts). Other publications, like *Outside* magazine and *National Geographic Traveler,* also publish lodging round-ups from time to time, focusing on niches like wilderness lodges or eco-friendly resorts. (See the sidebar on page 5 for Web addresses of these magazines and other publications that cover travel.)

Pros: Magazines and newspapers offer a fresher perspective than guidebooks, keeping up on hotels that are opening or that have recently been remodeled. These sources also tend to put together some ambitious features that take advantage of the whole staff's expertise, like the best beach resorts in the Caribbean or ten moderately priced hotels in New York.

Cons: Searching for that needle in a haystack — like a classic hotel in Budapest — can be a chore.

Visitor and tourist bureaus

Most tourist bureaus list hotel options on their Web sites, though local and regional agencies tend to include more information about lodging than sites representing a whole country. (For tips on finding these sites, see page 19.) If you're headed to a destination that isn't a travel hot spot, universities, corporations, or other institutions in the area sometimes maintain lists of nearby hotels and may post them on line.

Pros: The local visitors bureau or chamber of commerce can be a good source to turn to if you're going to an area that isn't covered thoroughly by guidebooks or you're booking late. These organizations often know which hotels or inns still have rooms available when it seems as if the entire city is sold out.

Cons: Don't expect to get an opinion about the hotels these groups list (they aren't supposed to play favorites), and the information offered about each hotel tends to be sparse — often, simply names, addresses, and phone numbers.

Brands you trust

If you've had a good experience with a particular hotel chain, there's something to be said for sticking with what you know. More than one traveler has told me that whenever it's an option, they always stay at the Four Seasons because they know they won't be disappointed. Of course, such luxury accommodations aren't in everyone's budget, but this strategy can work for less expensive brands as well.

There are also a few hotel associations that offer a similar type of brand affiliation to independently owned hotels. Leading Hotels of the World (lhw.com) and Small Luxury Hotels of the World (slh.com) are two membership organizations that hotels pay to join (they have to meet the group's standards first). Both associations are on the luxury end of the spectrum, but if you're looking for a high-end hotel, especially in a foreign country, these can be useful sources to browse.

Pros: Choosing a brand you know is one way to avoid unpleasant surprises; also, if you join a hotel chain's frequent guest program, you may get other perks, like an upgrade, a better room assignment, or a discount.

Cons: There's a lot of franchising in the hotel industry, especially in the middle and budget end of the market, which means that there's not always a consistent level of service at hotels that share the same logo.

On-line message boards

If you'd prefer a personal recommendation but your own network can't help you out, one way to expand your circle, at least virtually, is by visiting some of the message boards where travelers hang out on line. (See the sidebar on page 16 for a list of options.) You can either browse through messages that have already been posted about a destination — these boards are typically organized geographically — or post your own message, asking whether anyone can recommend a good hotel wherever you're going. There are also a few Web sites that specialize in feedback about hotels.

TripAdvisor (tripadvisor.com) has been around the longest, collecting customer reviews of thousands of hotels worldwide; you can browse its listings by destination (to see which hotels are most popular in a particular city) or search for a specific hotel (to see what other people have to say about it). HotelShark (hotelshark.com) also publishes hotel reviews from past guests, though it doesn't cover as many properties as TripAdvisor or have as many opinions about each hotel. HotelChatter.com is a newer site, designed more as an industry blog. It posts news about hotels that are opening and feedback from travelers who have stayed at places that are generating buzz. You can search its database for information about hotels in your destination, but cities and travel hot spots are more likely to turn up results.

Pros: If more than a few people have submitted feedback about a hotel, common themes start to emerge, so reading reviews can be a good way to find out the real scoop — like the rooms are dingy or the pool is next to a parking lot.

Cons: When you don't know the person offering an opinion, it's difficult to gauge whether it's a source you can trust; a negative review may have been written by a disgruntled employee or an overly picky guest, and a positive review may have been submitted by the hotel manager's son. Also, feedback about the same hotel is sometimes contradictory — a glowing recommendation followed by an all-caps rant about the service and décor.

Agencies that book hotels

Travel agencies that handle hotel reservations can also be useful for researching your options, though they're generally not the most objective source of feedback, since their main goal is to sell lodging. Expedia, Orbitz, Travelocity, and similar sites tend to be innovators on the technology front, offering tools to make it easier to narrow your search to a particular neighborhood, price range, and star rating or to hotels that have certain amenities, like a pool, a gym, or high-speed Internet access in each room.

There are also on-line agencies that focus exclusively on hotels, like Hotels.com and Quikbook.com, which specializes in independent and boutique hotels. Another site, FiveStarAlliance.com, focuses exclusively on reservations for four- and five-star hotels, and TabletHotels.com aims to be a booking tool for unique hotels around the world, with an emphasis on style and ambience. (For more about these sites, see the sidebar on page 133.)

Pros: On-line agencies are trying to make it easier to find a hotel that suits your needs, and companies that specialize in lodging may list options you wouldn't come across anywhere else.

Cons: You won't see everything that's available in a particular city — these sites include only the hotels they get paid to sell, and each agency usually has different inventory. And some sites might tell you that a hotel is sold out even if you could get a room by booking direct. Agencies also have a tendency to highlight the hotels that pay the highest commissions and don't tell you what's good and bad about each hotel — though some are adding customer reviews to their results.

How to Get the Best Rate: On-line Agencies, Hotel Web Sites, the Phone

Once you've decided on a hotel or at least narrowed down your options, the next hurdle is figuring out how to get the best rate for your stay. As with plane tickets or cruises, there's no standard price for a hotel room, so guests in identical rooms during the same weekend may have paid wildly different rates — which they'll end up discovering during a conversation by the pool, ruining someone's vacation.

Although it's tempting to think that where you book has the biggest impact on price — and that if you search enough Web sites, you'll find the best deal — a lot of other factors are at stake. Here are some strategies you can try to make sure you're not the guest who overpaid.

Shop around

When you're booking a hotel room, you basically have two choices: make your reservation either through an agency or directly with the hotel. Although there used to be big price differences depending on where you booked, those gaps aren't as common, or as large, as they once were. Although many of the bigger hotel chains have adopted "best-rate guarantees," promising that you'll get the lowest rate for a room if you book direct, agencies often insist on being able to sell a hotel's lowest rates, too, and have their own rate guarantees, so you may find more or less the same price wherever you look. It's still worth comparing rates from a few sources, because sometimes an agency will have a lower price, especially for hotels that aren't part of a big chain. And if you're not set on a place to stay, agencies don't all have the same *selection* of hotels, so you may find a cheaper option at a different site.

Book early

As with airline tickets, the earlier you make your hotel reservation, the more likely you'll get a lower rate. Hotels do sell out during peak travel times, so if you wait until the last minute to book a room, you may find only expensive suites available — or no empty beds at all. Some hotels discount rooms at the last minute but tend to sell those rooms through sites like Priceline or Hotwire, which don't reveal which hotel you'll be staying at until after you commit to the deal. (For more on using these sites, see page 76.) Many hotel reservations can be canceled without penalty up until a few days before your stay, so when you first start shopping, book a rate you can cancel; then keep looking around for a better deal.

Prepay for your stay

In recent years, many hotels and travel agencies have begun offering the deepest discounts if you agree to prepay for your stay. These rates are sometimes available only on line, which is why they're often called "Internet rates." The main drawback of prepaid rates is that they usually can't be canceled or changed without a stiff penalty (often a charge equal to one night of your stay), and some can't be canceled at all. But if you're sure that your plans won't change or you're willing to take a chance, booking a prepaid rate is one way to save.

Try negotiating

You may also get a better rate by calling the hotel and asking for a discount (try the front desk rather than the toll-free number for the chain). A survey conducted by *Consumer Reports* magazine found that its reporter got a lower rate nearly half the time by calling, but that strategy depends on occupancy rates, who picks up the phone, and your negotiating skills (it doesn't always work for me). Hotels are generally more willing to cut a deal when they have a lot of empty rooms to fill, but if you're a repeat guest or planning a longer stay, that may help your case. You may also get better advice over the phone about discounts, special packages, or other ways to save — though again, that depends on how helpful the representative is on the other end of the line.

Try different dates

Hotel rates also vary depending on when you're traveling — both the time of year and the day of the week. For vacation destinations, rates are higher when most people want to travel: holidays and when the weather is at its peak (winter months for beach resorts and ski towns, summer for European cities). Rates are also higher on weekends for places that attract leisure travelers, but that rule of thumb is reversed in cities dominated by business travel, where you'll often find lower weekend rates. (So for a stay that extends from Wednesday through Saturday in a big city, you'll probably pay a higher rate the first two nights of your trip.) In other words, don't assume the first rate you see is a standard price, especially at a big hotel.

Compare room types

One thing Internet booking has revealed is the complicated way hotel rooms are classified, with some larger hotels offering dozens of room types, often with cryptic names like *traditional, standard, deluxe, quality, executive,* or *superior,* not to mention the occasional *guest room* or *parlor suite.* (One traveler told me that he once arrived at an expensive hotel and was told — as if he should have known — that a "superior standard room" didn't have a bathtub, just a shower. "How am I supposed to understand their hotel gobbledygook?" he complained.) All these different room types correspond to different rates, so assume that every question you're asked when you're booking — like "What type of bed do you need?" or "Do you want to be on a high floor or a low floor?" — affects the price you're quoted, so if you're pinching pennies, before you answer, ask whether there's a price difference. And if a bathtub is important, get that hotel gobbledygook translated.

See whether you qualify for a discount

Hotels frequently offer discounts to members of organizations like AARP or AAA, government workers, or companies that have negotiated special rates for their employees. If you book on line, it's not always clear how to get these discounts, so if not, call the hotel and ask. But these discounted rates aren't always the lowest ones available, so be sure to compare prices. And if you book a rate based on some type of affiliation, be prepared to show proof of membership or employment when you check in; some hotels are getting stricter about verifying that guests qualify for the discounts they claim. Also, if you're attending a wedding, don't assume that the rate offered to guests of the bride and groom is the lowest available — often, it's not. And if you're the one getting married, it may not be in your best interest to mention the word "honeymoon" when you make your reservation (wait until after you've locked in a rate). Hotels see dollar signs when newlyweds call, so often you'll overpay for a honeymoon package versus booking your own massages and ordering a bottle of champagne.

Ask about extra fees

One of the most frustrating things about comparing prices for hotel rooms is that most Web sites quote room rates without including

WHERE TO CHECK HOTEL RATES

Here are some of your options for comparing hotel prices and what each option is best for, though once you've narrowed the field, you should always check the hotel's Web site, too (or call), because you may get a better rate by booking direct. Although the comparison sites often turn up roughly the same rate for the same hotel, they'll usually offer different choices for whatever city you search, so it's worth shopping around to compare your options, especially if you're flexible about where you stay.

HOTEL SPECIALISTS

- **Five Star Alliance** (fivestaralliance.com). Despite its name, Five Star Alliance is actually more inclusive, booking four- and five-star hotels in the United States and abroad. Its goal isn't to compete on price but rather to show travelers what's available at the upper end of the market and to offer more detailed information about each hotel. It's a good choice if you want to compare luxury hotels without weeding through dozens of budget brands.

- **Hotels.com** (hotels.com). Owned by the same parent company as Expedia and Hotwire, Hotels.com is the specialist of the family, though its search tools aren't as sophisticated as what Expedia offers. Hotels.com shows a wide range of hotel options for major cities, but it's still only a subset of what's available in that market, and it's less useful outside urban areas. You probably won't find any deals for the larger chains, but rates are more competitive for independent hotels.

- **Lodging.com** (lodging.com). Not as big a player as the other hotel specialists, Lodging.com is owned by the same company as Orbitz and tends to have more hotels in the budget market. You'll find the largest selection of options in cities in the United States, though you can also search for places to stay in popular destinations in Canada, the Caribbean, Europe, and Mexico. It's worth a stop to compare prices or to see other options, but its search tools don't match what the big agencies offer.

- **Quikbook** (quikbook.com). Quikbook specializes in independent and boutique hotels, so it's a good site to check if you're looking for something different in an urban market. Quikbook's focus is mostly large cities in the United States, though it also books hotels in vacation destinations like Florida and Arizona. Unlike some of its competitors, Quikbook doesn't require prepayment for many of its lowest rates, and it steers clear of the pop-up ads and upselling the big agencies tend to embrace.

- **Tablet Hotels** (tablethotels.com). Tablet Hotels is a booking service that focuses on unique hotels around the world, with an emphasis on style, ambience, and design. That doesn't mean that all the hotels listed are hipster hangouts; Tablet Hotels also includes many classic and traditional hotels and rates each property's atmosphere, from "quiet" or "secluded" to "happening" or "lively." The site itself is well designed, and it's a good source to find boutique hotels, though most tend to be pricey.

ON-LINE TRAVEL AGENCIES

- **Expedia** (expedia.com). Traditionally, Expedia has been the leader in hotel bookings, offering a wide range of listings and more information about each hotel than you'll find elsewhere. For most hotels, that means lots of photos and sometimes illustrations showing room layouts or virtual tours of public areas. But sorting through all the options Expedia displays can be overwhelming, and the company is aggressive about upselling — trying to get you to book a city tour, a car rental, and a flight with your hotel. Some of Expedia's packages are a good deal, but its à la carte prices aren't as competitive as they once were. Also, if Expedia says that no rooms are available on the date you selected for a particular hotel, try another source (the hotel may not be sold out; it's just that Expedia doesn't have any rooms left to sell).

- **Orbitz** (orbitz.com). Orbitz has some of the best search tools around for finding a hotel, and its clean page design makes it easier to sort through your options (there's less clutter than you'll find on other sites). One especially useful tool is the site's mapping feature, which shows where each hotel is located on a map displayed above the results; hotels disappear from the map as you select a price range and the neighborhood you want. Rates for the larger chains won't necessarily beat the price you can get by booking direct, but you may find better deals for independent hotels.

- **Travelocity** (travelocity.com). Like the other on-line agencies, Travelocity displays a lot of options when you search for a hotel. Although the various tools can help you narrow a long list of results, these features aren't as sophisticated as those offered by Expedia or Orbitz. One plus: Travelocity shows AAA's diamond rating for the hotels in its results, lending the ratings more credibility than other sites' homegrown (often inflated) stars. Lately, the company has been trying to position itself as a customer service champion, but travelers will ultimately be the judge of whether that's more than a marketing slogan.

DISCOUNTERS

- **Hotwire** (hotwire.com). If you're not picky about where you stay, Hotwire may offer lower rates than you'll find elsewhere, especially if you're not traveling at peak times. The catch is, you don't find out the name of the hotel you're staying at until after you book. Hotwire lets you select a city, neighborhood, and your travel dates, then shows you information about various hotel options, including amenities, price, and star rating, but not each hotel's name. That's revealed only after you commit, at which point it's too late to change your mind. Hotwire is best for U.S. cities, but it's also expanding abroad, including destinations in Canada, the Caribbean, Europe, and Mexico.

- **Priceline** (priceline.com). With Priceline, you select a city, your travel dates, a neighborhood, and star rating and then name the price you want to pay. If one of Priceline's hotel partners accepts your offer, there's no backing out, but if no one goes for your bid, you can try again later. More recently, Priceline has started offering a traditional hotel booking option, but its prices aren't as competitive if you choose that route. (For more about using Priceline or Hotwire, see page 76.)

- **LastMinute** (lastminute.com). Formerly called Site59, this site specializes in last-minute packages, so in order to book a hotel, you also have to book either a flight or a car rental. But if you're traveling on short notice, these packages may be cheaper than what you'd pay just for a hotel somewhere else. Most of these packages are for travel in the United States and Canada. (See page 79 for more about last-minute travel.)

taxes and fees. And with taxes on hotel rooms averaging about 13 percent, plus all the extra fees hotels charge — not to mention the fees some agencies charge to make a reservation — you're likely to see a huge jump between your initial quote and the final total on your bill. So when you compare prices, ask whether there are any other fees, besides tax, that aren't included in the room rate. Some of the things hotels may charge extra for are parking, use of the gym, Internet access, an in-room safe (whether or not you use it), turn-down services, newspaper delivery, and even housekeeping. (Resorts sometimes bundle these charges together as a daily "resort fee" automatically added to your bill.) Some hotels are more aggressive than others about this à la carte pricing, so that may influence where you choose to stay. And if you aren't told about extra fees in advance, don't be shy about asking to have them taken off your bill.

Hotel Cancellation Policies: Rules Vary, Depending on Where You Book

Back in the more service-oriented days of travel, it used to be standard practice for hotels to allow guests to call as late as their check-in day and say something like, "Gee, we don't really feel like driving in to the city this weekend, so we'd like to cancel our reservation." More often than not, there was no penalty for flaking out at the last minute, but in recent years, hotels have gotten a lot less forgiving about these kinds of cancellations, charging penalties when guests back out at the eleventh hour.

Fair enough. If a guest scheduled to arrive on my doorstep called to cancel as I was putting away the mop and vacuum cleaner, I'd be happy I had a clean house but still irritated about the change of plans (and that's with no money at stake). What's frustrating for travelers is that there's very little consistency within the industry about when those penalties kick in and not very clear disclosure about them.

Although it's impossible to sum up every hotel or travel seller's cancellation policy, here are some factors that influence any penalty you may have to pay.

- *The seventy-two-hour rule.* In many cases, if you cancel a hotel reservation at least seventy-two hours before your check-in time, you won't be on the hook for any penalties charged by the hotel. That three-day window varies — you may be able to cancel forty-eight, twenty-four, or even a few hours before arrival penalty-free, and that cut-off point may be a week with a B&B — but as a general rule, seventy-two hours is a safe bet. If you cancel after that deadline, whatever it is, expect to pay a penalty of at least a one-night charge (plus tax), or as much as the entire stay.
- *Discounted Internet rates.* If you book certain discounted rates through a hotel's Web site or an on-line travel agency, you may be subject to a stiffer cancellation penalty — or you may not be allowed to cancel at all. If you have to prepay for your stay (instead

of paying at check-out) or you're booking some kind of "special" rate, those are both tip-offs that the cancellation policy is probably more strict. As one hotel executive told me, "The customer gets a lower rate in exchange for losing that flexibility." So don't go for these deals unless your plans are set in stone.

- *On-line agency penalties.* In addition to whatever penalty the hotel charges, most on-line travel agencies impose their own cancellation fees. Hotels.com, Expedia, Orbitz, and Travelocity typically charge a $25 penalty no matter when you cancel your hotel reservation (there are exceptions, but this penalty applies to most rooms they sell). Quikbook charges a $10 fee for cancellations to prepaid reservations.
- *No refunds.* Discount travel sellers like Hotwire and Priceline have a very simple policy about cancellations: They don't offer any refunds, and they don't allow any changes to reservations. Because you have to prepay with both of these sites, you won't get any money back if you cancel.
- *Holiday travel.* You may also encounter stricter rules if you're staying at a resort or traveling during the holidays. In either case, the penalty-free cut-off date for cancellations may be weeks or months before you're scheduled to arrive. That's because hotels in vacation destinations tend to sell out during the holidays, and empty rooms in remote locations are difficult to fill at a late date.
- *Early-departure fees.* Besides tightening their cancellation penalties, hotels have become less tolerant of early departures. If you don't stay for the number of nights you reserved, you may have to pay for your whole reservation anyway or be charged an early-departure fee — say, one night of your stay. If you book through a third party, you'll probably have a tougher time getting a refund for any unused nights than if you book directly with the hotel.

Understanding Hotel Ratings: One Rater Says Three Stars; Another Says Four

One of the ways many of us decide which hotel to stay at is the number of stars next to its name. "Well, it's a four-star hotel, so it must be pretty nice," you've probably thought to yourself — if not boasted to a friend.

But as it turns out, hotel ratings are a very subjective — and controversial — business, and there's very little consensus about what all those stars actually mean. So before you pay top dollar for what you *think* is a four-star hotel or tell your traveling companion about the luxury lodging you've booked, here's what you need to know about hotel ratings and all the grade inflation that's been going on in the industry.

Mobil and AAA: The gold standard

The two pioneers in the ratings business are Mobil and AAA, both of which have been evaluating hotels for about fifty years — originally as a service to drivers looking for advice on where to pull over and catch a few winks. Mobil rates hotels on a star system (see mobiltravelguide.com), whereas AAA uses diamonds (see aaa.com/diamonds), with five being the top rating in either case. But even with similar evaluation processes, Mobil and AAA don't always come up with the same rating for a hotel — though there's certainly a lot of overlap between their lists.

For the hotels they evaluate, both companies send inspectors who look at criteria like whether there's a pool, if room service is available around the clock, and how the bathroom is stocked (cheap shampoo and a thin shower curtain or fancy brands and plush towels). For top-tier hotels, Mobil and AAA also do an incognito service evaluation, judging things like the check-in process, how housekeeping responds to requests, and whether the concierge desk is merely courteous or goes the extra mile. (Lest you think that it's time for a career change, insiders say these inspectors have a tough job.)

For the most part, hotels consider these two rating systems "the gold standard," and some executives lose sleep anticipating their release every year — if not their jobs, should a star or diamond suddenly disappear. But as Internet booking has taken off, a number of on-line travel agencies have started assigning their own hotel ratings, with a tendency to hand out stars more freely than the old guard.

Travel agency ratings: Stars and more stars

Expedia, Hotels.com, Hotwire, Orbitz, and Priceline are among the sites that have developed their own rating systems, typically using stars to differentiate between hotels at the upper end of the spectrum and those with less exacting standards. Bucking that trend, Travelocity displays AAA's diamond ratings for many of the hotels listed on the site, but uses its own ratings for hotels AAA hasn't evaluated.

The problem is, many of these sites don't fully disclose how they come up with these ratings, other than to say that they take customer feedback and other rating systems into account. Although most do post a page explaining each star category, it's often easy to miss — and so cursory, it doesn't really help differentiate between a hotel that's merely passable and one that stands out. And to say that grade inflation is an issue on the Web would be an understatement — some sites even use half stars, so a four-and-a-half-star rating has become sort of the A− given to a wide range of hotels.

Where this really becomes an issue is when you're booking on Priceline or Hotwire and don't know which hotel you're getting until after your credit card has been charged. You may be willing to pay $175 a night for what Mobil or AAA considers a four-star hotel, but if the hotel that accepts your offer is a four-star hotel only in Priceline's universe, that's a different story.

The bottom line: Look closely at the ratings on-line travel agencies assign, and compare them to other sources before you boast about your sweet deal to a friend — or promise your spouse that you've booked a luxury hotel.

Customer ratings: The people's choice

A travel executive once compared AAA and Mobil's ratings to the Academy Awards, and ratings based on customer surveys to the People's Choice Awards — which struck me as a pretty good analogy. But within the realm of customer feedback, there's a further distinction: Ratings based on surveys of hundreds or thousands of travelers and the less statistically sound — if more entertaining — feedback you can find on the Web.

The leaders in the more formal category are magazines like *Condé Nast Traveler* and *Travel + Leisure,* which survey readers annually about their favorite hotels and publish the results. (See page 85 for more about these lists.) Zagat Survey Guides — best known for restaurant reviews — publishes two guidebooks based on similar customer surveys: *Top U.S. Hotels, Resorts & Spas* and *Top International Hotels, Resorts & Spas.* All these sources are good for getting a sense of how a lot of travelers felt about a particular hotel, though they cover mostly the upper end of the market.

For more unfettered opinions about a wider range of hotels, check some of the Web sites mentioned on page 128 that let visitors post hotel reviews, like TripAdvisor (tripadvisor.com) or HotelShark (hotelshark.com). Although the opinions posted at these sites are sometimes all over the map, they're often the only way you'll find out whether one wing of a hotel is undergoing renovations or whether there's a cutthroat competition for beach chairs at a particular resort.

International hotel ratings: Stars aren't the same

In some foreign countries, especially in Europe, a government agency determines hotel ratings, generally based on objective criteria like whether there's an elevator in the hotel, phones in the bathrooms, and king-size beds for guests who like to stretch out. In other words, these ratings aren't necessarily based on service evaluations, and they may not correspond to the rating systems used in the United States. (What's considered a four-star hotel in another country may be only a three-star hotel in America.)

For an opinion that does take service into account, Michelin (viamichelin.com) is the European counterpart to Mobil and AAA (Michelin also publishes guidebooks). You have to register to access its hotel listings on line, but it's worth the few minutes it takes. The Web site offers useful search tools to find hotels throughout Europe, with clear maps showing where each hotel is located, what amenities it offers, and its rating — represented by icons ranging from a small building (indicating a "comfortable hotel") to a large building (representing a "top-class comfortable and pleasant hotel").

Finding a B&B or Inn: Places for Travelers Who Like to Feel at Home

The idea of staying at a bed and breakfast tends to elicit strong reactions among travelers, many of whom associate B&Bs with floral bedspreads, patterned wallpaper, and rooms with themed names (say, the Lavender room or the Great Gatsby suite). Although that stereotype isn't entirely inaccurate — many *are* decorated in a style reminiscent of *Little House on the Prairie* — you can also find B&Bs that look more like they were inspired by the pages of Pottery Barn, *Martha Stewart Living*, or L.L. Bean.

In fact, some establishments that serve a morning meal go to great lengths to avoid calling themselves a bed and breakfast, preferring terms like *inn, lodge, guest house,* or *ranch.* And outside the United States, the same type of accommodation might be called something else entirely: *pensione* or *agriturismo* in Italy or a *chambre d'hôte* in France.

So I'm using the term *bed and breakfast* loosely here and somewhat interchangeably with *inn,* basically referring to a smaller establishment where the owner is involved in day-to-day operations and breakfast is served to guests. That usually involves some amount of mingling with your fellow travelers — a draw or a drawback, depending on your perspective — and generally closer quarters than you'll find at most hotels.

These types of places don't necessarily show up on Web sites that list bigger hotels and resorts, so here's how you go about finding them — and how to make sure that the one you choose is a good fit for you *and* your traveling companion. I'll avoid stereotyping along gender lines, but B&Bs don't always appeal to both members of a couple traveling together. They also don't necessarily welcome guests who travel in strollers, so best to ask before bringing the kids. (For more tips on choosing a B&B, see the sidebar on page 143.)

Where to look

If you want more of a traditional bed-and-breakfast experience, a good place to start is BedandBreakfast.com, a site that claims to list more than 25,000 B&Bs, inns, and guest houses around the world, though most are in the United States. The site is well designed, with good search tools, photos, and clear summaries of relevant details, so you can tell at a glance whether the place welcomes children (some quite explicitly don't), the price, and how many rooms it has. BedandBreakfast.com also takes reservations, but you may be able to negotiate a better price by booking direct.

Another Web site, BBOnline.com, lists about five thousand B&Bs and also handles reservations. Although it has a less polished feel than BedandBreakfast.com, it's worth checking for a second opinion. With both sites, B&Bs have to pay to be listed, so if you limit your search to these two sources, you'll miss out on places that didn't join.

Other sources

Another strategy is to do an Internet search for your destination and "bed and breakfast" or "inn," which often turns up links to local lodging or B&B associations, as well as listings for specific inns. The Professional Association of Innkeepers International (paii.org) also has links to state associations, which list member B&Bs. Look for the link to "Other Associations" in the site's Resources section.

Besides sites that specialize in the bed-and-breakfast market, you can get information about these types of accommodations from more general lodging sources. TripAdvisor.com, best known for its hotel reviews, also posts feedback about B&Bs and inns, and both AAA and Mobil rate B&Bs.

Another way to find alternatives to a big hotel is by tracking down a local visitors bureau (see page 19). Staff at these agencies probably won't tell you which inn has drafty rooms or the best breakfast in town but may know about places that aren't listed in any of the directories.

There are also guidebooks that specifically cover bed and breakfasts, often focusing on a particular region, like the northeastern United States. But some of these books require establishments to pay a fee to be included, so before you buy one, try to find out whether you're getting an editorial or financially driven selection.

WHAT TO ASK: CHOOSING A B&B

Booking any place you've never stayed at before is always a bit of a gamble, but in some sense, the smaller the establishment, the bigger the risks. With a large hotel chain, there's usually some consistency within the brand and more options to change rooms if the sink backs up or your neighbors are having a fight at 2 A.M.

Then again, at many B&Bs, the owner is the person dealing with your request, and service is often a priority. But the best way to make sure that a B&B or an inn is a good fit is to ask lots of questions before you commit. Here's a cheat sheet you can use as a script.

- *How many guest rooms are there?*
  This is sort of a Goldilocks question, so what number feels "just right" to you may vary from the norm (about eight rooms on average for B&Bs). If there are only two or three guest rooms, that may be too intimate for your tastes, whereas a couple dozen rooms may mean less attentive service and a breakfast of cold toast and cafeteria-style scrambled eggs.

- *Will you have to share a bathroom?*
  Some people don't mind sharing a bathroom, but even if you're open to the idea, it's worth asking how many people will be jockeying for a shower in the morning and how far the bathroom is from your room. (Not to mention whether there's a "water closet" separate from the shower queue.)

- *What's for breakfast?*
  If the breakfast spread is important to you, don't be shy about asking what type of food you can expect. The offerings can vary from a selection of day-old pastries, coffee, and juice made from concentrate to the proprietor's famous pecan pancakes served with eggs, bacon, sausage, fresh-squeezed orange juice, and toasted homemade bread. (If a B&B touts a special recipe on its Web site, that's usually a good sign.)

- *What time can you eat?*
  Another detail worth inquiring about is *when* breakfast is served. Sometimes, the window of opportunity is limited and may not coincide with your schedule, especially if you like to sleep in. On the flip side, I once stayed at a B&B the night daylight savings time took effect — turning a three-hour time difference into four — and got reprimanded for sneaking into the kitchen and making coffee before the cook showed up. (Another

quirk of some B&Bs: Inadvertently — or deliberately — breaking a house rule can make you feel as though you're ten years old all over again.)

- *Can you get Internet access or watch TV?*
  You're less likely to find in-room televisions or Internet access at a hundred-year-old inn, so if watching the news or checking your e-mail is a priority, ask about your options before you check in.

- *What's the cancellation policy?*
  B&Bs sometimes have more restrictive cancellation policies than you'll find at a big hotel chain, requiring more advance notice if you have to cancel. Rules and penalties vary, so ask when you book.

- *Are extra guests allowed?*
  Since B&Bs often occupy older buildings, the rooms tend to be smaller than what you'd find in a modern hotel. That may mean there isn't space for a cot or a crib in some guest rooms, so if you're traveling with an extra person (or two), ask about the sleeping arrangements well in advance — and if you're planning to bring the kids, make sure that children are welcome.

- *Are there any common areas besides the dining room?*
  If it's a rainy day or you don't feel like venturing out, you may not want to spend an entire afternoon cooped up in your room. Some B&Bs have other common areas where you can read a book, watch TV, or just lounge, so if communal space is important, ask where guests are welcome to hang out.

- *Is there a curfew?*
  Most B&Bs don't have a formal curfew, but some do lock the doors after a certain time at night or at least discourage you from staying out until the wee hours and then waking everyone else when you tromp up the creaky wooden stairs and run water through old pipes. You might also be subject to a curfew if you stay at a hostel or a place that borders on a hostel experience, especially abroad (see the sidebar on the facing page for more about budget lodging options).

- *Is the rate negotiable?*
  You may be speaking directly with the owner when you call to make a reservation, which means that there might be some wiggle room on the rate. Whether you can talk yourself into a better deal depends on the economy and your negotiating skills, but it's worth asking, especially if you're a repeat customer, traveling off-season, or planning a longer stay.

HOSTELS: BUNKING ON A BUDGET

If you're traveling on a tight budget, staying at a hostel is an option worth investigating — especially if you're attracted by the idea of spending just $20 or $30 a night for a place to rest your head. Although hostels have a reputation as crash pads for the college backpacker set, there's a wider range of options than the dormitory-style bunks many people associate with the hostel experience, including rooms for one or two people instead of eight or ten. And with the Internet, you can even preview the accommodations before you pack your bag.

A good place to start is Hostelworld.com, an on-line service that takes reservations for more than nine thousand hostels and budget hotels around the world. It's a well-designed site, with detailed descriptions, photos, and ratings for each listing; past guests rate the hostel's location, cleanliness, security, and staff and can also post comments.

Another option is Hostelling International USA (hiusa.org), the U.S. affiliate of the Hostelling International network, which has its own Web site (hihostels.com). To stay at some of these hostels, you have to become a member (annual fees range from $18 to $28, depending on your age); others let you pay a nominal one-time fee instead.

Renting a House or Condo: Finding and Evaluating Rental Options

Staying in a hotel certainly has its appeal: Someone else makes your bed every morning, you get fresh towels every time you take a shower, and in the best of all worlds, there's a pool with a hot tub and sauna. But for some trips, what you really want is the comforts of home — well, someone else's home — with multiple bedrooms, a kitchen so you don't have to eat out all the time, and a living room where you can kick back and relax. Also, renting a house is sometimes a more affordable way to travel and often gives you the feeling of really living in a destination rather than being surrounded by tourists in an area populated mostly by hotels.

With so many on-line services popping up that list vacation properties for rent, it's gotten much easier to find rental options. That said, a lot of the homes posted on the Internet are rented by owner, instead of an agency, which puts more of a burden on you to make sure that your vacation isn't fodder for a story you tell about the house rental from hell.

Here are some tips on finding a place to rent, whether you choose to work with an agency or negotiate directly with the owner. (For tips on what to ask when renting, see the sidebar on page 149.) In popular destinations, the best places get snapped up quickly, so don't wait until June to start looking for a Fourth of July beach house.

Working with a rental agency

Before the Internet, most people thumbed through the classifieds to find rental properties or tracked down an agency that handled vacation rentals wherever they planned to go. It's safe to say that many of those print ads have migrated to on-line listing services, but plenty of travelers still opt to work with an agency — especially if they're traveling somewhere they've never been before.

One of the advantages of working with an agency is that it lends some security to the process: the person you're dealing with presumably knows the market, has seen the places you're considering, and can tell you the pros and cons of each one. You also have someone to turn to if the hot water heater stops working, and because an agency stakes its reputation on happy customers and repeat business, it's less likely to place you in a dump. But agencies take a cut of the rental fee, which means that the properties they handle often cost more than ones rented by owner. They also tend to represent just a fraction of the properties available in an area, so you may have to try multiple agencies to see a range of options.

To find a rental agency, call a real estate office at your destination, which may refer you to a company that specializes in vacation rentals (real estate companies that handle home sales don't necessarily deal with rentals). A local visitors bureau or chamber of commerce can also refer you to a rental agency, or try searching the Internet for the name of your destination and "rental agency" or "vacation rental." Most companies that manage vacation properties have Web sites, so you can browse through photos and descriptions of the homes they have available.

WHERE TO FIND RENTAL PROPERTIES

Here are a few Web sites that offer some of the most extensive listings of houses, condos, cottages, and apartments for rent, mostly in the United States but some overseas destinations as well. These sites list primarily homes available for rent directly from the owner, but some rental agencies also post properties on these sites.

CyberRentals (cyberrentals.com)
Great Rentals (greatrentals.com)
Rentalo (rentalo.com)
Vacation Rentals By Owner (vrbo.com)
VacationRentals.com (vacationrentals.com)

Renting directly from the owner

Your other option is to explore some of the Internet services that list vacation homes for rent, mostly by owner, in destinations all over the world (see the sidebar above for details). Owners pay a fee to post their properties on these sites, but you can browse the listings for free (although sometimes, you have to register in order to send a message inquiring about a rental).

The main advantage of an on-line service is that it offers easy access to a wide selection of properties. Some of the bigger services list thousands of places for rent, including Victorian houses on Cape Cod, ski cabins in Colorado, villas in France and Italy, beach houses in Mexico or the Caribbean, and even the occasional "mansion" (at least, according to the owner).

But these services provide a forum just for listings — they don't verify the accuracy of the information owners post (or even confirm that the property exists), and they don't assume any liability for the rental. You contact the property owner directly and negotiate all the arrangements yourself. Although some rental agencies also post their own properties on these services, most of the listings are posted by the owner.

Compared to other travel Web sites, many of these on-line rental services feel pretty homegrown (several did start as hobbies), and the quality of the listings varies widely. Some owners post detailed descriptions of their homes, with lots of photos and calendars showing which days or weeks are available for rent. Other owners may take a more minimalist approach or choose primarily photos that highlight the surrounding area more than the actual house (or vice versa).

Also, some owners are lackadaisical about responding to inquiries — maybe ignoring someone who asks about renting the house for a week they've already booked or who mentions that they're traveling with five kids, two cats, and three dogs. So if you don't get a response in a few days, assume that the house isn't available, and move on.

Renting a house abroad

For overseas rentals, working with an agency is often the best way to go. Although you can find many ads on the Internet for homes in other countries that are rented by owner, a cross-border transaction can get complicated, if not linguistically and culturally a challenge. Although many ads are written in passable English, if a bit off topic (Italians, I've noticed, have a tendency to write more about the history of the region and its connections to famous people — say, Leonardo da Vinci — than the house), any language barrier becomes a real issue when you're working out the terms of the rental.

Companies that handle foreign rentals typically specialize in a particular region, so you have to search the Internet with that in mind. Try the name of the city, town, or region you want to visit, plus lots of variations on phrases like "rental agency" or "vacation rental." Depending on the local lingo and the type of house you want, "villa" or "cottage" may turn up more results, and in England, they go on holiday rather than taking a vacation, so "holiday rental" is your best bet.

In some destinations, you may even find a rental agency that is run by American expats — such as locogringo.com, a booking service that arranges rentals in Mexico's Riviera Maya region. There are also U.S.-based companies that handle overseas rentals. Rentvillas.com and VillaVacations.com are two agencies that coordinate rentals in Europe; to find others, an Internet search is the best way to go.

RENTING SIGHT UNSEEN: WHAT TO ASK

Many listings don't exactly tell you everything you want to know about the place they're advertising, but that doesn't mean you can't ask for more details, or more photos. Here are a few things you should investigate about a possible rental before you agree to a deal and what to get in writing before you show up. If the owner (or your rental agent) seems evasive, unresponsive, or unwilling to answer your questions, that usually bodes trouble, so go with your gut feeling if you're having doubts. Even if you're desperate to find a place, it's not worth getting entangled with someone you don't trust.

THE PROPERTY

If the pictures show the house only from a distance or have no view of the outside at all, ask for the shots you want. And if the description says "sleeps eight," find out whether everyone can sleep in a bedroom or whether some guests will be drawing straws for the pull-out couch. Other issues to investigate: how many bathrooms have showers, how well the kitchen is equipped (especially if you plan to cook), whether there's a washer and dryer, and how close the neighbors are. As for any other features mentioned in the ad — like a beach, lake access, or a pool — get details. The more you ask, the less likely you'll be disappointed.

THE AREA

It's easy to get wrapped up in details about the property and overlook what's outside the front door. Be sure you understand where the house is located, and ask about nearby services, like restaurants, shopping, and a grocery store. If you're driving, make sure that parking is available; if not, find out about transportation options. And if you have any health concerns, it's a good idea to ask about nearby medical facilities — there won't be a concierge to help you find a hospital.

PAYMENT

If you're planning to travel off-season or stay for several weeks, there may be negotiating room on the asking price — but don't assume that the owner will take whatever you offer. (And if a deal seems too good to be true, there's probably a reason the price is so low.) You'll usually have to pay a deposit up front, but get the terms of the rental in writing before you send any money. The lease should specify your rental dates, the price you agreed to, when the final payment is due, and the cancellation policy, as well as any additional charges, like a cleaning fee, local taxes, utilities, or a security deposit. If possible, pay with a credit card, which gives you some protection if the deal goes south. Some homeowners accept plastic, as do some rental agencies.

REFERENCES

If you know anyone who lives near the house you're considering, your best bet is to ask that person to take a look at it or at least drive by the property. Another option is to ask for references from past renters or a company that provides a service for the owner (like a lawn service or a gardener). They may not offer much information about a client's home, but at least you can verify that it exists and has some connection to a company in the area. You can also look up the home's address at a site like MapQuest — but ultimately, you have to follow your gut. If the owner communicates only via e-mail and cell phone and won't give you a work number or the street address of the home, find another option.

LOGISTICS

Once you've settled on a rental, make sure that you have clear directions to the property and a way to contact the owner (or rental agency) during your stay if anything goes wrong. Many owners leave detailed instructions at the house, covering issues like using the appliances, where to take the garbage, and how to work the fireplace — not to mention brochures about what to do in the area — but it doesn't hurt to ask whether the owner typically leaves some type of renter's guide.

Doing a Home Exchange: With the Web, House Swaps Catch On

Before I did research for an article about home exchanges, I assumed that people who chose this vacation option were mostly travelers on a budget, trading modest, inconveniently located homes. But as soon as I started browsing the listings at home exchange Web sites, I nearly whipped out a digital camera, fluffed up my pillows, and posted my own listing — ready to trade my New York apartment for a vine-covered villa in Tuscany, a house on the coast of Maine, or any number of Caribbean condos.

Swapping homes is a practice that started among teachers looking for ways to economize during their summer vacations; interested swappers subscribed to print catalogs listing potential trading partners around the world. But as home exchange services migrated to the Internet in the 1990s, the concept caught on with a wider range of travelers — including people who could afford a nice hotel but would rather trade their not-so-modest digs for an equally comfortable home somewhere else.

There's just one catch: You have to be willing to open up your home to strangers who may set a sweaty drink glass on your heirloom coffee table or run your good chopping knives through the dishwasher. But if the thought of such transgressions doesn't make you shudder, there may be a villa in Italy with your name on it.

Which brings up another caveat: If you don't live near a destination other people want to visit, you may not find as many takers interested in your offer to swap. Home-exchange services tell you not to assume that no one would want to stay at your house in suburban Ohio — you may find someone who wants to visit relatives nearby — but the reality is, homes in more popular travel destinations generate more offers.

How it works

These days, most home exchanges are facilitated by a few services that operate primarily on line: HomeExchange.com, HomeLink, and Intervac are three of the biggest (see the sidebar on page 152 for details). Despite some differences among these services, they basically do the same thing: provide a place for people to post listings describing their homes (with photos), where they're interested in traveling, and a way to contact potential exchange partners.

The main difference is that HomeExchange.com lets nonmembers contact members who have paid to join and post a listing (fees for these services are about $65 to $100 per year), which means that you can browse through its listings and send inquiries to prospective swap mates without joining. HomeLink and Intervac, which have both been around for more than fifty years, let only members view their listings, which they publish on line and in print catalogs. The advantage of joining and posting your own listing is that you're likely to connect with more people; also, some people are more comfortable swapping with other members.

HOME EXCHANGE SERVICES

The top three home-exchange services all claim to have between 5,000 and 10,000 paying members; despite squabbling over which organization is actually "the largest," they're all big enough to offer a wide range of exchange partners all over the world. The other services are smaller but may be worth checking out.

- **HomeExchange.com** (www.homeexchange.com)

- **HomeLink** (www.homelink.org)

- **Intervac** (www.intervac.com)

- **Other options: Digsville** (digsville.com), **Home Base Holidays** (home base-hols.com), and **Vacation Homes Unlimited** (exchangehomes.com)

Testing the waters

If you browse the listings at HomeExchange.com, you'll probably be tempted to give it a go. The options available run the gamut from apartments in major cities like New York, Paris, Chicago, Sydney, and Rome to houses in more pastoral settings like the south of France, the Caribbean, Tuscany, or California's Napa Valley.

Don't be discouraged if you send out a bunch of inquiries and don't hear back from everyone; some people don't bother to reply if they're not interested in what you have to offer. Europeans often want to exchange for two or three weeks — which isn't always an option for Americans with a paltry two weeks of vacation — but within the United States, weekend exchanges aren't uncommon, especially among people swapping a second home.

As for security concerns, people who run home-exchange services say that they've never heard of anything being stolen from a member's home during an exchange (which doesn't mean it's never happened) and that any problems people report tend to be minor issues like a broken dish or less than accurate information about the home (an apartment wasn't quite as close to the beach as described). Although none of the services vet members or take responsibility for anything that goes wrong during an exchange, they all offer tips on checking out your prospective partner and agreeing on terms (see the sidebar on the facing page for advice).

TIPS FOR A HAPPY HOME EXCHANGE

Letting guests stay in your home while you're away is always a bit nervous making, especially if you're particular about cleanliness or your blood pressure rises when someone messes up the TV settings by using the wrong remote. That's even more of a gamble when you're handing over the keys to a stranger, so here are some tips to help ensure a smooth swap.

- *Be specific.* Like Internet dating profiles or auction listings, descriptions in ads for house swaps sometimes exaggerate the appeal of the offering. Press for details on phrases like *on the beach, walking distance to town,* or *sleeps four* — and if you don't see a photo of that *ocean view,* ask the owner to e-mail you one.

- *Ask for references.* Even if you have the interviewing skills of an FBI interrogator, don't just rely on the homeowner's honesty; ask for phone numbers of past exchange partners, and check them out. (Even if it's an international call, spring for the expense rather than relying on e-mail, which is easy to forge.) When dealing with first-time exchangers, get other types of references if possible.

- *Check your insurance coverage.* Most homeowner's insurance policies cover guests staying in your home, but check your policy or call your provider to be sure. Some exchanges also include use of a car; before you hand over your keys, check your auto insurance coverage.

- *Sign an agreement.* Most home-exchange services offer sample agreements that members can use to outline the terms of the swap. Among the things you should put in writing: who's responsible for cleaning, whether use of a car or a computer is included, how any damage to the home will be handled, and what happens if one of you backs out.

- *Leave detailed instructions.* Leave a note on the kitchen table with instructions on minor matters like whether your plants should be watered and whether you'd prefer that your fluffy white bath towels not be used down by the dock. Protocol dictates that these nitpicky requests be accompanied by helpful hints like restaurant recommendations, the closest gas station, and public transportation options and often a welcoming gift like locally made honey or a bottle of wine.

- *Enlist a friend to check up.* Some people choose to leave their keys with a friend, who can both unlock the door and serve as a caretaker/spy. Especially if you'll be in another country, it's good to have someone on the home front who can step in if the refrigerator stops running or your guests lock themselves out of the house.

Browser Beware: Photos and Descriptions
May Be Much Nicer Than Reality

I once made a reservation to stay at a ranch in northern California after admiring photos on the Web that made it seem like the place had an ocean view. Never mind that I knew the area well enough to figure out that no building in that town could possibly look out over the Pacific — I saw the blue water sparkling in the photo, and I was seduced. (Our actual view: a dusty driveway and an equally dusty horse corral.)

As far as I'm concerned, every photo that appears on a travel Web site should be accompanied by a warning: "Accommodations are not nearly as nice as they appear." (Although there are certainly exceptions to this rule — I've also seen unflattering photos of hotel rooms and wondered, "Is this really the best they could do?") With text, I think it's often easier to see through the exaggerations — maybe because the writing generally isn't very subtle. But even so, it seems that everyone has a tale to tell about staying at a place that wasn't exactly as billed.

So whether you're renting a condo, booking a B&B, or reserving a room at a fancy hotel, it's wise to take everything you see or read with a grain of salt — especially if it doesn't come from an independent source. Here are some tips that can help narrow the gap between expectations and reality and hopefully prevent unpleasant surprises when you arrive. (For a list of words that should trigger skepticism, see page 157.)

Know your acres and miles

When talking about property in rural areas, it's not uncommon for people to use the term *acres* — as in, "Our bed and breakfast sits on six wooded acres outside town . . ." To a city slicker, that certainly *sounds* bucolic, but once you venture beyond a world of seven-hundred-square-foot apartments and restaurants with eight inches between tables, six acres is not that large. (It takes 640 acres to add up to a square mile, so on 6 acres, you're not exactly getting away from it all.) Do the math if you're told that a hotel is "half a mile from the beach" (that's a long walk in flip-flops) or "ten blocks from the civic center" (How long are those blocks?). And if the descriptions are somewhat vague — for instance, "close to the beach" or "within walking distance of downtown shopping district" — press for some real numbers.

Consult your own map

Sometimes, a hotel, inn, or travel agency will include a small map on its Web site, showing where the property is located. But it's always a good idea to consult an independent map — either on line or the old-fashioned fold-out kind — so you can really judge things like how close you'll be to a subway stop or the nearest restaurant. The hotel's map may be a bit selective in what it displays, showing only the main streets, so what seems like two or three blocks could actually be ten or fifteen, and a busy highway may not appear at all. It's also a good idea to get as much information as possible about the neighborhood. For instance, train and bus stations are often in grittier areas, so if a hotel is "near the train station" or "by the bus terminal," that's not necessarily a selling point. (Although in some cities, like Amsterdam, trains do pull up to a perfectly acceptable part of town, so being near a transportation hub isn't always a drawback.)

Read the reviews

If you're planning to stay at a hotel or a resort, check for reviews from past guests at Web sites like TripAdvisor.com or HotelShark .com. (You may find feedback about an inn or B&B, too.) Another option is to do an Internet search for the name of the hotel or owner, which might turn up a comment on a past guest's home page or blog. Customer feedback, often anonymous, can be maddeningly contradictory, so look for reviews that include positive and negative comments, and give more weight to recent opinions, since hotels change over time.

Call a neighbor

When I lived in San Francisco — where it can be completely foggy in one neighborhood and sunny twenty blocks away — my room-mate taught me a trick: To find out what the weather was like at the beach, we called a restaurant nearby. That won't help you predict the weather during your vacation, but if you're traveling to a small town, chances are that someone who works at a restaurant or other business nearby could give you the lowdown on your lodging options. The trick is finding someone willing to chat, so if you do yoga, try calling a local yoga studio or if you're planning to ski, a ski rental shop. They'll want your business during your visit, so they may try to score points by giving you advice.

Ask about the amenities

It's one thing to read that a hotel has a pool or that a house is on a lake and quite another to find out whether these features really match whatever vision you've conjured up. The Olympic pool de-scribed on a hotel's Web site may have only two lanes for laps (Did the photo show the entire pool or only a corner with an attractive woman in a bikini?), and the lake touted by a rental agency may be a muddy weed-filled pond. You may not be able to get anyone to fess up about shortcomings — and the amenities advertised might live up to your expectations — but if photos seem strategically cropped or tightly shot, resist the urge to fill in the blank.

Assume that the weather will be worse

Certain people freely admit to being weather jinxes: bringing rain or unseasonably low (or high) temperatures wherever they go. These people are in the minority, though, because the rest of us as-sume that if we're going to the beach, it will be sunny and seventy-nine degrees every day. After all, that's how it looks in the photos. There's nothing wrong with being optimistic, but you can avoid a major disappointment by making sure that you're not renting a house during hurricane season or when the black flies keep every-one indoors. In the real world, these things happen on vacation — but not in any of the photos that enticed you to leave home.

WORDS TO THE WARY

It's not so much that travel sellers lie, but they have a tendency to commit lesser sins, like exaggeration or omission. Here are some words and phrases that should trigger skepticism — or at least a closer look.

- *Ceiling fan:* In theory, it seems like a soothing way to fall asleep, but it can also mean that there's no air conditioning in a place where nighttime temperatures never drop below "unbearable."

- *Charming:* Usually flattering when used to describe people but with room décor, it can mean patterned wallpaper, busy upholstery, and an excessive use of knick-knacks adorning tables and shelves.

- *Cozy:* Translated into square footage, often means tiny guest rooms and a tendency for noise to pass easily between them.

- *Garden room:* Usually, the opposite of a room with an ocean view, but that garden may be a small patch of grass alongside the parking lot.

- *Hip:* Typically used to indicate the influence of a high-priced designer, but it also tends to signal insufficient lighting in rooms, impractical furniture, and guests who won't be sympathetic when your toddler has a meltdown.

- *Mosquito netting:* Where there is mosquito netting, there are mosquitoes.

- *Remote:* Sometimes, getting away from it all means that there's nowhere else to go for dinner when you find out that the chef's cooking is tasteless or that the gift shop charges double what you'd pay anywhere else.

- *Renovated:* The thing about renovations is that they never seemed to end on a specific date (or on schedule), so if a place has been "recently renovated," make sure that you're not going to be in the middle of a construction site when you're trying to relax.

- *Rustic:* May mean wood paneling and furnishings from L. L. Bean, or that the radiator clangs like a fire alarm and the pipes tend to freeze.

- *Secluded:* Also described as "private" but runs the gamut from plenty of space between bungalows to a hedge separating you from your neighbor's late-night fun.

- *Shared bathroom:* Sharing is generally good, but sharing a bathroom with six or eight other guests may turn your entire vacation into a competition over hot water and toilet privileges.

- *View:* Frequently means that from some vantage point, there's a view — just not from the window in your room (though perhaps from the window in your bathroom, if you stick your neck out far enough).

6 Cruises

FOR A LONG TIME, the joke about cruising was that it was a travel option favored by the "newly wed or nearly dead," but the industry has been hard at work to give that image a makeover — with some success. Now, the glossy ads you see for cruise lines show young couples embracing against a railing at dusk, kids splashing in the pool, and attractive passengers across the age spectrum cavorting on jet skis, scaling rock-climbing walls, and taking brisk walks around the promenade deck. (Even the *Love Boat* didn't have this much action.) Bingo, blackjack, and show tunes — though still on board most ships — don't play a big role in the marketing message. The goal is to convince more people to give cruising a try, especially families and younger travelers.

Thus baited, I took my first cruise, along Alaska's Inside Passage, and did in fact make the leap from the skeptical camp to those who have tried cruising and would do it again. The main appeal: The cruise lines are on to something when they say that it's a less stressful way to travel: no decisions to make about finding a restaurant or hotel, no fights over which route to take in the rental car (unless you rent one on shore), no packing up and relocating if you want to visit multiple places in one trip. And if you like being around water, you may find that you get your money's worth just taking in the view on deck.

That said, I found that some of the stereotypes about cruising are still alive and well — starting with the fact that there weren't many passengers younger than fifty on my ship, and the on-board entertainment *was* mostly song-and-dance routines and magic tricks. Certainly, plenty of people on board loved those shows — and the casino and the bingo tournaments — but different cruise lines offer different experiences, so it's important to choose one that's a good fit.

The goal of this chapter is to help you do just that, as well as figure out when and where to book a cruise to get the best deal, how to
decide whether you should book shore excursions through the
cruise line or go it alone, and where to find on-line cruise communities that can answer more of your questions about vacationing at
sea — and some you probably wouldn't think to ask.

Cruise Lines 101: An Overview of Your Options

If you've never cruised before, the first thing you need to know is
that not all cruise lines are created equal. Although several lines are
owned by the same company, and most of the larger ships have the
same basic footprint — a casino, spa, pool, gym, several dining
rooms, and a theater with a heavy dose of glitz — like siblings, two
cruise lines can have the same parents and similar DNA and still attract entirely different crowds.

Even within the same cruise line, each ship has its own personality, based on size, age, where the ship sails, and the mix of passengers on board, not to mention when the redecorating team last
visited. So booking a cruise is more than a matter of simply comparing prices; choosing a ship that's a good fit can really make or
break your trip.

Here's an overview of how the major cruise lines stack up, based
on categories the industry uses that generally reflect how much you
can expect to spend.

Mass-market cruise lines

There isn't a consensus about what to call cruise lines at the more
economical end of the spectrum, so you may hear them referred to
as *mass market, resort, mainstream,* or *contemporary* (whatever that
means). These cruise lines tend to appeal more to families, single
travelers, and younger passengers, in part because of their lower
prices, and generally sail larger ships that feel like floating resorts,
with more restaurant choices, more pools, and a more casual atmosphere on board.

- *Carnival Cruise Lines* (carnival.com). Carnival refers to its fleet as "Fun Ships" — others might use the phrase "party boats" — but either way, there's no doubt that Carnival attracts a younger crowd. On Carnival cruises, you'll find more single people and more families with young children, so it's not the company to choose if you're bothered by kids splashing in the pool or a more boisterous crowd at the bar. Its ships tend to be big (most carry more than two thousand passengers), but its prices are comparatively low. Carnival also owns Holland America, Princess, Cunard, and several smaller cruise lines, but each line offers a different experience on board.
- *Disney Cruise Line* (disneycruise.com). As you might expect, Disney ships cater to families, with an emphasis on the type of entertainment the company is known for on shore: aiming to please not only children, but also the parents who pay the bills. Mickey Mouse, Goofy, and other characters make appearances from time to time, but even so, Disney's ships have less of a theme park feel than other lines in this category, starting with more of a classic ocean liner design. Its cabins are larger than the industry average, to accommodate families bunking together, and there are lots of programs for children and teens and even babysitting for toddlers and infants. But Disney has only a few ships, so its itineraries are limited, sailing mostly to the Bahamas and the Caribbean, often with a stop at Disney's private island, Castaway Cay.
- *Norwegian Cruise Line* (ncl.com). NCL is best known for pioneering the concept of freestyle cruising, which means you can eat in any restaurant with your choice of dining companions whenever your stomach starts to grumble, instead of being assigned to a particular table at a set time. Some people like this flexibility; others say that it creates chaos, but it's indicative of the company's more casual approach. You won't find as many men wearing tuxedos in the dining room (or even suit jackets), and NCL's ships can feel more like theme parks — with a waterslide by the pool, a sculptured palm tree on deck, and paintings on the side of the hull. NCL's prices are generally affordable, which attracts a budget-minded crowd.

- *Royal Caribbean* (royalcaribbean.com). Royal Caribbean ships come in two sizes: big (more than two thousand passengers) and bigger (more than three thousand), and the company's fleet of megaships continues to grow. Royal Caribbean projects an active image — its motto is "get out there" — and on board many of its ships, you'll find ice skating rinks, in-line skating, a miniature golf course, and rock-climbing walls, as well as video game arcades and other dedicated hangouts for teenagers and younger children. As the name suggests, the Caribbean accounts for a big chunk of its itineraries, but the company also sails to Alaska, Canada, Europe, Hawaii, Mexico, and other destinations.

Premium Cruise Lines

Cruise lines in the premium category cost more than the mass-market brands, but you generally get better food, bigger cabins, more attentive service, and a less crowded feeling on board. The premium lines also offer a wider selection of longer itineraries and not as many three- or four-day trips as the more budget-minded brands. Although many of these cruise lines are reaching out to families, renovating their ships to create special areas for kids, you generally won't find as many young children aboard.

- *Celebrity Cruises* (celebrity.com). Celebrity is owned by Royal Caribbean, and an executive at the company once told me that if he wanted a romantic vacation with his wife, he'd pick Celebrity but that if they were taking the kids, he'd opt for Royal Caribbean. Celebrity's cuisine consistently gets high marks (compared to other premium cruise lines), and the company tries to cultivate a more sophisticated image, emphasizing a different style of entertainment — Cirque du Soleil performs on board — a more formal dress code in the dining room, and more elaborate health clubs and spas. Celebrity's shore excursions are also somewhat more exotic than the industry norm, with a special category of "Xpeditions" that offer some unique experience, like a tour of the NASA-Johnson Space Center led by a former astronaut or a snorkeling tour of a shipwreck, though often with a high price tag attached.

- *Cunard Line* (cunard.com). Some consider Cunard a luxury cruise line — and its service, cuisine, and décor are arguably a cut above the rest of the premium brands — but its ships are much larger than other luxury lines, so the on-board experience is more like what you'll find on the premium ships. Best known for its transatlantic crossings between Southampton, England, and New York, Cunard also sails itineraries in Africa, the Americas, and Europe. Its newest ship, the *Queen Mary 2,* carries more than 2,600 passengers, whereas the older *Queen Elizabeth 2* carries about 1,700. Cunard emphasizes the sophistication and quality of its on-board experience, partnering with Canyon Ranch to develop the spa on the *QM2* and various well-known chefs as advisers on its restaurants.

- *Holland America* (hollandamerica.com). A Dutch company that sails with a mostly Indonesian and Filipino crew, Holland America offers a more traditional cruise experience, catering to a slightly older clientele. Although its fleet tends to be older, too, the company launched a campaign in 2004 to renovate its ships, with new mattresses and bedding, more spaces for kids' activities, and an updated décor. On deck, its ships still have a more classic feel — more wood, less fiberglass and chrome — with teak deck chairs and plaid lap blankets welcoming quiet repose.

- *Oceania Cruises* (oceaniacruises.com). Less well known than other premium cruise lines, Oceania has been sailing since only 2003, when the company took over two 684-passenger ships from Renaissance Cruises (which went out of business). Oceania gave the ships a makeover and has since added a third similarly sized ship to its fleet, offering a more intimate on-board experience than its bigger competitors in the premium category. Chef Jacques Pépin serves as Oceania's executive culinary director, and all three ships have several dining rooms to choose from. Oceania primarily sails to destinations in the Caribbean, Central America, Europe, Mexico, and South America.

- *Princess Cruises* (princess.com). The cruise line popularized by the TV show *The Love Boat,* Princess still retains its all-American image — a cruise line for everybody, that sails practically everywhere. Most of its ships are big, roughly two thousand to three thousand passengers, and generally newer, with a more modern look. Princess also offers a flexible dining option, with more alternative restaurants: an Italian bistro, a steakhouse, or a southwestern grill. The Princess fleet of more than a dozen ships sail to destinations that span the globe.

Luxury cruise lines

Not surprisingly, luxury cruise lines cost more — how much more varies, depending on the ship, its itinerary, and whether you can find a deal. But for the higher price, you get top-of-the-line cuisine; bigger, more stylish accommodations; and a crew that really does go out of its way to anticipate your needs, then indulge them. The luxury lines generally have smaller ships, too, and a more refined feeling on board. They also tend to offer longer itineraries and include more in the basic cruise price, like soft drinks and sometimes alcohol.

- *Crystal Cruises* (crystalcruises.com). Crystal's ships carry about one thousand passengers each, and nearly all of the cabins face outside, many with balconies. Crystal offers itineraries all over the world — including some world cruises that last several months. Its casinos are run by Caesars Palace, and gambling is generally a popular activity on board, though if you're not in the mood to place a bet, Crystal's ships also offer classes that range from acting or creative-writing workshops to estate planning, cooking, and wine appreciation.
- *Regent Seven Seas* (rssc.com). Formerly known as Radisson, the rebranded Regent Seven Seas operates ships that carry between three hundred and seven hundred passengers; on the larger boats, all the cabins are suites with balconies. Its itineraries span the globe with what the company describes as an "upscale but not uptight" atmosphere (translation: a more casual approach than you'll find on other luxury lines). Regent offers open-seating dining, meaning that you can choose your table, dining compan-

ions, and dining time, and the basic cruise price includes tips, wine with dinner, and an in-suite bar.

- *Seabourn Cruise Line* (seabourn.com). Seabourn offers one of the most intimate and exclusive cruise experiences — each ship carries just two hundred passengers, and all the cabins are suites. With fewer people on board, cruising with Seabourn can feel more like traveling on a wealthy friend's yacht (well, with lots of other friends, too): The crew remembers your name, and the chef prepares each dinner to order — not the assembly-line approach typical aboard ships with thousands of passengers. Seabourn's cruises have a high price tag but include alcoholic drinks, tips, and one shore excursion with the base fare.

- *Silversea Cruises* (silversea.com). Silversea is known for pampering its passengers (between three hundred and four hundred on each cruise), starting with a complimentary glass of champagne when you board. Alcohol and tips are included in the price of the cruise, and like other luxury lines, there is little of the commercialism you'll find on the mass-market or premium cruise lines. (The company's spokeswoman is Isabella Rossellini, and its tag line: "intimate Italian cruising.") All Silversea ships have a wine cellar, open-seating dining, and exclusively outside cabins, most with verandas, and with Silversea's Personalized Voyages program, you can even design your own itinerary, embarking and disembarking at selected ports.

Specialty cruise lines

Besides the major cruise lines, which account for the vast majority of sailings worldwide, a number of companies offer a different approach to cruising — mostly, on a smaller scale. These specialty cruise lines typically use much smaller ships, sometimes sailboats, and travel to destinations huge liners can't navigate, with an emphasis on adventure and exploring more remote parts of the world. That is, you're more likely to spend your evening listening to a lecture about the environment than playing blackjack or watching a performance of Broadway show tunes. Prices vary but are often comparable to what the luxury lines charge.

- *Cruise West* (cruisewest.com). Cruise West's small ships carry about one hundred passengers to Alaska, Baja Mexico, Costa Rica, and Panama — with an emphasis on discovering nature and a casual dress code. Its smaller ships can get closer to glaciers or travel narrower waterways than the big cruise lines can, and the company emphasizes that nature, not a lounge act, is the main entertainment on board. But don't expect to pay backpacker prices for the more outdoorsy experience Cruise West offers; its cruises generally cost more than those in the premium category.
- *Lindblad Expeditions* (expeditions.com). Lindblad calls its cruises "expeditions," specializing in out-of-the-way destinations like Antarctica, Arctic Norway, Central America, and the Galapagos Islands, though it also offers itineraries in Alaska, Baja California, the Caribbean, and Europe. Most ships carry fewer than one hundred passengers, with a laid-back, explorer's approach to travel. On-board naturalists and other experts serve as guides, and the emphasis is on wildlife and nature, though these expeditions generally have a high price tag.
- *Windstar Cruises* (windstarcruises.com). Windstar's main distinction is the wind that powers its fleet of luxury sailboats, though motors are used, too, so you won't be stranded when the wind dies down. The yachts carry 150 to 300 passengers to destinations in the Americas, the Caribbean, and the Mediterranean (including the Greek Isles), in a style that the company describes as "casual elegance."
- Other companies are American Canadian Clipper Line (acclsmallships.com), Peter Deilmann Cruises (deilmann-cruises.com), Star Clippers (starclippers.com), and Swan Hellenic (swanhellenic.com).

Narrowing the Fleet: Choosing an Itinerary, Ship, and Sailing Date

Booking a cruise is sort of like shopping for a car: You have to choose from the options available, and the company you like best may not offer exactly what you want when you're ready to spend.

With a cruise, the line you like best may not sail where you want to go, or the ship you have in mind may not be weighing anchor when you want to travel. (It's not like buying a plane ticket for the dates you want to fly; you have to sail on the captain's schedule.) So you can either pick a destination and find out which companies sail there or choose a cruise line (or ship) you like and see what itineraries are on the upcoming schedule.

Many travel agencies that sell cruises let you do both types of searches on their Web sites (see page 159 for advice on buying a cruise), or if you know which cruise line you want to sail, you can look up itineraries at its Web site. Once you know your options, resist the urge to pick a cruise based solely on price; you should consider a few other factors that might trump the bottom line.

What to ask

The first time I booked a cruise, I spent a lot of time figuring out which ports I wanted to visit along Alaska's coast, making the itinerary the focus of my choice. So there were lots of questions it didn't occur to me to ask — and because I was booking with a discounter, the agent didn't spend much time discussing my options.

Among the surprises: Our cabin had orange paisley bedding and turquoise carpeting, the average age of the passengers was well over fifty, and the show lounge looked like it had been designed when John Travolta could still fit into slim trousers. (The ship was given a makeover shortly after we sailed, which is probably why we got such a great price.)

So as you narrow down your options, here are some questions you should explore to avoid similar surprises at sea.

- *How old is the ship?* A newer ship isn't necessarily better, especially if you're after a more traditional maritime experience (no waterslides or paintings on the ship's hull). But if a ship is ten years old, the décor may feel quite dated — and on vacation, we all want to feel like we've left our worn-out carpeting behind. If age is an issue, seek out feedback from other passengers or photos that reveal how the public areas and cabins *really* look (see page 183 for sources you can check).

- *How big is the ship?* Even within the same cruise line, ships come in different shapes and sizes, so check how many passengers — and crew — will be on board. Sailing with two thousand or three thousand other people is very different from sailing with one thousand or several hundred, especially when it's time for dinner or you're disembarking at a small port. (You sometimes have to queue to get on and off the boat.) With several ships docking at the same time in some locations, you're never going to feel like Lewis and Clark, but a 1,300-passenger ship does manage to feel less massive than one carrying twice that number.

- *What's the itinerary?* Even if you know that you want to cruise in a specific region — say, Alaska — you'll have many different itineraries to choose from. In Alaska, some ships sail round-trip (returning to the same city you depart from — typically, Vancouver or Seattle), whereas others do a one-way voyage (usually, between Vancouver and Anchorage). Also, each ship makes various stops along the way, so if you've got your heart set on a particular port, that may influence which cruise line you book. (For more on departure ports, see the sidebar on page 168.)

- *How often is the ship in port?* Another factor to consider is how much time you want to spend at sea. If you'd rather spend most of your days on shore, exploring various ports — or if you're worried about getting seasick (see the sidebar on page 170) — a long ocean crossing isn't the best choice. You also won't get much of a change in scenery, though some people like the idea of being out in open water most of the time, and there's usually plenty of activity to keep you from getting bored.

- *How long is the cruise?* If you've never cruised before, an itinerary longer than seven days may be too much for your first experience at sea, and if you're prone to motion sickness, even a week can be a gamble. Then again, a three- or four-day cruise may make you feel like you barely had time to unpack or may not be offered in the region where you want to travel. So test out your sea legs with a shorter cruise before booking a two-week trip around Europe.

- *What can you do on board?* Most cruise lines offer a wide range of activities on board their ships, including traditional cruise pastimes and a few things you wouldn't expect to find at sea, like a

SAILING FROM YOUR HOME PORT

Cruise lines are adding a growing number of itineraries that depart from ports more people can reach by car, hoping to attract new customers by eliminating the cost of plane tickets and the hassle of air travel. Florida is still the point of departure for the largest number of passengers — Miami, Port Canaveral, Ft. Lauderdale, or Tampa — but cruises also depart from Galveston, Los Angeles, New York, San Diego, San Francisco, Seattle, and other smaller ports. If you're near a coast and are flexible about where you go, you may find an appealing itinerary leaving from a port within driving distance — which is one way to keep costs down.

skating rink or a planetarium. Almost every ship has a gym, a running or walking track, a pool, a spa, a computer center, a library, and a movie theater, not to mention a casino and a place to play bingo or cards. But more cruise lines are diverging from the norm, offering wine tasting or cooking classes and athletic facilities, like driving ranges and mini–basketball courts. You'll also find lots of lectures on the daily schedule, ranging from naturalists and scientists talking about wildlife or geology (a big draw in Alaska) to authors or photographers discussing their work.

Selecting a Cabin: Inside, Outside, High Deck, or Low

Unlike a hotel room, a cabin on a cruise ship is assigned to you the day you make your reservation — in fact, you can visit the cruise line's Web site, find the deck plans for your ship, and see your exact location on board. But actually, that's something you should do *before* you put down a deposit, because that deck plan also shows how close you'll be to the elevator or the stairs (convenient but sometimes loud) and whether you'll be in earshot of noise coming from the engine room, the kitchen, a nightclub, or a running track on the deck above. (See the sidebar on page 172 for tips on upgrading your stateroom.)

Besides noise issues, your cabin's location also affects the cost of the cruise — one ocean view cabin, it turns out, is not like the others (on cruises, there are a dizzying number of price categories). Here are some of the decisions you'll have to make when choosing a cabin, most of which will influence not only your travel experience but also the final total that shows up on your credit card.

Ocean view or inside cabin

Springing for an ocean view or outside cabin gets you a room with a view, but you should ask a few things about what you'll see outside your window. For starters, find out whether you'll have a window or a porthole; there can be a big difference in size. You should also confirm that there isn't a lifeboat or other object blocking your view; some cruise lines actually sell ocean view cabins that have an "obstructed" view — an issue your travel agent should, but may not, raise. Also, ask whether your window looks out on a promenade; despite tinted glass, you may not feel comfortable with the curtains open — and smokers hanging out by the railing probably isn't the view you paid extra to see.

An inside cabin costs less, and some people find the savings worth sacrificing a view and natural light, figuring that they won't spend much time in their cabins. But before you're swayed by that argument, consider that cruise cabins are generally much smaller than a typical hotel room (a standard size is about 120 to 170 square feet). If you're claustrophobic, work ten hours a day in a windowless office, or are taking a cruise in large part for the scenery, this isn't the place to economize.

Upper or lower deck

The bigger the ship, the more decks it has, and which one you're on matters for a few reasons. Lower decks are more stable, which is better if you're susceptible to motion sickness, but you're farther from the decks where the dining rooms, pools, and other public spaces are typically located. That means more time waiting for the elevator or climbing stairs, which is why lower decks tend to be cheaper, but some people consider that distance from potentially noisy areas a draw.

FEELING SEASICK: AVOIDING IT, TREATING IT

For some people, even the thought of going on a cruise is enough to bring on a queasy stomach and visions of spending your entire vacation close to a bathroom — if not up on deck in a not-especially-romantic position gripping the railing. Although newer ships are built with stabilizers to minimize the effects of the waves, getting seasick is still one of the hazards of cruising, and many people find that it takes a day or two to adjust to being at sea. (Even though I've spent a lot of time boating on large lakes in Michigan, during my first cruise I discovered that my usual comfort around water didn't translate into the "sea legs" you need to overcome an ocean's bigger waves. That said, I experienced only slight nausea, and it passed after a day.)

Motion sickness is caused by conflicting sensory signals going to your brain: You feel like you're standing still, but your inner ear senses that the ship is rocking from side to side. Sometimes, you can alleviate the problem by going up on deck or looking out the window, which adds another sensory signal to the mix (your eyes confirm that yes, indeed, you're moving).

There are also various homeopathic, over-the-counter, and prescription remedies for motion sickness that all seem to have their share of champions — and for each fan, it seems, an equal number of skeptics — so finding one that works may be a matter of trial and error. One natural option for suppressing nausea is powdered ginger root, available in most health food stores (ginger in soda, tea, or candy isn't as effective, doctors say). You can also buy elastic wristbands that apply pressure on a point below your palm; Sea Bands (or other brands) are available in drugstores for less than $10 and are an accessory you'll certainly see on board.

Moving into the medicine cabinet, the most commonly used over-the-counter medications for motion sickness are antihistamines, such as Dramamine (diphenhydramine) and Bonine (meclizine), which also cost less than $10 and are usually available on the ship. The downside is that they typically cause drowsiness and shouldn't be mixed with alcohol, which can put a damper on your vacation plans.

Another option is a patch that delivers a dose of a drug called scopolamine through your skin. Typically worn behind the ear, this remedy requires a prescription from a doctor, so you have to buy it before your trip; you also have to start wearing it before you experience any symptoms, since it takes several hours for the medicine to be absorbed.

Your doctor can give you more personalized advice. Or check the cruise message boards, which offer tips that don't come with an M.D. but are based on lots of first-hand experience trying various options.

Bow, stern, or midship

The middle of the ship is more stable than the front or the back (that's the bow or the stern, in maritime lingo), so you'll pay a premium for a cabin located midship. If you're worried about getting seasick, it's probably worth it, though middle cabins tend to fill up early, so you may not have much choice if you book late. Otherwise, choose your location based on what you want to be near — say, the main dining room or perhaps the gym to work off all those four-course meals and midnight buffets. Also, you may hear more engine noise at the back of the ship, and if you're booking a cabin with a balcony, the front of the ship is generally windy.

Port or starboard side

On some cruises, it may not make a difference whether you're on the port (left) or starboard (right) side of the ship, especially if the ship isn't traveling in a straight line. But if you're sailing along a coast, one side of the ship will face the sea and one will face land — and the sun always sets in the west — so if you have a preference about your view, consider geography when you book. But which side of the ship you're on usually won't affect how much you pay.

Balconies and suites

If you feel like splurging, the two main ways you can improve your accommodations are springing for a balcony or a suite (or both). Balconies, often called verandas, generally add at least $100 a night to the price tag and vary in size and the amount of privacy they offer, so you may be able to see — or hear — your neighbors, and vice versa. Although one balcony is more or less like any other on the same ship, suites come in a range of sizes but typically have a sitting area separate from the bedroom. The nicest suites (think "penthouse") may have multiple bedrooms and bathrooms, a private porch (perhaps with a Jacuzzi), and a dining area and sometimes butler service to make sure that no request goes unanswered. On some ships, the higher cabin classes also have their own bars, dining rooms, or lounge areas, so big spenders can socialize away from the masses.

UPGRADING YOUR CABIN

As with airplane seats, it's sometimes possible to upgrade your cabin, but it helps if you're a preferred customer or are willing to pay extra to trade up. Your travel agent may offer you a free or discounted upgrade when you book, either because of a special deal the agency has gotten from the cruise line or your history as a loyal customer. You can also buy what's called a cabin guarantee, which means that you reserve a cabin category but are not assigned a specific cabin. The cruise line guarantees you'll be assigned a cabin at least in the category you reserved, but you may get a free upgrade to a better category. The risk is, if you don't get upgraded, you *could* end up in a worse cabin than if you had picked a stateroom when you booked.

Another option is to call your travel agent or the cruise line a few weeks before sailing and see whether you can pay extra for a better cabin. You may be able to upgrade for less than what you would have paid for a nicer stateroom when you made your reservation, since cruise lines often discount cabins just before the ship sails. You can also try to negotiate an upgrade once you board the ship, when it's too late for the cruise line to sell empty berths. But the ship may be fully booked, or the front desk may not want the hassle of a cabin change while everyone is boarding, so the last-minute approach is a long shot.

How Cruise Pricing Works: When and Where to Get the Best Deals

Unlike other travel purchases, the vast majority of cruises are still sold by travel agents, but there's still a big do-it-yourself element involved in the shopping process. That's because cruise prices vary, depending on who's doing the selling — with the same cabin on the same ship sailing on the same date commanding different prices, depending on whom you call (and when you buy).

So if you don't want to find out that you overpaid — when your table mate lets slip that he or she got a similar cabin for a song — you still have to shop around. Also, many travel agents who sell cruises expect you to know exactly which cruise you want to book before you call, which means that you have to do a lot of the legwork yourself. But whether you buy a cruise through a travel agent or on your own, the price will not include some extra expenses (see the sidebar on the facing page for examples).

WHAT'S NOT INCLUDED

Cruise lines promote their products as all-inclusive vacations, but in reality, you can expect to spend about 25 percent to 30 percent more once you're on board (not including airfare to get you to the port). Here are some of the things you'll pay extra for on most cruises, though luxury lines include some of these items in their basic prices. These on-board expenses are charged to your cabin — it's generally a cashless society at sea — so it's easy to get carried away when you're not pulling bills from your wallet.

- *Alcohol:* Except for a few of the luxury lines, most cruise lines charge for beer, wine, and liquor. Expect to pay a bit less than you would for a drink in a bar or a restaurant ($4 to $6), but prices vary, depending on the cruise line and your fondness for fine wines and top-shelf liquor.

- *Airport transfers:* When you book your cruise, many travel agents will offer to sell you airport transfers, but they're not usually included in the ticket price. Ask the agent to break out this cost to make sure that you're not getting overcharged. Anything more than $25 per person each way usually isn't a deal, since you'll be climbing onto a big tour bus, and taking a cab may be cheaper — and quicker — for two people.

- *Classes:* Lectures offered on board cruise ships are generally free, but some lines charge for certain gym classes — like yoga or Pilates (about $10 each) — or special events like cooking seminars ($40 or so).

- *Gambling:* No, your cabin steward isn't likely to leave a stack of chips on your nightstand to curry favor (though you may get a chocolate on your pillow). What you spend (or win) depends on your luck at the tables and whether you have a heavy hand at the slots.

- *Internet access:* Cruise lines have been touting their on-board Internet services in recent years, which typically include a cybercafé where you can log on using public computers or sometimes a wireless network you can tap into from your own laptop (mostly in designated public areas but sometimes in your cabin as well). Prices range from $0.35 to $0.75 per minute, which can quickly add up to far more than you pay at home. You can save money by checking e-mail at a cybercafé in port (which often charges just $0.10 a minute), and some public libraries offer free Internet terminals. Guidebooks or the ship's crew can tell you where to look on shore.

- *Laundry:* Some of the bigger ships offer self-service washers and dryers (for a fee), but for full service, you'll have to pay per item charges that may make you consider rolling up your shirt sleeve to hide a stain on the cuff ($5 to clean a shirt, $2 for underwear, other items $2 to $10).

- *Photos:* If you're camera-shy, one of the more surprising experiences on board most cruises (except the luxury lines) is how often the ship's photographers try to take your photo: when you board, at dinner, during the lifeboat drill (when everyone dons life preservers), each time you disembark, and countless other times throughout the cruise, which can feel like being pursued by paparazzi. The ship's photographers post these photos daily, selling them for $10 to $20 each — and people do indeed buy them, despite having their own cameras on board. One new twist: Some cruise lines will download and print pictures from passengers' digital cameras, for about $0.40 per photo.

- *Shore excursions:* The biggest hit you'll take in terms of on-board expenses is what you'll spend to go ashore. Excursions offered through cruise lines range from $50 to $350, with a city tour at the bottom end and options like helicopter rides or fishing expeditions at the top; some companies are marketing even more extravagant adventures for prices that can easily reach the four-digit mark. (See page 179 for ways to save by making your own arrangements in port.)

- *Soda:* Most cruise ships charge about $2.50 for a soda, even at meals, so if you (or your kids) have a carbonated craving, consider buying one of the unlimited-soda cards some lines offer (about $25 to $35 for a seven-day cruise).

- *Specialty coffee drinks:* Your basic cup of coffee is still free, but if your taste runs more toward cappuccino or espresso, you'll generally pay for that extra jolt of caffeine, since many cruise lines charge ($2 to $3) for fancy coffees.

- *Spa treatments:* The spa-ification of the travel industry has swept through cruise lines, too, so besides getting your nails and hair done, you can get all sorts of spa treatments on board. Options range from a basic massage to more eclectic offerings: aromatherapy, reflexology, or an invigorating scrub. Prices are comparable to what you'd pay on land — about $25 to $45 for manicures and pedicures or $100 for a fifty-minute massage.

- *Tips:* Cruise passengers used to get complicated directives indicating whom they should tip (the waiter, the cabin steward, the maitre d', and so on) and how much, but that resulted in a frustrating exercise in gathering small bills and distributing these tips before disembarking. Now, most lines add a standard fee for tips to each passenger's bill (about $10 per day, per person). You can usually adjust that amount up or down when you settle your account.

The myth of the advertised price

Price differences among agencies are a relic of an era when cruise lines routinely allowed travel agents to sell cruises at a discount, which agents were able to do by rebating a portion of their commission to the customer. But a few cruise lines have begun to put the kibosh on this practice, adopting policies that prohibit agents from selling their cruises for lower than the company-approved price. Among them: Royal Caribbean, Celebrity, and Carnival (which originally just forbade agents from *advertising* lower prices). Plenty of agencies still offer discounts, especially on cruise lines that don't care or that look the other way, but as the industry rebounds from its post-9/11 slump, more companies are getting stricter about controlling their prices.

What does all this mean for travelers? It's definitely worth shopping around when you're booking a cruise, because in many cases, you'll find that different agencies quote different prices — which can also vary from what the cruise line charges if you book direct. And when agents can't discount the basic cruise fare without breaking the rules, some will offer customers other deals, like a coupon for on-board spending, free airport transfers, or a free cabin upgrade. So don't assume that the initial price you're quoted from an agent is the best price you're going to get: It's always worth negotiating as you shop around.

Discounters versus full-service agencies

The agencies most likely to offer rebates — or generally the lowest prices — are known as discounters, and many of them have the word *cruise* in their names (see the sidebar on page 177 for examples). If you book through a discounter, you'll usually save money, but don't expect a lot of hand-holding as you mull over which cruise to buy. Many of these agencies expect you to know which cruise you want when you call, or at least to have narrowed the field to a few options. And in a way, it's a fair trade: They're sacrificing some of their commission to save you money, so you should expect less service in return.

That's not to say that you won't get any help from discounters —

they want repeat customers, after all — but if you really have no idea which cruise line is a good fit or even where you want to go, you're probably better off working with a full-service agency. Agencies that do a lot of business with one cruise line may get special deals for their clients or offer extra perks on board, like a private cocktail party or a special shore excursion. But agents sometimes get a higher commission from certain cruise lines, which can influence which ship they recommend, so if the person you're working with isn't giving you a range of options, take your business somewhere else. (For tips on finding a travel agent, see page 83.)

You can also buy directly from the cruise line, but that's often the most expensive way to go, and you don't get the benefit of working with an agent who can give you advice about various companies. One way you may save by booking direct is if you make a reservation for your next cruise before you disembark, since most cruise lines offer deals on board their ships while you're enjoying the moment. They also have special programs for past passengers, which sometimes include extra amenities or discounts.

When to buy and when to sail

The other variable that determines how much you'll pay is how far in advance you make your plans. One rule of thumb is that the earlier you buy a cruise, the less you'll pay, since the cruise lines generally raise their prices as it gets closer to the departure date. But they also have a tendency to *lower* their prices as a sailing approaches if the ship isn't full, sometimes announcing a last-minute sale. (Unlike airlines, cruise lines aim to set sail at full capacity, so they'll drop their prices to fill empty berths.) So in reality, the best time to buy is *either* early or late.

Of course, waiting for a last-minute sale can be risky: There may not be one, so you're either stuck paying a higher price, or you may not be able to get the cruise or cabin category you want. (Popular destinations do sell out.) In general, the cruise lines don't offer as many late discounts when times are flush, so if the travel industry is booming, that's probably not the time to gamble, especially if you're celebrating a special occasion or want three cabins all in a row.

CRUISE DISCOUNTERS

If you're a savvy traveler and know more or less which cruise you want to buy, cruise discounters will generally offer the lowest prices. Keep in mind that any agency that sells cruises advertises enticingly low prices — "from $699 per person" — but that's usually for an inside cabin, a less desirable sailing date, or an old ship (or all of these); the cost is bound to be higher for the cabin, ship, and itinerary you want. Also, advertised prices don't always include taxes, fees, and port charges, so make sure that the prices you're comparing include those costs. Here are some cruise discounters worth checking out as you shop around.

- Cruise 411 (cruise411.com)
- Cruise Brothers (cruisebrothers.com)
- Cruise.com (cruise.com)
- Cruise Direct (cruisedirect.com)
- Cruises 'N More (cruises-n-more.com)
- Cruises Only (cruisesonly.com)
- Cruise Value Center (mycruisevalue.com)
- ICruise (icruise.com)

But if you're flexible about *when* you travel, and if you don't mind taking a chance on the weather, you can save money by working the calendar. Like destinations, cruises have high seasons and low seasons, so if you travel at the beginning or end of a season — say, June or September for Alaska or late spring for the Caribbean and Mexico — you'll pay less than if you cruise at peak times.

The Web versus the phone

Many travel agencies offer two ways to book a cruise: on line or on the phone. If you've been on a dozen ships and know the ins and outs of cruise pricing, you may find that Internet booking works just fine. But for most people, especially first-timers, you're much better off talking to an agent. A cruise is a complicated purchase, and most Web sites I've tried don't offer the best tools to buy one.

That said, the Web is a great resource for researching itineraries, ships, and prices, and it does make it easier to shop around. In fact, a site called CruiseCompete.com lets you enter the sailing you're considering; then travel agents post their lowest price for the cruise and cabin category you want. CruiseCompete sends you an e-mail saying that a new "bid" has been posted, then it's up to you to decide whether to follow up on the agency's offer. If more cruise lines adopt standard prices, that service won't be as useful (since agents would all have to sell cruises for the fare dictated by the company), but in the meantime, it's worth a shot once you know which cruise you want.

Airfare, Shore Excursions, and Land Tours: Buying from the Cruise Line or Going It Alone

When you book a cruise, you'll have to make a few other decisions about your purchase (besides that age-old question, Can I really afford this trip right now?). Namely, you'll have to decide whether to buy your airfare through the cruise line or on your own, prebook any shore excursions the cruise line offers, and opt for a pre- or postcruise land tour — escorted trips to sights farther inland from wherever you begin or end your cruise (say, visiting Machu Picchu while you're all the way down in South America).

There's no one-size-fits-all answer to these questions — after all, maybe you've already been to Machu Picchu — but here are some factors to consider as you research your options.

Airfare: Getting to the ship on time

If you have to hop on a plane to get to the ship, you'll be asked whether you want to buy your airfare through the cruise line's program (known as "cruise air") or purchase your tickets on your own. Cruise lines negotiate special rates for their customers with various airlines, but that may not be the lowest fare available for the route you need to fly, so compare prices before you decide.

The main advantage of buying your airfare through the cruise line is that the company assumes responsibility for getting you to the ship on time — or helping you catch up to the ship if your flight is delayed and you literally miss the boat. If you buy your own air-fare, you're on your own, which is why some people who book their own plane tickets plan to arrive a day early and spend the night in a hotel.

But buying "cruise air" has some drawbacks, too: You don't find out your flight itinerary until a couple weeks before your departure (and cruise lines often don't book the most direct routes), and you may have less recourse to get credit toward a future flight if you have to cancel your trip. Policies vary, so ask when you book.

Shore excursions: Group tours versus going solo

After you book your cruise, another choice you'll have to make is whether to prebook any of the shore excursions the cruise line offers. These range from guided city tours — sometimes with a gimmicky hook like hula dancers or a lumberjack show — to fishing expeditions, helicopter rides, scuba diving trips, and hikes (you'll find more active options these days).

If you're looking for an alternative to the tour bus but don't necessarily want to break a sweat, cruise lines are crafting more excursions that promise some type of unique experience — like a behind-the-scenes tour of a museum led by an art expert or a side trip in a private jet. Not surprisingly, these special outings often come with a hefty price tag, exceeding the $50 to $350 per person you can expect to pay for most other excursions.

You can usually save money by making your own arrangements, either before your trip or once you arrive (you'll find lots of tour operators hanging out around the docks). The on-line cruise communities listed on page 185 are a great source of advice about what to do and how to save money in various ports, and so are many of the resources listed in chapter 2 of this book.

Most ports have a visitor's center not too far from where the cruise ships dock, and often these agencies hand out free maps of city walking tours. To venture out of town, it's often more economical (and more liberating) to rent a car or hire a taxi rather than pay top dollar for an organized excursion, which tends to move at the pace of the slowest person in the group — often, the shutterbug who wants to take just one more photo.

The main advantage of buying a cruise-sanctioned shore excursion is that the ship isn't going to sail if forty passengers are still on a tour bus that got a flat tire. But if your rental car breaks down, you may reach the dock just in time to watch the ship pull away, so leave plenty of time to get back on board.

Either way, try to make some of your plans ahead of time — not necessarily six months before your cruise but at least a few weeks before you set sail. For one thing, if you're planning to rent a car or book a private tour, it's often easier to do that from home (most tour companies that operate in cruise ports have Web sites). And if you want to book any excursions through the cruise line, popular options sometimes sell out quickly, and that mad rush to snap up a space on the first day of your cruise isn't the most relaxing way to begin your voyage. Just be sure to ask about cancellation penalties whenever you book anything in advance.

Back on land: Pre- and postcruise tours

Another option cruise lines offer is the chance to join an escorted tour inland before or after your cruise. At first glance, this may sound appealing — after all, if you're traveling all the way to Alaska, why not see Mt. McKinley and Denali National Park while you're there?

But if you're used to a more independent style of travel, you may chafe at being herded on and off trains and buses with dozens of other people, not to mention all the stops for bathroom breaks or souvenir shopping. Before you book a cruise tour, think carefully about how you like to travel — you can almost always plan a similar trip on your own. (For advice on deciding whether a group tour is right for you, see page 31.)

Deposits, Cancellation Policies, and Refunds: What to Know Before You Book

Buying a cruise is often a big investment, and if you book your trip well ahead of your sailing date, a lot of things can happen before it's time to pack your bags. That's why most travel agents will offer to sell you some type of travel insurance, which doesn't *guarantee* that you'll get a refund if you have to cancel but allows you to get your money back under certain circumstances.

Here's what you need to know about paying for a cruise, what happens if you have to cancel, and what insurance covers if bad luck spoils your plans.

Deposits and cancellation penalties

When you book a cruise, you typically have to pay a deposit when you make your reservation. The amount varies, depending on the cruise line, the length of the cruise, and your sailing date, but it's about $250 to $350 per person for a seven-day cruise (and a bit more for longer cruises, holiday sailings, or luxury lines). Final payment is usually due between sixty and ninety days before your departure, but if you're buying at the last minute, you'll pay the full price at once.

What happens if you have to cancel depends on how much you've already paid and when you call to back out. With most cruise lines, if you cancel before your final payment is due, you'll get all your deposit back. But if you made your reservation through a travel agent, the agency may charge some kind of cancellation fee regardless of the cruise line's policy, so be sure to ask about that before you book.

Once you've paid in full, penalties kick in if you have to cancel, on a scale based on how close it is to your departure date. As a general rule, if you cancel within a month after your final payment is due, you'll lose only your deposit. If you cancel seven to thirty days before your departure, you'll typically lose 50 percent of your total payment, and if it's within a week before your sailing, you'll typically lose 100 percent of what you paid (ditto if you're a no-show when the ship sails).

But cancellation policies vary — and they're subject to change — so check with your cruise line or travel agent for specific rules. You should also ask about cancellation policies for prepaid shore excursions, airfare, and land tours, which often involve other penalties.

By all accounts, cruise lines do enforce these policies, so don't assume that the cruise line will bend the rules if there's a death in the family or you're suddenly hospitalized. That's why cruise lines and travel agents encourage passengers to buy trip cancellation insurance, which is something you should consider if your plans are subject to change — or you have a lot of money at stake.

Trip cancellation insurance

Almost anyone you buy a cruise from will offer you some kind of trip cancellation insurance — whether you book through the cruise line, a travel agency, or a discounter. Trip cancellation insurance typically reimburses you for most of the penalty you'd have to pay if you cancel, but you can also buy a more comprehensive travel insurance policy, which also covers things like medical emergencies during a cruise, lost luggage, or expenses if you miss a flight and have to pay for a hotel.

Like airlines, cruise lines assume liability for only a paltry sum if they lose your luggage — in some cases, as little as $100 per passenger — so if you don't have a homeowner's policy or other insurance that fills the gap, travel insurance may be a worthwhile investment. (See page 71 for more details about travel insurance.)

The most important thing to understand about travel insurance and many trip cancellation policies is that they usually cover cancellations only for certain defined reasons — like a serious illness or a death in the family or other unexpected circumstances. With most policies, you can't cancel just because you changed your mind about the trip. Although some cruise lines do sell policies that let you cancel for any reason, that's more the exception than the rule — and if you don't cancel for a covered reason, you may be offered a credit toward a future cruise instead of a refund.

Refunds if the price drops

Sometimes, cruise lines will refund the difference if they lower the price for the exact category of cabin you purchased, but it's up to you (or your travel agent) to keep track of the going rate and request a refund. If you haven't made the final payment for your cruise, you generally have more room to negotiate; if the cruise line won't give you a refund, the company may offer you other compensation, like a credit toward on-board expenses, so it's worth keeping an eye on the price after you book.

Where to Find Cruising Advice: Ship Reviews, Itineraries, and Message Boards

Most travelers are eager to share their experiences with others headed somewhere they've been, but people who enjoy cruising take that habit to a whole other level. They don't just want to tell you about their cruise; they want to convince you to try one.

At a cocktail party, such enthusiasm can become overbearing, but with on-line forums, you can walk away at any time. And that's precisely the attraction of some of the cruise communities that have sprung up on the Web: You can find answers to all your questions about cruising, without the awkward experience of trying to extricate yourself from a conversation that's gone on too long. And if you do want to stay up until the wee hours reading about cruise itineraries and ports of call, you won't run out of material to fuel your insomnia.

Where cruisers hang out on line

The two Web sites that have become the leading communities for cruisers are CruiseMates.com and CruiseCritic.com. Both offer articles for first-timers as well as old hands, covering basic topics like what to expect on board, the best ships for families, and how to deal with seasickness (see the sidebar on page 170 for advice), as well as more insider news about the industry, including previews of new ships and which itineraries hit the best ports of call.

These articles are written by regular contributors who spend a lot of time on cruise ships — some of whom used to work in the cruise industry. But it's the message boards and ship reviews submitted by readers that are the real draw, offering some of the frank opinions you won't find anywhere else — except maybe in the buffet line on board.

Both sites organize their message boards by topic, so you can browse discussions about a particular destination, cruise line, or even a specific ship. The regional threads focus mostly on what to do in various ports, like the best place to snorkel in Cozumel, whether to take a helicopter or a float plane tour in Alaska, or where to find a luau in Honolulu — the type of information you won't necessarily get from a travel agent, especially if you book through a discounter.

On both sites, you can find specific advice for certain demographic groups — families, first-timers, gay and lesbian travelers, or singles — and boards dedicated to practical topics like what to pack, tipping etiquette, cruise cuisine, shore excursions, and health. There are also plenty of offbeat discussions about topics like whether a dress could be "too sexy" to wear on board, or what to do to keep a sleepwalker inside a cabin at night, so if you have a question you can't get answered anywhere else, these forums are the place to go.

Sorting through the ship reviews

The other useful feature these communities offer is a place for cruise enthusiasts to read and post ship reviews, which you can browse by itinerary or cruise line. CruiseCritic has an especially useful way of organizing and summarizing ship reviews submitted by members, which are peppered with blunt comments like "Our butler was worthless," "The bed was sorta lumpy," or "I did not appreciate being called 'sweetie' constantly." (There are plenty of positive comments, too, but it's the rants about things like a passenger talent show gone awry that make for the best reading, especially late at night.) And unlike hotel reviews, cruise reviews are generally long enough that you can tell whether you're dealing with someone whose tastes match your own. In fact, some people post such detailed reports about their cruise, you start to wonder whether they had time to do anything except take notes. (For more about where to find these and other Web sites of interest to cruisers, see the sidebar on page 185.)

FOR MORE ABOUT CRUISING. . .

Here's a list of Web sites worth checking out if you're thinking about taking a cruise, but if you're more of a print person, there are plenty of books that can help you choose a cruise and tell you what to expect on board. A good general guide to buying and taking a cruise is *Econoguide Cruises,* by Corey Sandler, but you can also find guidebooks that cover specific regions or ports of call.

CRUISE COMMUNITIES

- **CruiseCritic** (cruisecritic.com). This site is a useful source for ship reviews, message boards, and help finding a cruise, though some of the articles are less critical than you'd expect from the site's name. But the ship reviews submitted by members are well organized and easy to browse.

- **CruiseMates** (cruisemates.com). One of the best on-line sources for advice about cruising, this site offers ship reviews, news about the cruise industry, message boards, and a wide range of articles for both experts and first-timers.

INDUSTRY ASSOCIATIONS

- **Cruise Lines International Association** (CLIA) (cruising.org). CLIA is primarily a marketing organization for the industry, but its Web site offers a few features that are also useful for travelers — namely, profiles of member cruise lines and concise facts about various ships, as well as search tools to find a cruise or a travel agent who specializes in cruises.

- **International Council of Cruise Lines** (ICCL) (iccl.org). This organization represents the cruise industry on policy issues, so on its Web site you can find information about issues like safety, security, and health at sea, along with news about the industry's activities on the environmental front.

HEALTH ISSUES

- **Access-Able Travel Source** (access-able.com). A lawsuit about the accessibility of cruise ships to passengers with disabilities reached the Supreme Court in 2005, shining a spotlight on what the industry is doing to accommodate passengers with special needs. This Web site describes what services various cruise lines offer to passengers with vision, hearing, or physical impairments, including how many wheelchair-accessible cabins you'll find on various ships. Most cruise lines also cover this topic on their Web sites and provide a number you can call for more info.

- **CDC's Vessel Sanitation Program** (cdc.gov/nceh/vsp). The Vessel Sanitation Program of the U.S. Centers for Disease Control and Prevention conducts unannounced inspections of cruise ships twice a year and publishes the results on line. So if you're concerned about cleanliness, you can see how a particular ship fared on its most recent inspection; the CDC also offers information about norovirus outbreaks and other health topics of interest to cruise passengers.

7 Rental Cars, Trains, and Buses

IF YOU'RE LIKE MOST travelers, you probably book your plane ticket and hotel a couple months before your trip and then a week before your departure date, realize that you forgot to reserve a car. With trains, you may not bother making a reservation at all, since you can often just show up at the station and get a seat on the train you want.

One reason these reservations tend to fall by the wayside is that there's not much choice involved in the process. Most travelers aren't picky about which company they rent a car from, and the cars are all pretty similar, so it's not like you have to confer with your traveling companion and ask, "So what do you think about this midsize four-door?" With trains, the only choices you have to make are whether it's worth paying more for a better seat or a faster ride.

Another relevant factor is the Internet, which has made it much easier to research your options and compare prices. With sites like Expedia, Orbitz, and Travelocity, you can quickly compare rates from all the major car rental companies, and the Internet has also taken much of the mystery out of riding the rails, making it possible to look up timetables and in some cases buy tickets for trains all over the world.

But even though the research process is pretty straightforward, technology still hasn't banished a few issues to the annals of "things we don't have to worry about anymore." Deciding whether you need car rental insurance practically requires the services of a lawyer, and you still have to keep up your guard to make sure that your final bill isn't double the price you were quoted.

This chapter offers advice on both of those topics, as well as what to consider when renting a car in a foreign country and how to avoid every renter's worst nightmare: long lines at the counter. As for trains, it may be easy to find schedules before your trip, but it isn't always easy to decipher them, especially in a foreign country. This chapter covers what you need to know to understand those timetables and how to decide whether your best option is a plane, a train, a car, or a bus.

Reserving a Rental Car: How to Get the Best Rate

Booking a car over the Internet has gone from being the most frustrating part of on-line travel planning to one of the easiest tasks to cross off your to-do list. A few years ago, it was a different story. None of the on-line travel agencies included taxes and fees in their price quotes, and if you clicked over to a car rental company's Web site, the situation wasn't much better: Companies buried these fees under vaguely titled links like "Important Local Policy Information." Companies also had a reputation for padding customers' bills with all sorts of extra charges, most of which you never found out about until you returned the car.

Although many of these surcharges are still around (see the sidebar on page 192 for examples), at least now you're more likely to learn about them up front, especially if you book on line. Expedia, Orbitz, and Travelocity all offer what they call "total pricing" (does anybody ever want to know just the *partial* price?), displaying rates that include mandatory taxes and fees, not just a daily or weekly rate. Most car rental companies go a step further, displaying total prices as well as charges for options like insurance, an additional driver, prepaid fuel, or a child safety seat — information you may start seeing on the agencies' Web sites at some point.

All this means that you should be able to book a car in the time it takes to microwave a bag of popcorn — well, maybe two bags of popcorn. Here's how to decide where to click the buy button and how to keep your total bill from inflating like a bag of Orville Redenbacher's with extra butter.

Where to book: Agencies versus suppliers
For comparing rates, your best bet is still one of the on-line agencies — Expedia, Orbitz, or Travelocity. Some of the travel search en-

gines mentioned on pages 91–93 also offer search tools for car rentals, but so far, those sites are better for comparing flights.

Although they often have the same prices for car rentals, the big three agencies don't necessarily display the same number of companies. Orbitz tends to offer more choices than either Expedia or Travelocity, in a format that makes comparing prices easier, but that could change over time.

You'll get pretty much the same rate whether you book with an agency or through the car rental company — the agencies charge about $5 more per rental — but booking direct has a few other benefits. For starters, car rental companies do a better job of outlining all the fees they charge and usually post information about current promotions and sales that you won't see anywhere else. You're also more likely to be able to use a discount code if you book direct — say, if you qualify for a corporate rate, are a AAA member, or saw a discount code in an ad.

It's been a longstanding policy that you can usually cancel a car reservation without penalty at any time, but the on-line agencies have been getting pretty aggressive about cancellation fees, so if you reserve a car through an agency, make sure that you can cancel it without getting charged.

As for booking on line versus by phone, there's usually not a price difference, but you'll get a clearer breakdown of costs and fees on your computer screen. Wherever you book, make sure you get a receipt sent to you via e-mail — and print a copy. That way, you'll have a paper trail if you show up at the counter and the price is mysteriously higher than what you booked.

Booking tips: How to save

Many car rental companies now tout a "best-rate guarantee," promising that their Web sites always have the lowest prices for their cars, but these same rates often show up on other sites, too, give or take a few dollars, so you'll no longer find huge price differences based on where you book a particular car (though there are still differences between what Budget, Hertz, other agencies charge). (For more about comparing car rental companies, see the sidebar on page 190.) Here are some other ways to trim the fat from your total bill.

COMPARING CAR RENTAL COMPANIES

Car rental companies tend to fall into two price ranges, discounters and full-service agencies, but don't think of these as hard-and-fast lines. Sometimes, Hertz may be cheaper than Dollar, or Payless may turn out to be the most expensive choice, so you can't always predict who will have the lowest rate, and better service doesn't always correspond to a higher price.

Besides the companies listed here, most of which have locations worldwide, there are also lots of independent agencies that rent cars. To find out who operates where, check a guidebook or try Carrentalexpress .com, which displays rates from more than three hundred independently owned companies, mostly in the United States.

Sometimes, these local businesses are cheaper or have more flexible rental polices — and may even rent by the hour — but if you're renting from a smaller operation with a name like Joe's Jalopies, check out the company's reputation before you sign on the dotted line.

DISCOUNTERS

- Budget (budget.com)
- Dollar (dollar.com)
- Enterprise (enterprise.com)
- Fox (foxrentacar.com)
- Payless (paylesscarrental.com)
- Thrifty (thrifty.com)

FULL-SERVICE AGENCIES

- Alamo (alamo.com)
- Avis (avis.com)
- Hertz (hertz.com)
- National (nationalcar.com)

Reserve early. Procrastination won't cost you nearly as much with a car rental as it does with a plane ticket or a hotel, but you'll usually get a better deal if you plan ahead, especially if you're renting abroad. Also, agencies do run out of cars during busy times, so if you need an SUV for a spring-break ski trip or a minivan for the Fourth of July, *carpe mus* (Latin for "seize your mouse"). There's really no reason not to make a reservation early, since you can usually cancel without penalty if you find a better deal later on.

Try for weekend or weekly rates. Weekend rates are usually lower than renting during the week, but a good trick to remember is that weekend rates are often available as early as Thursday at noon and extend through Monday morning, so you may notice a price difference simply by shifting your pick-up time — for instance, to Thursday at 12:30 P.M. instead of 11:00 A.M. To qualify for a weekly rate, you usually have to keep the car for at least five days, so if you reserve a car for a week and return it on the fourth day you may get charged the higher daily rate.

Compare rates at different locations. One feature I wish the on-line agencies offered is the ability to compare rates at different locations in or near a city — say, the airport and any office downtown. Usually, you have to do separate searches to see rates at more than one location, but it's worth checking, especially if you're debating where to pick up the car. There's generally a surcharge for airport rentals, but in some cities, like San Francisco, rates are higher downtown, where it's expensive to lease office space and park all those cars. In New York City, you can often save money by renting a car in nearby suburbs instead of in the city — but that means a train or bus ride to pick up the car.

Use a discount code. Coupons for car rentals take a predictable journey through my house: They show up with credit card bills or frequent flier statements, then gather dust with other piles of paper until I rediscover them, find out they've expired, and throw them out. But if you're more organized, the discount codes printed on coupons, in ads, or available with a corporate, AAA, or AARP rate can sometimes save you money on a car rental. You can also try searching for discount codes on the Internet, using a phrase like "Avis and coupon and code" — coupon clippers sometimes go to the trouble of sharing these codes on line. These rates often have blackout dates, though, and they're usually good for only limited times and locations; also, they're not necessarily the lowest rates available, so you should double-check prices without entering a special code.

Compare rates for extra charges. This tip may fall under the cate-

ADDING UP THE EXTRAS

Besides the base rate you'll see advertised for a rental car — a low $19 a day or $120 for a week — here are some of the other charges that can make your final bill a whole lot higher. When companies cite "total prices," they're usually including taxes and fees everyone has to pay; other charges are based on options you select. Note that some of these are daily fees, whereas others are per rental.

- *Taxes:* State and local governments are notorious for taxing tourists who come to town, and car rentals are a prime target. The worst offender? Texas, where you'll pay an extra 50 percent to 70 percent in taxes and fees if you rent a car at airports in Austin, Dallas, or Houston. Nationwide, the average is about 25 percent. Some of these taxes fund projects like local stadiums, while others are fees that car rental companies are required to pay but pass along to their customers, like a "concession recovery fee" for airport rentals or a "vehicle license fee" you probably pay for your own car.

- *Insurance:* If you choose to buy insurance from the car rental company, you can easily double or even triple your total bill. Many people already have coverage for car rentals through their personal auto insurance, homeowner's insurance, or credit card; see page 199 for advice on how to tell whether you're covered.

- *Extra equipment:* All states have laws requiring children under a certain age to be strapped into a car seat, even in a rental car, so unless you bring your own, expect to pay about $8 a day to rent one. You'll also pay extra for luggage or ski racks, tire chains, and GPS navigation systems. You should reserve any of this equipment when you book the car.

- *Additional driver:* Most companies charge extra if you want to authorize anyone else to drive the car; this fee is usually about $7 per day, though some companies cap it at $35 or so per rental. Some companies waive their additional-driver charge if you book a AAA or AARP rate, join a frequent-renter program, or the second driver is a work colleague or spouse. Policies vary, so this is one fee you may be able to avoid by shopping around.

- *Underage driver:* Anyone under the age of twenty-five who has tried to rent a car knows that the last milestone on the road to adulthood isn't turning twenty-one but being able to rent a car without paying an eye-popping surcharge. Most companies charge renters younger than twenty-five a daily fee that ranges from $10 to $100 per day, depending on the location, but $30 is about average, and some agencies won't rent to anyone under twenty-one. You may be able to avoid this fee if you're renting a car on a corporate account or through a local agency; try carrentalexpress.com to find one.

- *Drop-off fees:* If you rent a car in one location and drop it off somewhere else, most companies charge an extra fee for these one-way rentals. Surcharges vary, depending on the company and the distance between your destination and your starting point, but may be as low as $50 if you're driving from Los Angeles to San Francisco or several hundred dollars if you're traveling across the United States — or even more if you're renting overseas and want to drop off the car in a different country. But in some cases, you won't have to pay a drop-off fee if the company is trying to relocate part of its fleet from one location to another.

- *Frequent-flier miles:* If you choose to earn frequent flier miles for your car rental, most companies now charge a fee — about 50 cents a day — for the privilege of adding a few hundred miles to your account.

- *Gas:* Car rental companies charge two different rates for gas: a prepaid option, which means that you can return the car empty and pay a set rate for a full tank of gas (maybe 25 percent higher than market price), or an even higher rate (often double what you'd pay at the pump) if you don't opt for the prepaid rate but return the car with the tank less than full. Rates vary, but neither option is a deal.

gory of "Who would ever bother to do that?" but if you have to pay any extra charges, it's worth comparing prices for these fees, since companies don't always charge the same rate for extra options. You probably won't find a huge price difference for things like insurance or a car seat, but some companies don't charge for an additional driver — or waive the fee for AAA members, a work colleague, or a spouse — so you may be able to save on these fees by shopping around.

Check prices for different car types. Some sites let you select a car type when you search for a rental, but you're better off seeing all your options. That's because a smaller car isn't always the cheapest way to go; you may find a special on a bigger car, so scan the whole list before you decide (the options aren't always listed from lowest to highest price).

Make sure that your rate includes unlimited miles. If you're renting locally, booking a promotional rate, or doing business with an independent agency, you may not get unlimited miles. Car rental companies have gotten better about disclosing any mileage restrictions when you book, not just burying them in your contract, but it's still a detail you should double-check, since extra-mileage fees can lead to serious sticker shock. You should also find out whether there are any restrictions on where you can drive. Some companies use GPS technology to monitor their cars' whereabouts, so you could get hit with a hefty penalty if you violate any rules against crossing state lines.

Watch out for cancellation charges. Some car rental companies reserve the right to charge a penalty if you don't cancel at least twenty-four hours before your scheduled pick-up time, so ask about the cancellation policy when you book the car. These fees are more common if you're traveling during a holiday, reserving a minivan or an SUV, or renting abroad, but if you hold a reservation with a credit card, you risk getting charged if you're a no-show. On the flip side, some companies automatically cancel your reservation if you don't pick up your car within two hours of your scheduled arrival time, so if your flight is delayed, call and let the company know.

Try Hotwire or Priceline. If you're flexible about which company you rent a car from, you may be able to get a better deal by booking through Priceline or Hotwire (see page 76 for advice). Compare rates elsewhere first, because unless you can save at least $40 on the rental, it's not worth the trade-off of an inflexible cancellation policy, since neither site lets you make any changes after you book, and you don't get a refund if you have to cancel.

Check your bill. Another way to avoid overpaying is to check your receipt after you return the car and your credit card bill once your statement arrives. Disclosure about extra fees has generally improved, but there's a lot of franchising in this industry, so you may find that a less reputable location slips an additional charge onto your tab — for gas, a ding in the windshield, or insurance you thought you declined. You should definitely fight any fees you think were improperly assessed (see page 287), but you have to notice them in order to demand a refund.

Renting a Car Abroad: Where to Book, Potential Potholes

It's sort of a toss-up as to which is more challenging: arranging a car rental for a trip abroad or actually driving it once you pick it up. A few years ago, I met my parents while they were traveling in Italy, and the stories we keep retelling about that trip all seem to involve the rental car: finding the office to pick it up in Rome, described as "right next to the Spanish Steps," in the way that a building could be considered "right by Times Square" in New York; navigating the winding roads of the Amalfi coast, where a missed exit led to a nail-biting detour up and over a mountain; and returning the car to the airport at 4:00 A.M., which involved another treasure hunt to find the box to drop off the keys after hours.

Which isn't to say that we should've skipped the car; in a country like Italy, there are amazing places that you just can't see unless you hit the road. But driving in a foreign country isn't for the faint of heart: The road signs are in a different language (if there are signs at all), speed limits are often flagrantly ignored, and even the most detailed maps — or the best navigators — can't always provide a clear answer to the question, "Is this the exit we want?"

Meanwhile, booking a rental car for a trip overseas involves its own set of challenges. Here are some strategies to help minimize headaches, both during the booking process and on the road, and advice to ensure that your bill isn't triple the cost you planned on.

Book by phone
The Web is great for comparing prices and finding companies that rent cars abroad (see the sidebar on page 196), but once you're ready to book, pick up the phone. International rentals raise a lot of questions most Web sites don't answer very well — like how many people, with luggage, fit comfortably in an Alfa Romeo 156 or whether the rental office will be open on a public holiday. If you book by phone, you also have the opportunity to negotiate on price — and with an overseas rental, companies are sometimes more willing to bargain.

INTERNATIONAL RENTALS: WHERE TO BOOK

All the major U.S. car rental companies also arrange rentals for trips abroad, though your choices will vary, depending on where you're going. You can check your options and compare rates at sites like Expedia, Orbitz, or Travelocity or see what kind of deal you can get through Hotwire, which books car rentals for Mexico, the Caribbean, and major cities in Europe.

Usually, you'll save money on an international rental by making your reservation before your trip — the earlier, the better — but if you're not sure you'll need a car or you need one for only a few days in the middle of your stay, another option is to book through a local agency once you arrive. Guidebooks usually list car rental agencies that operate in the destinations they cover, including major brands and local options, and sometimes indicate which is the most economical way to go. If you rent through a local agency, make sure that you understand all the costs and rules involved — which isn't always easy when you're dealing with language barriers.

A couple of agencies in the United States specialize in European rentals, as well as other destinations around the world. These agencies work with both U.S. and foreign car rental companies, so you may end up renting from a company like Sixt, a big rental agency in Germany.

- **Auto Europe** (autoeurope.com). Based in Portland, Maine, Auto Europe is an agency that arranges car rentals for more than four thousand locations worldwide, working with both local and multinational suppliers. Its Web site is easy to use — clearly showing the hours of each rental location and which ones are at the airport versus in the city or near a train station. Auto Europe also owns kemwel.com — a former competitor — but regardless of where you book, you're dealing with the same company.

- **Europe By Car** (europebycar.com). Europe By Car is kind of an anachronism in the travel industry — a company that encourages customers to call. Based in New York, it's a family-run business that arranges rentals primarily in Europe, but with options in 40,000 locations, what's considered Europe is pretty broad. The agency works with about twenty car rental companies throughout Europe and also handles short-term leases for Renault and Peugeot (see the sidebar on page 197).

Ask about additional charges

Price quotes for foreign car rentals don't always include *all* the taxes and fees you'll have to pay, so when you're comparing rates, ask whether there will be any additional charges — and then ask a second time, just to be sure. Taxes can run as high as 20 percent to 25

SHORT-TERM LEASES FOR LONGER RENTALS

If you're planning to stay in Europe for a month or more, a short-term lease may be the way to roll. Rather than renting, you actually lease a brand-new car. These leases are priced based on a fixed fee for the first seventeen days and a daily charge from then on; insurance is included, though you may have to pay other additional charges.

Renault Eurodrive (renaultusa.com) and Peugeot Open Europe (peu geot-openeurope.com) are the two main options for a short-term lease in Europe. Both companies offer several dozen pick-up and drop-off locations in Belgium, France, Germany, Great Britain, Italy, the Netherlands, Portugal, Spain, and Switzerland, though you're allowed to drive in other countries as well.

You can get more information from Renault or Peugeot or from Auto Europe (autoeurope.com) or Europe By Car (europebycar.com), both of which handle leases as well as rentals. A lease is most economical if you need a car for at least three weeks, but compare rates with what it would cost to rent one.

percent in some countries, which you may be able to minimize by not picking up your car at a train station or an airport. Make sure that there isn't an extra fee for mileage, and double-check your insurance coverage for international rentals (see page 199). In some countries, like Italy, insurance is mandatory, so you have to pay for it even if you're covered by your own policy. Once you make a reservation, ask the company to e-mail you a quote that itemizes all these charges.

Compare rates for various pick-up points

The cost of a car rental can vary pretty dramatically in different countries, so if you're planning a multinational road trip, compare rates to see where it's most cost-effective to pick up your car. Drop-off charges are another issue to consider: It may be cheaper to book two separate rentals and fly or take the train from one country to another. But if you do plan to cross a border in a rental car, make sure that it's allowed — and that you have the paperwork you'll need for the car. Rates can also vary between airport and city locations, so check whether it's cheaper to take a taxi into town and pick up your car there. That way, you'll also avoid parking fees while you're in the

city and be better adjusted to the local time zone once you get behind the wheel.

Choose your car wisely

Although it's gotten easier to rent cars abroad with automatic transmission, manual transmission is generally cheaper and sometimes
your only option. But if your most recent experience shifting gears
took place in a parking lot when you were seventeen (as in my case),
you're probably not in shape to take on Germany's autobahn. In
countries where you'll be driving on the left side of the road, that
means shifting with your left hand, too, so think twice about manual transmission in England, unless you're ambidextrous. As for
car size, smaller is often better in countries where streets are narrow and parking spaces are tiny, so even if you're offered a free upgrade, that's a gift you may want to turn down. But don't get a tiny
car if you'll be on the highway a lot — you'll want some pick-up for
that autobahn.

Check age restrictions

Some countries — or the car rental companies that do business
abroad — don't allow people above a certain age to rent a car. These
age limits vary but can be as young as seventy years old, so if
you've already celebrated that birthday, ask whether there are any
age restrictions when you book. (The company may not check your
age until you pick up the car, so better to know if that's an issue
up front.) If you're over the limit, don't assume that it's a national
policy — another company may have a different maximum.

Get detailed directions

Make sure to ask for clear directions to your car's pick-up and return location, especially if it's not at the airport. On our trip to Italy,
the rental office that was supposedly "near the Spanish Steps"
was actually off a street way above the Spanish Steps and not well
marked. You should also consider buying a road map before you
arrive (see page 223). The maps car rental companies give out
are often not much help when you're navigating city roads, since

they tend to leave out smaller streets and critical details like one-way arrows.

Supplemental Insurance: When You Need It, When You Don't

One of the most stressful aspects of renting a car is deciding whether to accept or decline all the insurance options you're offered, usually as you're standing at the counter and wondering whether your credit card or auto insurance covers all the dire possibilities the agent is describing. If you gamble that you're covered, you're probably left wondering whether you're wrong, especially if the agent raises his or her eyebrows and says something like, "Well, as long as you're *sure* about that . . ." And if you decide not to take a risk and opt for the extra insurance, you can easily end up paying twice as much for the rental. Either way, there's a lingering uneasiness as you walk away from the counter — not to mention the first time you slam on the brakes to avoid another car.

Some companies reward employees for selling insurance, so don't count on getting objective advice from an agent as you're weighing your options. The best way to avoid buying insurance you don't need — or exposing yourself to a potentially expensive liability — is to make a few phone calls before your next trip and find out whether you have coverage through your own insurance policies or your credit card.

Demystifying car rental insurance

One of the things that makes car rental insurance so complicated is that insurance laws are different in every state, and companies offer different options depending on where you're renting a car. Making matters more confusing, each company uses different names for the policies it sells, so even if you get a handle on Hertz's options in Hawaii, that may not help you when you rent from Alamo in Alabama.

That said, all those cryptic names and abbreviations boil down to a few basic choices, which are outlined here, along with advice on how to figure out whether you're already covered.

Loss or damage to the car. If you have an accident in a rental car, you're responsible for the cost of repairs and possibly whatever fee the company charges for "loss of use" while the car is being repaired, even if the accident wasn't your fault. You're also responsible for the value of the car if it's stolen. Car rental companies sell various waivers that either limit or release you from this responsibility, but before you accept any of these options, make sure that you understand exactly what's covered. And keep in mind that any waiver you purchase is voided if you're driving recklessly or violate the terms of your contract — say, by driving out of state or turning over the wheel to an unauthorized driver.

Often called: Collision damage waiver (CDW) or Loss damage waiver (LDW).

Cost: $9 to $25 a day.

Other options: All Visa cards, most American Express cards (except student cards), and some MasterCards (including gold, platinum, or world cards) cover loss or damage to a rental car, but only if you use that card to pay for the rental and usually up to a limit of $50,000. Also, coverage from a credit card is secondary, meaning that you first have to seek coverage through your own auto insurance, which may also cover loss or damage to a rental car — although the limit might be below the value of the car you rent (say, if you drive a junker and rent a car with 12,000 miles on the odometer). Some credit card companies or auto insurers may limit the length of rentals covered to fourteen days or a month and may not cover rentals in other countries. (Australia, Ireland, Israel, Italy, Jamaica, and New Zealand are among the countries that are often excluded.) And some credit card companies don't cover "loss of use" charges.

Do you need it? Chances are, your credit card or auto insurance offers some coverage for loss or damage to a rental car, at least in the United States. If not, this is an option you should probably spring for.

Liability for damage or injuries you cause to others. If you cause an accident, you're also responsible for damage to anyone else's car or property, not to mention any injuries or lawsuits that result. States have different rules requiring car rental companies to include a minimum amount of liability insurance with every rental, but that probably won't cover all the expenses you're liable for if you have a bad accident. To bridge the gap, most companies offer some type of additional liability insurance you can buy.

Often called: Additional Liability Insurance (ALI), Supplemental Liability Insurance (SLI), Supplemental Liability Protection (SLP), or Liability Insurance Supplement (LIS). A related option, called Uninsured Motorist Protection (UMP), provides coverage if you're injured in an accident caused by an uninsured driver.

Cost: $6 to $13 a day.

Other coverage: Most credit cards don't offer liability protection for rental cars, but many auto insurance policies do. Call your insurance company and find out whether your policy offers liability coverage for rental cars — and how much.

Do you need it? Ask how much liability coverage is automatically included when you rent the car (this varies by state). If you don't have additional liability coverage through your own auto policy — and you may not, since some people opt for low liability coverage to keep their premiums down — it's up to you to decide whether you want more liability insurance than you have on the car you drive at home.

Injury to you or theft of your belongings. Two other types of insurance car rental companies offer are coverage for any injuries sustained by you or other passengers in an accident; sometimes including an accidental-death benefit, and coverage if anything is stolen from the car. All these benefits are capped at a maximum dollar amount, which may be quite low, so if you're considering either option, find out what these limits are. Some car rental companies bundle these two options, so you may have to buy them both if you want either one.

Often called: Personal Accident Insurance (PAI), Personal Effects Protection (PEP), Personal Effects Coverage (PEC), or Personal Accident and Effects Protection (PAE).

Cost: $3 to $11 a day.

Other coverage: If you have homeowner's or renter's insurance, you may be covered if anything is stolen from your rental car, though you'd probably have to pay a deductible first. And if you're injured in an accident in the United States, your medical bills would probably be covered by your health insurance policy — though many policies, and Medicare, don't cover you at all when you're traveling abroad (see page 219).

Do you need it? If you're renting a car in the United States, it's almost never worth paying for either of these insurance options, since you're probably already covered through other sources, and the limits on the benefits car rental companies offer are generally very low. These provisions also tend to include a lot of loopholes. For instance, if the car is robbed, some policies cover only the driver's possessions, not anyone else's luggage. But theft protection is sometimes mandatory in countries where break-ins are a problem.

Express Pick-Up Programs: Skip the Line, at Least Some of the Time

For people who rent cars frequently, the worst pick-up line in the world isn't, "Do you come here often?" or "Haven't we met somewhere before?"; it's a long line of customers waiting to pick up a rental car, everyone impatient to grab the keys and get going. Sometimes, luck is on your side and you can step right up to the counter, but if you're the last person off the shuttle bus or there's one employee behind the desk dealing with a high-maintenance customer, you can find yourself cooling your heels for a whole lot longer. My personal record was a nearly hour-long wait to pick up a car at Oakland airport — not including the trip on the shuttle bus to get to the lot — which is what finally drove me to investigate the membership programs most car rental companies now offer.

The main incentive? Joining these programs means that you can go straight to your car at some locations, without stopping at the counter (you find out which car is yours either on the bus or by checking a sign once you get to the lot). In other cases, you still have to go to the counter, but at least you get to wait in a special express line for members. At smaller airports or city offices, you may have to queue with everyone else — not every location is set up to give members a red carpet welcome — but at most airports, you can expect to be on your way much more quickly than the rest of the crowd.

Another incentive to join these programs is that most companies send a coupon for a discount or free upgrade on a future rental with your membership materials, and if you provide your e-mail address when you sign up, you can opt to get news about other promotions. (See the sidebar on page 204 for a list of companies that offer membership programs.)

These loyalty programs were originally designed for business travelers, but even if you don't rent a car several times a month, it's worth joining, especially if there are a few companies you typically rent from. Most of these clubs are free, and you can sign up on line — it took me about forty-five minutes to fill out forms for four different programs.

Most companies ask for your address, phone number, date of birth, driver's license, and credit card information, along with your preferred car type and insurance choices, though you can change the preferences you have on file when you make a reservation — say, if you need a minivan for a family vacation instead of the midsize car you usually rent for work. Once your preferences are on file, booking a car is easier, too, since you don't have to enter all this information each time.

My only complaint about the sign-up process is that with some car rental companies, you will be required to check a box agreeing to terms and conditions outlined in a "master rental agreement" — a sixty-two-page document from Avis, and a seventy-five-page document from Budget — a volume of legalese that no one could realistically be expected to digest, let alone understand (which is why these electronic agreements are often deemed unenforceable by the courts).

Even so, the first time I got to skip the line — fittingly, back at Oakland airport, on a holiday weekend when there were dozens of people waiting in line — I practically skipped to my car, I was so thrilled.

FOR MEMBERS ONLY: QUICKER PICK-UP LINES

Here are some of the car rental loyalty programs you can join if you're looking to limit your time in line at the counter. Most are free, but Hertz and National charge an annual fee, which probably isn't worth paying unless you rent from either company often.

Program name	Cost	Member benefits
Alamo Quicksilver (alamo.com)	Free	Special member lines at more than 50 U.S. locations (mostly at airports)
Avis Preferred (avis.com)	Free	Can go straight to your car at 1,400 locations or use express lines at counter; typically assigned the company's newer cars
Budget Fastbreak (budget.com)	Free	Can go directly to your car at about 1,400 locations; elsewhere, special lines at counter
Dollar Express (dollar.com)	Free	Dedicated lines at major airports; preprinted rental agreement ready at counter
Hertz #1 Club (hertz.com)	Free[a]	Access to express lines at 55 U.S. and Canadian locations; no additional-driver fee for spouse or domestic partner
National Emerald Club (emeraldclub.com); (nationalcar.com)	$50[b]	At most major airports you can go directly to your car; elsewhere, special lines at counter
Thrifty Blue Chip Express (bluechip.thrifty.com)	Free	Separate lines at most major U.S. airports; rental contract preprinted and ready at counter

a $50 annual fee for Hertz Gold membership, which lets you go straight to your car at some locations and qualify for discounts and free upgrades, based on how often you rent
b annual fee

Riding the Rails: Timetables, Reservations, and Tickets

One of my Top Ten Most Terrifying Moments in Travel was landing in Italy by myself at age nineteen — my first trip overseas — and making my way from the Milan airport to the train station and boarding the correct train to Florence. I had three heavy bags (yes, I overpacked, but I was staying for six months), which I dragged from the information booth to the ticket window, then to the *correct* ticket window, then all the way to the end of the platform, never quite sure I was on the right train or in the right car or what time we'd arrive in Florence.

That was back in the digital dark ages, before the Internet made it possible to look up timetables for pretty much any train in the world, which at least eliminates some of the anxiety of arriving at an unfamiliar station — tired, clueless, and burdened with baggage. Once you find the Web site of the train system you need (see the sidebar on page 207 for where to look), all you have to do is enter your departure city, destination, travel dates, and approximate travel time, and you get a list of all the trains that depart around the time you selected, with varying degrees of information about each one.

At a minimum, you can usually find out what time the train arrives, how many stops it makes, fares for various classes of travel, and what services are on board, like sleeping compartments or a dining car. Some railroad Web sites even let you make a reservation or buy tickets on line; you either pick up your ticket at the station, often from a kiosk, or the receipt sent to you via e-mail works as your ticket on board. And most of the major railroad Web sites are multilingual, so there's almost always an English-language option.

Tips for train travel

Even though life has gotten much easier for those planning to travel by train, it's not all a smooth ride. (If I wrote a book about trains, it would be titled, *Everything I Learned About Traveling by Train, I Learned by Doing Something Wrong.*) Here are a few tips on navigating some of the idiosyncrasies of train travel, both during the planning phase of your trip and once you're on board.

Thinking like a local. Although most railroad Web sites reach out to foreigners by offering translations in other languages, these sites are designed primarily for the local residents who use them the most. So you may find yourself baffled by choices like the six train stations in Paris or the national spelling for a city or town (for instance, the Italian Firenze, which we call Florence).

Plus, not all the pages on every site are translated into English, so if you click a link, you may find that the explanation you were looking for is given only in Dutch, French, or German. It's usually possible to muddle through and find basic information about schedules and prices, but be prepared for a few cultural hurdles as you click around — like the fact that prices are usually listed in the local currency. (Visit xe.com if you need help converting to dollars.) Also, many foreign sites ask for the date in day/month/year format, so make sure that you're entering those numbers in the correct order. And "return" is sometimes used to indicate a round-trip ticket, versus a "single," or one-way, price.

Deciphering train lingo. Once you pull up a train schedule on the Web — or, for that matter, at the station — the differences among the trains you can choose from aren't always obvious. Some of the faster, premium trains operating in Europe are the AVE, Eurostar, ICE, Talgo, Thalys, and TGV, which generally travel between countries; and intercity trains are usually the faster trains within a country (as opposed to a "local" option, which may stop at every town along the way). The more a train costs, the faster it's likely to travel, so use price and travel time as your guide.

Choosing a seat (or a bed). Trains are still a very class-based form of travel, but the class differences aren't consistent around the world. A first-class ticket usually buys you a bigger seat and more room to spread out and sometimes cleaner bathrooms, meal service, and better-dressed traveling companions, but these distinctions can vary quite a bit from country to country — and from train to train. In a second-class car, sometimes called tourist or standard class, there are more seats and more people, but if you're used to the tight squeeze on an airplane, second class on a train may feel spacious by comparison.

For overnight travel, you can pay about $30 extra for a "couchette," a bunk bed that folds down from the wall (usually there are six bunks to a compartment, so you'll most likely be bunking with strangers), or you can opt for a "sleeper" compartment, which has fewer, more comfortable beds and sometimes a sink. Prices for sleeper compartments vary, depending on the train and the size you reserve; they usually accommodate one person (a single) or two people (a double), and you have the option of locking the door.

Deciding whether you need a reservation. Buying a ticket for a train doesn't guarantee you a seat; if you want a confirmed seat assign-

FINDING TRAIN SCHEDULES

The easiest way to find train schedules on line is to do a search for your destination (country, state, or city) and the phrase "train schedule"; the site you want is likely to show up on the first page of results. Many countries have a national railroad system or at least a common Web site with schedules, so you can almost always find all the timetables you need in one place. Other options: Try railfaneurope.net, which links to train schedules for most of Europe, or raileurope.com, which sells rail passes and point-to-point tickets for many European trains (though you'll pay more than if you wait to buy your ticket after you arrive).

Many specialty and tourist trains have their own Web sites, like the Eurostar (eurostar.com) train, which passes under the English Channel, or the White Pass & Yukon Route Railroad (wpyr.com), which offers excursions from Alaska up to the Yukon Territory in Canada. Railserve.com provides links to many of these specialty and tourist trains, as well as timetables for passenger and commuter trains worldwide.

If you're looking for a shortcut, here are Web sites for some of the main railroad systems around the world, all of which offer an English option. You may have to hunt around for a link that says "English" or look for a graphic of the British flag — apparently, the international symbol for "English," at least on line.

Australia: Rail Australia (railaustralia.com.au)
Canada: Via Rail Canada (viarail.ca)
France: Société Nationale des Chemins de fer Français (SNCF)
(sncf.com)
Germany: Deutsche Bahn (bahn.de)
Italy: Ferrovie dello Stato (trenitalia.com)
Japan: Japan Railways Group (japanrail.com)
Spain: Renfe (renfe.es)
United Kingdom: National Rail (nationalrail.co.uk)
United States: Amtrak (amtrak.com)

ment, you have to make a reservation. For most shorter trips, it isn't really necessary, but if you're traveling on a Friday or a Sunday or during a local holiday, it's a good idea to make one. Otherwise, you may find yourself standing the whole way, or you'll have to buy a first-class seat just to sit down. For some premium or overnight trains, a reservation is mandatory.

In Europe, a reservation costs a few dollars more than the price

BUYING RAIL PASSES

Buying a Eurailpass used to be a rite of passage for college students headed to Europe, not to mention travelers beyond college age planning an extended European tour. Despite competition from low-cost carriers, these passes are still for sale, though the choices have proliferated like toothpaste flavors since my backpacking days.

You can now buy dozens of different rail passes for travel within a single country, two adjacent countries, several neighboring countries, or most of Europe; variations allow unlimited travel during a certain time period or a specific number of travel days during a similar window (say, ten travel days within two months). There are also passes that combine rail travel with a few days of car rental (a Rail 'n Drive pass) and discounted passes for groups of people traveling together, seniors, or youth. Frankly, the permutations are so dizzying, you really do need a travel agent to help you sort them out.

Most rail passes must be purchased before your trip or at least outside the country you're visiting. Rail Europe (raileurope.com) is the main agency that sells European rail passes to Americans, but you can purchase them through other travel agencies as well. The European guidebook guru Rick Steves offers advice on his Web site about buying rail passes, which his company also sells (see ricksteves.com/rail). And Europe isn't the only place you might consider a pass: Australia, India, and Japan also offer passes for their railroads.

But don't get talked into buying a rail pass before you've considered other options. Unless you're planning to move around a lot, it's often cheaper to buy separate train tickets or even flights, so compare prices before you commit. Also, these passes aren't good for every train — you can't use a pass to travel between France and Britain, for example, and you'll have to pay a surcharge if you want to take some faster trains. Be sure you understand all the terms and conditions — there's a lot of fine print to decipher.

of your ticket and can usually be made sixty to ninety days ahead of time. Although some railways let passengers make reservations on line, the process isn't always clear-cut if you don't understand the local language (this is where the English translations have a tendency to trail off). If you'll be in Europe a few days before your train trip, you can make a reservation at the station once you arrive. Another option is to buy your ticket through Rail Europe, a U.S. agency that sells tickets and rail passes for European trains (see the sidebar on the facing page for more about rail passes), but you'll pay a bit more for this peace of mind.

Understanding the rules of the railroad. For people not used to taking trains, figuring out rail travel protocol is usually a matter of trial and error. You board the train and take what you think is an empty seat, only to have some other passenger come along to claim it. Or you inadvertently sit down in a first class seat until the conductor unceremoniously sends you back several cars to second class, which at that point may be standing-room only. To avoid such mishaps, look for a "1" or "2" on the side of the car when you board; when you're in doubt, the first-class cars are often toward the front of the platform, but your best bet is to ask someone before you get settled. If you have a reservation, it will indicate a car and a seat number.

You should also make sure that you're in a car that's going to your destination, since some cars get detached and sent in a different direction en route. The conductor may not read your ticket carefully, so risk the public humiliation of confirming where the train is going — better to reveal your tourist status than to end up in the wrong country. Besides, befriending the conductor helps ensure that you don't miss your station. I was once traveling with friends in Spain, and we would have slept through our stop if the conductor hadn't roused us and started tossing our bags onto the platform. We barely made it out the door, dazed and barefoot, before the train started pulling away.

Travel tips. If you look up timetables on line, double-check that information locally when you arrive, since the Web site may not be completely up-to-date, or the schedule may have changed after you looked at it. You should always get to your platform on time, but don't assume that you'll arrive at your destination exactly on schedule; despite politicians' aspirations to "make sure the trains run on time," some countries, including the United States, haven't achieved this goal. If you're taking a local train, try to avoid rush hour, and if smoke bothers you, look for a nonsmoking car (though don't be surprised if other passengers ignore the "no smoking" sign near the door).

Timetables usually indicate whether a dining or bar car is on the train; if not, a vendor may pass through with a cart. In case there isn't any food service, it's always a good idea to bring your own water and snacks — especially if you're traveling alone and don't want to leave your luggage unattended. Theft is definitely an issue on trains, so if you're likely to nod off, one simple deterrent is to wrap a strap around the luggage rack, which at least makes it difficult for someone to grab your bag and dash off.

Trains, Planes, Cars, and Buses: How to Decide Which Way to Travel

One of the luxuries travelers enjoy in the twenty-first century is an abundance of transportation options. There's not only one way to get from here to there: you often have several winged or wheeled options to choose from.

Cost is frequently a deciding factor when you're weighing whether to fly, drive, take the train, or hop on a bus. But it's not the only variable you should consider, especially in a foreign country where everything is cheap compared to the prices at home. Here are some other issues to factor into your decision, particularly if you're traveling in a place where the transportation infrastructure is less developed.

Reliability
Depending on where you're traveling, a plane may be more reliable than a bus or a train — or vice versa — but this is definitely a factor you should investigate, especially if you're planning a tightly choreographed schedule. I once spent a couple of extra days in a small town in Bolivia, waiting for the dirt runway to dry out so a plane could land. ("Some days, the plane come, some days, she don't," was how locals summed up regional air travel.)

Roads are also susceptible to rainstorms, not to mention more likely to suffer from disrepair, which can make train travel more dependable than driving or taking a bus. So don't assume that just because there is a road, it's always passable — some close for weeks at a time. (I've also encountered that surprise.) In remote areas, buses are more likely than planes, or even trains, to experience break-downs, so be prepared for that wrinkle in your schedule.

To find out about road conditions and the pros and cons of vari-ous transportation options, guidebooks are generally a good source. So are the on-line message boards listed in the sidebar on page 16, where you can get advice from other travelers.

Safety

It's easy to overlook differences in safety standards around the world until you're climbing aboard a bus that looks like it's well be-yond an optimal retirement age or a plane that was built before you were born. Although it's impossible to say which form of transpor-tation is safest in every country, traffic accidents cause more in-juries and fatalities among travelers than other issues we worry about, like terrorism or SARS.

Taking the train is generally a safer option than driving or taking a bus, and train stations are less prone to crime than bus stations in many parts of the world — though both are places you should keep your guard up. In Rio de Janeiro, I ignored my hotel's advice and went ahead with my plan to take a bus to a town north of the city; even the taxi driver was worried about dropping me off at the sta-tion by myself. Nothing happened, but in retrospect, I should have opted for the car service my hotel offered, so the moral of that story is: Follow the locals' advice about safety concerns — even if it seems overly cautious.

For another point of view, the U.S. State Department covers road and aviation safety in the reports it publishes about most foreign countries (see travel.state.gov). These reports are worth reading if you're traveling to a less developed country and plan to fly on a na-tional airline or rent a car.

Comfort

It's tough to generalize about which is a more comfortable way to travel: train, plane, rental car, or bus. Often, the best way to find out is to ask around. On buses or trains, bathrooms may be putrid — or nonexistent — even in the United States, so if you're squeamish about restroom facilities, investigate this detail before you commit to a long haul. (One apparently regularly scheduled stop I experienced on a bus ride in Bolivia: a field by the side of the road.)

Strikes

Another issue to consider is the possibility of a strike, especially in European or other countries where unions are strong. This is more likely to be a problem with railroads, but strikes can also affect airlines and bus companies. There's not much you can do to avoid one, but if you have to get somewhere on time, pay attention to the news — strikes are usually announced ahead of time, which at least gives you time to come up with a back-up plan.

Additional expenses

If you're trying to decide whether you should rent a car for a trip, consider the cost of not only the rental but also gas, tolls, and parking, all of which can tip the scale in favor of a plane, a train, or a bus. AAA's fuel cost calculator (at fuelcostcalculator.com) can help you estimate how much you'll spend on gas for a trip within the United States; Viamichelin.com has a tool to estimate the cost of gas and tolls along routes in Europe. As for parking, some guidebooks give information about the cost of parking in the cities they cover, but you should definitely find out what your hotel charges. In New York and other big cities, some hotels charge more than $50 a day for parking, an expense that can quickly add up.

PART III

NAVIGATING

8 Pretrip Preparations

SOME PEOPLE START getting ready for a trip at 10 P.M. the night before their departure, pulling a suitcase out of the closet and throwing a load of laundry into the washer, while others have all their clothes laid out, neatly folded, well before it's time to go. If you're in the first category, you're probably tempted to skim over this chapter, so I'll give you the headlines and you can decide whether to read more: Your passport may not be valid six months *before* its expiration date, your health insurance probably doesn't cover you outside U.S. borders, your bank might put a hold on your credit card if you travel far from home, and if you really want to eat at a popular restaurant on vacation, you should make a reservation now.

As for the other topics this chapter covers — where to get maps and driving directions, how to find out which immunizations you might need, what to do to get your gadgets ready to go, and the best way to get to and from the airport — well, I'll assume that those kinds of preparations are of interest mostly to the folded-clothes crowd.

But one thing this chapter *doesn't* offer is packing advice. You already know that you should take half of what you think you'll need, but if you're inclined to pack seven different outfits for a week-long trip, nothing I say is going to change your mind.

Passports and Visas: New Rules — and Fees — When You're Crossing Borders

One of the first things you should do after booking a trip overseas is find your passport and double-check the expiration date. But don't think you can breathe easy if it doesn't expire for another four months and you're going to Brazil in three weeks.

Many countries, including Brazil, require your passport to be valid for at least six months beyond the return date of your trip, so if yours is due to expire sooner, they won't let you in (you may not even be allowed on the plane). Check with the embassy or consulate of the country you're visiting for specific rules, but it's a fairly common policy that catches many travelers by surprise.

U.S. passports: Higher prices, more rules

If you don't have a passport, you've got plenty of company — less than a third of American adults do — but you may be prompted to get one soon. As of late 2007, U.S. citizens are required to show a passport to reenter the United States by air, even from Canada, Mexico, and a few Caribbean countries where a driver's license or birth certificate used to be all you needed. At some point in 2008, U.S. citizens will most likely need a passport to renter the country by land or sea; check travel.state.gov for the latest rules. But the bottom line is: pretty soon, you're going to need a passport anytime you cross a U.S. border if you want to come back home.

If you have to get a passport for the first time, or are due for a renewal, you'll find that passport fees have gone up quite a bit in recent years. It now costs $97 to get a new passport ($82 for children under sixteen) and $67 to renew one, which you can do at more than six thousand places that accept passport applications, including post offices, courts, and libraries (see travel.state.gov/passport for forms and details). Another change is that in order to get a passport, children (even infants) must appear with their parents.

Don't put off this errand until the last minute: The typical processing time for a new passport or renewal is six weeks, although for an extra $60, plus shipping charges, you can shrink that down to two weeks. If you're traveling within two weeks, you can try to make an appointment to apply in person at a regional passport agency — there are thirteen in the United States — but you'll have to show proof of your upcoming departure date to get a slot and pay an extra fee. Another option is to work with an expediting service, a private company that offers last-minute passport and visa help (see the sidebar on the facing page for details).

IF YOU NEED A PASSPORT OR VISA IN A HURRY

In this day and age, of course there's a solution if you have to renew your passport or get a visa in a matter of days, not weeks or months. You can hire an expediter, a company that takes care of the in-person drop-off and pick-up duties for you, though you still have to fill out the appropriate documents and overnight your forms and photos to the expediter.

Expediter fees vary, depending on what passport service or visa you need and how quickly you need it, but typically range from $50 to $200, which is in addition to the cost of the passport or visa service itself. Here are a few companies that offer these services; you can find others by searching the Internet. (These companies are generally located in cities where there's a regional passport agency and many foreign embassies close by.)

All American Passports (allamericanpassports.com)
American Passport Express (americanpassport.com)
Passport Express (passportexpress.com)
Perry International (perryvisa.com)
Travisa (travisa.com)

Foreign travel visas: Also pricier, with more red tape

You don't need a visa to visit most countries, but you do if you're headed to Brazil, Cambodia, China, Egypt, India, Indonesia, Kenya, Laos, Russia, Turkey, or Vietnam. That's a partial list — and policies change — so check the State Department's Web site (travel.state .gov/foreignentryreqs.html) to find out whether your destination requires one. You can download a visa application and instructions from the U.S. embassy of the country you're visiting. The State Department's list includes links to these Web sites, or visit embassy world.com, a searchable database of embassies and consulates all over the world.

Because the State Department now charges $100 for foreigners to apply for a tourist visa (which isn't refunded if the application is rejected), some countries have responded by charging U.S. citizens the same fee. For instance, Brazil, Russia, and Turkey all charge $100 for a basic tourist visa, and Chile charges a $100 "entry fee," payable on arrival at the airport. Other countries, wary of discouraging tourism, charge about half that price.

Some countries have also gotten stricter about scrutinizing visa applications or have added more steps to the process, so don't wait until two weeks before your trip to apply for one — and make sure you follow the instructions to the letter. If you're traveling for work, you need a business visa, which usually involves different forms and fees. And some Middle Eastern or African countries will not issue you a visa or let you into the country if you have an Israeli stamp in your passport, so check the State Department's Web site for advice on working around this diplomatic dilemma.

How long it takes to get a visa varies by country, but a more pertinent factor is where you live. If you're near a major city, you may be able to visit a local embassy or consulate to apply for a visa in person — but even then, plan on a few hours or days of errands. Embassies and consulates usually have specific times when you can drop off or pick up your documents (make sure that the office isn't closed for a holiday, like Chinese New Year or Good Friday). You'll also have to get passport photos taken to submit with your application — subject to rules about how the shot is framed — and you may need to pay with a money order, since some embassies don't accept credit cards, cash, or checks.

If you don't live near a major city or don't have time to stand in line at the consulate, you can usually apply for a visa by mail. If that's not allowed or you're pressed for time, another option is to hire an expediting service to apply for a visa on your behalf.

Getting a visa at your destination

For some countries, like Kenya and Turkey, you may be able to get a visa at the airport or the border when you arrive. Check the requirements before you leave home — and make sure to bring whatever documents you'll need, including extra passport photos. On-line message boards (see the sidebar on page 16) are a good way to find out whether other travelers have had any problems getting visas in a particular country, rather than in advance. The main risk: You might not be granted a visa, in which case you'll have no choice but to turn back.

Immunizations and Health: Does Your Insurance Cover Travel Abroad?

If you're traveling abroad, another task you should add to your to-do list is to call your health insurance provider and ask whether you're covered if you twist your ankle doing the samba in Sao Paulo or develop chest pains in China. The fact is, most private health insurance plans, and Medicare, don't cover medical care you receive in a foreign country — even in an emergency — which is a detail many travelers don't find out about until they submit a claim that's denied.

If your plan *doesn't* cover you overseas, you can buy travel insurance that includes coverage for medical expenses (see page 71 for details) or take your chances and avoid any dicey dance moves or activity that might strain a troublesome ticker. In some countries, you may get lucky and be given free emergency care, but in most cases, you'll have to pay your bill before you're discharged. (When a friend was taken to a hospital in Mexico, even the ambulance driver asked for cash as she was wheeled into the ER.)

Even if you *are* covered overseas, you'll still have to pay out of pocket for any medical care you receive and submit a claim to your insurance company for reimbursement, though you may have to call and get approval from your provider within a few days after being treated. So another reason to call your insurance company before your trip is to get a phone number that works overseas; many insurance cards list only a toll-free number, which you can't necessarily call from another country.

Immunizations: When you need them, where to get them

If your health insurance doesn't follow you beyond U.S. borders, you may be more motivated to get any vaccines recommended for wherever you're going. The best source for advice on this topic is the Centers for Disease Control and Prevention, which has a whole section on its Web site devoted to travel health (see cdc.gov/travel).

The CDC leaves no virus unexplained or question unanswered, so you can scare yourself silly reading about outbreaks of rare dis-

TRAVEL HEALTH INFORMATION ON LINE

Here are a few Web sites where you can find more information about health issues that affect travelers or a doctor who specializes in travel medicine. Most major cities have travel medical clinics, but if you don't find a clinic near you through one of the organizations listed here, try calling a clinic in the same state and ask for a recommendation for a doctor closer to your hometown.

- **Centers for Disease Control and Prevention** (cdc.gov/travel). The CDC's Web site is the mother lode of health information for travelers. You can find out which vaccinations are recommended for the region you're visiting, learn how to avoid — and treat — traveler's diarrhea, check out the latest inspection reports for various cruise ships, and read up on diseases ranging from African sleeping sickness to yellow fever.

- **World Health Organization** (who.int/ith). Think of the WHO more as a source for a second opinion. It's not as comprehensive or well organized as the CDC's Web site, but you can download the latest version of its publication about international travel and health, which includes a list of vaccination requirements for various countries, information about infectious diseases, and advice on treating more common ailments like motion sickness, dehydration, and jet lag.

- **International Society of Travel Medicine** (istm.org). ISTM offers a directory of more than five hundred travel medical clinics in about forty countries; you can search for a doctor who specializes in travel health in or near your city. Listings include contact information, languages spoken, services offered, and a link to the clinic's Web site, if it has one.

- **American Society of Tropical Medicine and Hygiene** (astmh.org). ASTMH also offers a directory of travel health clinics you can search — by country or state, not by city. You'll find at least a few clinics listed for most states in the United States, including contact information, hours, Web addresses, and services offered.

- **International Association for Medical Assistance to Travelers** (iamat.org). IAMAT is a membership organization that offers a pocket-sized directory of English-speaking doctors working abroad (listings are organized by country). IAMAT reviews the qualifications of physicians listed in its network, and doctors agree to a set payment schedule. You can join for free, but donations are encouraged.

eases around the world. If you're a hypochondriac, best to head directly to the "Destinations" section and choose the region you're planning to visit, which will take you to a page explaining which vaccinations you should consider, whether you need antimalarial drugs, and any other health issues you might encounter.

Because the CDC's summaries cover a whole region — for example, all of Southeast Asia or southern Africa — you probably won't need every immunization recommended, especially if you're not going to rural areas where these diseases tend to be passed around. A doctor can help you figure out which ones you really need, but certain immunizations aren't optional; for instance, some countries require proof of a yellow fever vaccination before they'll let you across the border.

Also, some vaccines require multiple doses or should be given a few weeks before you arrive in an infected area, so try to schedule that doctor's appointment at least a month before your trip. But if you procrastinate, don't assume that it's too late to bother — some vaccines can be given with less lead time, which is better than skipping a shot entirely.

Your own doctor can probably give you any shots you need, but if you don't have a regular doctor or you want to talk to someone with more expertise in infectious diseases, try to find a doctor who specializes in travel health (see the sidebar on page 220 for where to look).

Other pretrip health tips

Even if you aren't traveling anywhere particularly exotic, one quick chore can save you trouble if you ever need medical treatment on the road. Send yourself an e-mail you can access from a Web account that lists your doctor's phone number, the names of any prescriptions you're taking, your blood type, and your insurance info — helpful in case your wallet is stolen or you don't usually carry this information around.

If you're taking any medications, resist the temptation to transfer your pills out of the original bottle into a more handy container, especially if you're going to another country. If your luggage is

A TRAVELER'S FIRST AID KIT: SUPPLIES FOR THE ROAD

For most trips, you probably don't need to drag along the entire contents of your medicine cabinet, since you can find many of these products in drugstores around the world. But if you're traveling off the beaten path or don't want the hassle of tracking down a pharmacy that's open on Sunday, here are some items you might want to take along.

At the very least, I recommend slipping a few Band-Aids into your carryon: I once waited ten minutes for a flight attendant to fetch a Band-Aid when I cut my finger on an airplane; then the airborne equivalent of a hazmat team descended to isolate the bloody napkin I was using and ceremoniously bandage my index finger. So, bring Band-Aids. That's my only packing advice.

Antacid
Antibacterial ointment
Antibiotics
Antidiarrhea medication
Antihistamine
Band-Aids
Blister pads or ointment
Decongestant
Ear plugs
Hand sanitizer
Hydrocortisone cream (to relieve itching)
Insect repellant (with DEET)
Laxative/enema
Motion sickness medication
Pain reliever
Sleeping pills (for jet lag)
Sunscreen

searched, you don't want to have to persuade a customs officer that the drugs you're carrying are perfectly legal, especially while you're surrounded by military personnel.

As for the more common ailments that plague travelers, there are a few items you might want to pack in case you wake up scratching a bunch of mosquito bites or battling a restless stomach (see the sidebar above). But in this day and age, you can pick up most of these products in a foreign drugstore, so if you're trying to travel light, you probably won't regret leaving the full first aid kit at home.

Maps and Driving Directions: When Not to
Trust a Computer for Help

I'm not sure what the travel equivalent is to the deserted-island question — you know, if you were stuck on a deserted island, what are the five items you'd want to have along — but one of my top five items for any trip would definitely be a good map. No matter who I travel with, I tend to be the navigator, the person in the passenger seat who misses half the scenery, squinting at little squiggly lines, or the one insisting at a street corner — waving a map for emphasis — that we need to turn *left* to get back to the hotel. (This is a role, I might add, that accrues plenty of blame for bad guidance but hardly ever any credit for a job well done.)

So it should come as no surprise that I like to pick up a map for my destination before I leave home, and I'm also pretty particular about getting good directions — though sometimes, you don't find out that you've been given *bad* directions until you're hopelessly lost. If you're similarly inclined, here are some tips on what to gather before you go and why you should double-check any directions you download on line.

Maps

Of course, you can buy a map pretty much anywhere you travel, but if you're setting off on a road trip or landing at an airport and picking up a rental car, it helps to have a map with you so you don't have to stop and buy one. The maps car rental agencies give out work in a pinch, but they often aren't detailed enough to help you navigate around a city — and sometimes don't even give great directions to return the car.

Most major bookstores sell maps for destinations all over the world, and if you're a member of AAA, you can get dozens of city, state, regional, and even some country maps for free, either by stopping by an office or ordering them on line. (You can order up to twenty-five maps at a time — as far as I'm concerned, that's reason enough to join.)

There are also lots of Web sites where you can look up digital maps by entering an address, landmark, or even just a city name (see the sidebar on the facing page for examples). These sites are great if you want to pinpoint the location of your hotel or see how far it is from a restaurant you're thinking about. But if you need a map to navigate around a city, buy one. It's just not possible to fit a lot of information on a Web page, so anything you print from the Internet will be either a bird's-eye view that doesn't show much detail or a street-level snapshot of just a few city blocks.

Directions

Ever since my mom sent me off to the dentist on my bike with the wrong street name as my destination — for the record, Chestnut is not the same as Chester — I've been a stickler about directions. In the unjust world of family lore, this has been interpreted as "bad with directions," but in fact, I'm just literal: If you tell me that the turn-off for your road is five miles past the schoolhouse, I'll turn around if I've gone seven miles and haven't seen your street sign, thinking I must have missed it the first time around (then I'll call and ask whether you've ever actually clocked that distance on your odometer).

So it's not surprising that I'm skeptical about the directions you can get from various Web sites, which let you enter a starting point and the address of your destination and then display directions and usually a small map of your route. Although these sites have gotten better since they debuted on line, they are sometimes just plain wrong, other times choose a route that no reasonably well-informed person would ever advise, and often use cryptic abbreviations for the roads they describe. They also tend to leave out critical details, like mentioning that you'll be entering a tunnel or crossing a state line.

That said, they *are* helpful for getting a general sense of how far it is from point A to point B — most sites include a total distance for your route and an estimated travel time — and some sites are getting better about details like translating the highway numbers stored in a computer into the more common names people use to refer to freeways and roads. Some sites also include updates about construction, back-ups, and road conditions, details most print maps can't tell you.

ON-LINE SOURCES FOR MAPS AND DIRECTIONS

Here are some of your options if you're looking for on-line maps or driving directions. These tools are handy if you don't have an atlas at your fingertips or are not driving very far, but if you're wandering around an unfamiliar area or embarking on a serious road trip, get a second opinion from another source. Besides these sites, you can get maps and driving directions from Google (maps.google.com), Microsoft (maps.msn.com), or Yahoo! (maps.yahoo.com). Each site offers slightly different features, so you may find one more useful than the others.

- **Automobile Club of America** (AAA) (aaa.com). You don't have to be a member of one of AAA's clubs to access its maps and driving directions on line (go to aaamaps.com). But if you are a member, you can also use its Internet TripTik feature, an on-line version of the TripTik strip maps the automobile clubs have offered for decades — which some people still find preferable. Fees for AAA clubs vary by region but are about $45 annually with a $10 initiation fee.

- **Mappy** (mappy.com). Although not quite as detailed as ViaMichelin, Mappy.com is another source for maps and driving directions in Europe, covering about twenty countries. You don't need an exact address to get a map, which is helpful if you just want to find out where a town is located in a country.

- **MapQuest** (mapquest.com). MapQuest is probably the best-known on-line source for maps and driving directions, covering primarily the United States and Canada, though you can use its atlas to get maps of countries all over the world. Its "find it" feature is also helpful, letting you look up landmarks, airports, or businesses when you don't have an exact address.

- **Rand McNally** (randmcnally.com). Rand McNally mostly sells maps and atlases — which you can order from its Web site — including road atlases and the ultradetailed Thomas Guides. The site also offers on-line maps and driving directions for destinations in the United States, though these tools aren't as sophisticated as what you'll find at other sites.

- **ViaMichelin** (viamichelin.com). ViaMichelin is your best source for maps and driving directions for destinations in Europe, not to mention ratings for European hotels (see page 140). Michelin's maps are very detailed, and its directions include approximate driving times, notations about roadwork, and even how much you can expect to spend on tolls and gas along your route.

But unless you consider getting lost part of the adventure of travel or you're already somewhat familiar with the area, it's best to supplement on-line sources with old-fashioned methods of finding your way: Bring a good map, and confirm the directions you get with someone who knows the route. Most hotels, airports, and other places you're likely to visit offer text directions on their Web sites, but if not — or if they just send you to another Web site for directions — you can always call.

Checking gas prices

The price of gas is one of those things that some people really track — driving miles out of their way to save two cents a gallon — and others just complain about as they're filling up at the most convenient pump. But if you want to scout out gas prices before you leave home, point your browser to GasBuddy.com, which lets you look up prices at stations in various cities in the United States and Canada. The information is submitted by GasBuddy's loyal following and includes each station's name and address, the price for a gallon of regular unleaded fuel, and the time the entry was posted.

But if you just want to know how much you'll spend on gas on a road trip, check out AAA's fuel cost calculator (accessible to non-members, too, at fuelcostcalculator.com). If you enter your starting point, destination, and the year, make, and model of your car, the site will tell you about how much you can expect to spend on gas — which can also help you figure out whether it would be cheaper to fly.

Money Matters: Why Your Bank Should Know Your Itinerary

When Walter Brooke told Dustin Hoffman in *The Graduate* that the future was in plastics, he wasn't referring to travel, but plastic has certainly made it much easier to spend freely around the world. No need to bother with traveler's checks or even exchange money if you're traveling abroad; now, you can get cash from an ATM machine in the local currency throughout much of the globe, and credit cards make it all too easy to overspend on everything from pasta dinners to Turkish rugs.

But those plastic cards we rely on sometimes cause their own hiccups, so here are some tips to help you manage your cards — and your cash — on the road. (As for managing your spending, you're on your own.)

Tell your bank where you're going

It may sound crazy to suggest calling your bank to say, "Hey, I just wanted to let you know I'm going to Thailand," but that phone call may save you a lot of hassle while you're far from home. With increasingly sophisticated fraud-detection systems monitoring activity on credit and debit cards, your bank might put a hold on your card if it suddenly detects an unusual spending pattern — say, a string of purchases in Bangkok instead of your usual charges around Boston.

If this happened while you were traveling in the United States, chances are you'd pick up a message from your bank, notifying you about a suspicious spending pattern and asking you to call. But if you're in the middle of China and don't get that message, your bank might put a temporary hold on your account until you call back to say that all is well. So if you're headed down a road you don't usually travel, tell your bank where you're going.

Scout out the ATM situation

Within the United States, you'd be hard pressed to find a town without an ATM, and in most cities, there's a machine on practically every block. But in other countries, you may encounter the occasional challenge as you search for an ATM or try to use one. For one thing, these machines don't always have an English-language option, which can make it difficult to figure out which buttons you're supposed to press or how much money you're actually taking out. (In Mexico, I once thought that I withdrew the local equivalent of $100, only to discover in a restaurant that I'd taken out 100 *pesos* — about $10.) I've also been in small towns overseas where the only

ATM regularly ran out of cash on weekends and have heard tales from other travelers who put their card in a machine that never spit it back out.

To avoid getting stuck without cash, take out plenty of money in the city or at the airport before you head anywhere remote. Another way to give yourself some peace of mind is to scout out the ATM situation before you leave home. Guidebooks usually tell you where you can find a machine, and airport Web sites sometimes describe where ATMs are located in the terminal. There are also Web sites that offer "ATM locators," like mastercard.com/atmlocator or visa.com/atms; if you enter a city name or address, you'll get a list of ATMs in the area.

Travel with backup
It's always a good idea to travel with two different credit cards — one in your wallet and one tucked away somewhere else. If you and your traveling companion each have one credit card linked to the same account, that doesn't count as backup; if one of you loses your wallet or it's stolen, you'll both be without plastic until your bank can get you new cards.

Check the exchange rate
Before you head off to a foreign country, take a minute to look up the exchange rate — xe.com has a handy tool that can help you figure out how much a dollar is worth in pounds, euros, pesos, and many other currencies. That way, you can avoid exchanging money at a bad rate or withdrawing more (or less) cash from an ATM than you meant to carry around. (See the sidebar on the facing page for information on foreign ATM and credit card charges.)

Take small bills
Even when the dollar is down in the dumps, you can get away with paying for a cab ride, tips, or small purchases with U.S. currency in many places, but that's not necessarily an option if you have to ask for change for a twenty. Even stateside, traveling with plenty of $1

FEES ON FOREIGN CHARGES

Most people expect to pay a fee when they get cash from a foreign ATM — usually, about $3 per withdrawal — but until recently, many travelers had no idea that they also paid fees to use a credit card to make purchases abroad. Since the 1980s, Visa and MasterCard have charged a 1 percent currency conversion fee on purchases made overseas, and many banks that issue credit cards added their own 2 percent fee to that amount. But most banks didn't itemize these fees on customers' statements, which led to a couple of lawsuits about the lack of disclosure.

Now, you're more likely to see these fees listed as a separate charge on your bill, which for most Visa and MasterCard accounts ends up being 3 percent of your total purchase. You may be able to find a credit card company that charges less — most likely, a smaller bank or credit union — but that 3 percent has become fairly standard. The one exception is American Express, which levies only a 2 percent currency-conversion charge.

bills will help you avoid awkward tipping moments — but better to ask the bellhop for change than not tip at all.

Get some foreign currency before you go

It's almost always cheaper to get foreign currency from an ATM at your destination, but if you'd rather have some cash in your pocket when you land, you'll generally get a better rate from a bank than at a foreign-exchange kiosk at the airport. One option is to stop by an American Express office, but some larger banks, like Citibank, Chase, or Bank of America — also sell select foreign currencies (but not at all branches, and you may have to have an account with the bank to use these services).

Another option is to order foreign currency on line — further proof that there really isn't anything you can't order on the Web. American Express (americanexpress.com/travellerscheques), Bank of America (bankofamerica.com/foreigncurrency), Travelex (travelex.com), and Wells Fargo (foreignexchangeservices.com), all offer services that let travelers order foreign currencies on line, typically for overnight or two-day delivery. You won't get the most bang for your buck, since these companies all charge some kind of delivery or service fee, so compare rates before you order — and make sure that you're home to sign for the envelope.

American Express also sells a prepaid card you can load with dollars or foreign currency, which you can use at ATMs or wherever American Express cards are accepted (see americanexpress.com/travelfundscard for details). This card is meant to be a modern alternative to traveler's checks (which Am Ex still sells), but you have to pay various fees to buy and use one, which makes it a more expensive option than a credit or debit card.

Making Reservations: What to Book Before You Arrive

One of the things that can make a vacation less than perfect is all the other people who had the same idea about where to go. In some resort areas or when times are flush, these crowds can mean tee times that are already taken, restaurants that are fully booked, and massages you can't get because the slots are filled with people who thought to call ahead.

Some hotels might nudge you to think about making these other reservations when you book a room or may send you an e-mail with a reminder a few weeks before your trip. But in case you don't get that prompt — or you're not naturally an advance planner — here are some things you may want to book (or at least research) before you arrive.

Restaurants

Some travelers take an ad hoc approach to dining out on vacation, relying on a hotel concierge, guidebook, or serendipity to lead them to a hearty plate of pasta or steak frites and a bottle of wine. But if food is an important part of your travel experience, you probably don't want to leave your dining decisions to the moment your stomach starts to grumble. And if you're vacationing in a popular destination during high season, you may need to make reservations ahead of time in order to get a table at a restaurant everyone says you *must* try.

Besides guidebooks, there are lots of resources on line that can help you figure out where to eat while you're away. Many newspaper Web sites offer a database of restaurant reviews you can search by cuisine and by neighborhood, so if you're going to San Francisco, visit sfgate.com/food; for New York City, try nytimes.com/dining (see page 5 for other publications). Zagat, well known for its customer surveys of restaurants, offers a searchable database of these reviews at zagat.com, covering destinations in Asia, Europe, and the United States. You have to pay to access the site — $5 for a thirty-day subscription or $25 for a year — but its search tool is worth the price of admission, allowing you to find, say, a Vietnamese restaurant near your hotel in Paris, then view a map showing exactly where it's located.

There are also on-line message boards devoted to discussions of food where you can get restaurant recommendations for even the most remote parts of the world. On Chowhound.com, I stumbled across a detailed response to someone's question about where to eat in Lithuania and Estonia, as well as a long report about the food in Myanmar. For true cuisine connoisseurs, Egullet.com is another site worth checking; you can find tips about restaurants in various cities by browsing through its forums. You can also get restaurant recommendations at some of the on-line travel communities listed on page 16.

Ferries
If your family has vacationed on an island like Nantucket or Martha's Vineyard for years, you probably already know that you need to make ferry reservations well before the summer crowds show up. But if you're a first-time visitor, this detail can catch you by surprise. Some ferry companies that serve popular vacation destinations start taking reservations months in advance, so don't assume that you can just show up at the dock with your bags — especially if you want to take your car. Most ferry companies have Web sites that list schedules, prices, and policies, and some even take reservations on line. If it's not clear from the Web site whether you need to book in advance, call and ask.

Tickets

For many events, you don't *need* to buy tickets before you arrive, especially if you don't care where you sit or can afford to pay top dollar for a show that's supposedly sold out (your hotel concierge can help). But if you've got your heart set on seeing an opera at La Scala in Milan or hearing a performance at Carnegie Hall, most cultural and sports venues around the world have Web sites where you can look up schedules and usually buy tickets — more often than not, with English translations. To find these sites, your best bet is to search the Internet for a specific venue, but there are also lots of more general Web sites devoted to the arts.

If you're going to New York and plan to catch a show, you can find out what's playing and how to buy tickets at Playbill.com or Theatermania.com, and TKTS (tdf.org/tkts) will tell you how to get discounted last-minute tickets once you're in town. The London Theatre Guide (officiallondontheatre.co.uk) is the official site for London's West End theaters and includes info about its own last-minute ticketing service. Before you leave home, it's even worth looking up museum Web sites, which sometimes sell entrance tickets on line. For instance, if you buy tickets in advance for the Louvre museum in Paris (louvre.fr), you can avoid the long line once you get to the museum — and the tickets can be used anytime. As with most advance-ticketing options, there's a surcharge for the service and a fee if you have the tickets sent to you in the United States (instead of picking them up after you arrive).

Spa appointments

Hotels, resorts, and even cruise lines have been making a big deal about their spa services in recent years — you've probably seen ads showing a photo of a sleek woman lying face down on a massage table, with scented candles, fresh flowers, and hot oil nearby. But on more than one occasion, I've sidled up to the reception desk at a resort, visions of relaxed muscles dancing in my head, only to find that the spa schedule was completely booked or that the only available appointment was at an inconvenient time. (This can even happen during low season, since resorts cut back on their spa staff

when they have fewer guests.) You may be able to get an appointment on the spot, but if a predinner shiatsu massage is critical to
making your vacation a perfect 10, book it in advance.

Sports

Many sports that people tend to do on vacation don't involve much
advance planning: A run on the beach, a few laps in the pool, or a
hike in the woods are all activities you can do when the mood
strikes (or not). But if you're thinking about trying out a sport that
involves any elaborate equipment or scarce facilities, especially at a
crowded resort, find out whether you need to book anything before
you check in. Tee times, tennis courts, dive boats, and any lessons
you want to take are a few things you should probably reserve in advance.

Even if you don't need reservations for your favorite sport, a little
research before you leave home can help you find a place to keep up
with your workout. For instance, SwimmersGuide.com offers a
searchable directory of swimming pools all over the world, listing
drop-in policies, prices, and even comments about how crowded
you'll find the lap lanes. And *Yoga Journal*'s Web site (yogajournal
.com) has a travel section with a searchable directory of yoga teachers and studios, if you want to take a class away from home.

Campgrounds

Campsites are another thing you don't always have to book in advance, but if you want to toast your marshmallows near the Grand
Canyon on Labor Day weekend or sleep under the stars just about
anywhere on the Fourth of July, you'd better start thinking about
reservations while it's still snowing outside. Although many campgrounds set aside a few sites for campers who show up the day
they're planning to stake a tent — these sites are assigned on a first-
come, first-served basis — most of the good campsites are reserved
as early as six months in advance. The challenge is figuring out how
to make a reservation.

The U.S. government has been trying to centralize its reservation services at one Web site, Recreation.gov, which will ultimately

take reservations for campgrounds managed by various federal agencies, including the National Park Service, the Forest Service, the Bureau of Land Management, the Bureau of Reclamation, and the U.S. Army Corps of Engineers. But until that site is fully operational, the two main reservation services for federally managed campgrounds are the National Park Reservation Service (reservations.nps.gov) and the National Recreation Reservation Service (reserveusa.com). To further complicate matters, these sites don't cover state and local parks, so for those campgrounds, your best bet is to search the Internet for the name of the park you have in mind and see whether you can reserve a campsite on line. Woodalls.com also offers a campground directory, listing facilities for both tent and RV campers.

Technology and Travel: Getting Your Gadgets Ready to Go

Remember when the only thing you packed in your luggage that had a plug was a hair dryer? Neither do I. Now, it seems impossible to leave home without a pile of gadgets weighing down your carryon and all those cords that get entangled en route — as if they spent the whole flight *trying* to weave themselves together, your iPod headset desperate not to get separated from your phone charger.

Even when you manage to steal away without your laptop or travel somewhere your cell phone doesn't work, that raises other challenges, like how to check e-mail or make calls while you're gone. Here's how to stay connected when you leave your hardware at home and how to make sure that your gadgets will work if you have to take them along.

Plugs, chargers, and converters

If you typically travel with several chargers, not to mention various adapters to recharge your devices in the car or on the plane, there is a way to lighten your load. A few technology companies make universal adapters, which can be used with wall sockets, cigarette lighters, and the special power outlets installed on some aircraft — and some of these gizmos can charge more than one device at a time.

The iGo Juice is one option popular with road warriors, but APC, Kensington, and Targus are other companies that make universal adapters. And if you plan to use your laptop or charge your cell phone while flying, stop by SeatGuru.com, which can tell you which aircraft seats are near power outlets and what type of adapter (if any) you'll need to plug in.

Electrical standards abroad. If you're traveling overseas, the best place to find out what type of electrical system is used at your destination is Kropla.com, a Web site compiled by a guy named Steve Kropla. Steve explains how to tell whether your laptop, camcorder, or electric razor can run on both the 100-volt and 220-volt currents used around the world or whether you'll need to buy a converter in order to get a clean shave in Barcelona. He also offers an impressive overview of plugs used worldwide — complete with illustrations — so you can look up which one is used at your destination and find out whether you'll need any adapters to fit your plugs into strange holes.

Internet access on the road

If you're traveling with a computer, the best place to find out what type of Internet access your hotel offers is the hotel's Web site, which should explain whether rooms and public areas have cable or wireless high-speed Internet access and whether there's a charge to log on. Fees of about $10 a day are pretty common, though some hotels offer Internet access for free, so if you haven't booked yet, shop around.

Finding wireless networks. To find out where you can tap into a wireless network away from home, two Web sites that list wi-fi hotspots in the United States and abroad are JiWire (jiwire.com) and WiFinder (wifinder.com), both of which let you enter a location to find nearby places where you can get a wireless signal — mostly, cafes and bookstores — and whether you have to pay to log on. If you're looking for a free ride, Metrofreefi.com and Wififreespot .com list where you can find a wi-fi network that doesn't charge.

Wireless service providers like Boingo (boingo.com), iPass (ipass

.com), and T-Mobile (t-mobile.com) also list their own hotspots on their Web sites, and some airport Web sites mention whether there's a wireless network in any of their terminals. In a pinch, look for a Borders, Kinkos, McDonald's, or Starbucks — all chains that have embraced wi-fi — and if you see lots of customers hunched over their keyboards in a cafe, there's a good chance that there's a signal nearby.

Using public computers. If you aren't traveling with a laptop, it's usually not that difficult to find a place to check your e-mail, especially in countries where most people don't have a computer at home. But if you want to scout out some options before your trip, Cybercaptive.com and Cybercafes.com list cafes or businesses that offer Internet access at public terminals. These places usually cost less than what you'd pay at a hotel business center or on a cruise ship, but if you really want a bargain, find a local library — many have computers you can use for free.

No matter where you log on to a public terminal or network, try to avoid any transactions that involve entering sensitive information like your bank account details or a credit card number. Public computers and many wireless networks aren't very secure, though I wouldn't worry about using one to check e-mail.

Cell phones around the world

Traveling abroad with a cell phone is still a challenge for many Americans, primarily because the standards used by most wireless companies in the United States aren't compatible with the technology that dominates other parts of the world. So to stay in touch overseas, you have three choices: (1) join that subset of Americans who have phones that work in other countries, (2) buy a second cell phone that you use only when you're traveling, or (3) rent a cell phone for your trip, either before you leave home or once you land.

Using your own phone. If you have a cell phone that works overseas, sometimes called a world phone, you probably already know it; if not, check with your service provider to find out where else your phone works. In most countries, you need a phone that works on GSM networks, which is the standard used in Europe and many other parts of the world (see gsmworld.com for details). T-Mobile and Cingular are the two main providers that operate GSM networks in the United States, but just because you're one of their customers doesn't mean that you have a GSM phone.

Even if your phone does get a signal abroad, U.S. service providers usually charge more than $1 a minute when you're in another country, for both incoming and outgoing calls, so before you call all your friends from Rome, find out what you'll be paying to chat about the ruins and fountains.

Buying a world phone. If you don't have a GSM phone but don't want to change your U.S. plan, you can buy a second phone to use when you travel abroad. Be sure to get one that's "unlocked," which means that you can pop out the chip (called a SIM card) and insert one that works at your destination. The SIM card is essentially the brains of the phone, so you can buy a prepaid card that comes with a phone number and a certain number of minutes (which you can refill).

Telestial.com is one company that sells SIM cards on line, but you'll pay a bit more than waiting until you land. In most countries, it's not tough to find stores that sell SIM cards — at the airport, a train station, or wherever cell phones are sold.

Renting a phone. There are also companies that rent cell phones for trips overseas, which may be your best option if you rarely travel abroad. Cellhire (cellhire.com), InTouch Global (intouchglobal .com), Planetfone (planetfone.com), Roadpost (roadpost.com), and Worldcell (worldcell.com) are a few options; they all charge about $40 to $60 per week for the phone rental, plus fees for your calls and delivery and return of the phone.

Per minute rates with a rented cell phone tend to be expensive, though some companies don't charge for incoming calls, and one advantage of renting a phone is that you find out your number before you leave home. (If you buy a SIM card at your destination, you won't know your number until you install the card.)

Phone cards. If you'd rather not mess with a cell phone, just buy a phone card, either before your trip or once you land. Phone companies in the United States usually offer cards that work overseas, but you'll get cheaper rates if you buy one of the prepaid cards sold at Costco or Wal-Mart or in airports, stores, or newsstands abroad. Besides long-distance rates, pay attention to charges for things like local calls and connection fees, where you can use the card, and how soon it expires.

Getting to and from the Airport: Know Your Options, Avoid Being Overcharged

In an ideal world, we'd all get dropped off at the airport by a loved one who was happy to serve as a chauffeur and then picked up by someone offering an equally enthusiastic welcome. But in real life, getting to and from the airport is often a lot more stressful — involving a crowded bus ride, a car service that shows up late, or a race against the clock to park your car and make it to your gate on time.

It can also be expensive. In fact, with the deals you can get for some plane tickets, it's possible to spend almost as much money getting to and from the airport as you spend on your flight. (I once scored a $200 fare to fly from New York to San Francisco, only to blow about $150 on three taxis and one airport shuttle.)

If you're looking for ways to economize, more airports now have decent train connections to city centers (see the sidebar on the facing page for examples), and these trains are sometimes faster than traveling by road. But even if a train isn't an option, you can save yourself money — and anxiety — by investigating the transportation situation at your destination before you leave home. Here's where to get those details, along with advice on finding the cheapest lot if you have to park your car.

Airport Web sites: Why you should bother

Airport Web sites are sort of the supporting actors of the on-line travel landscape — overshadowed and sometimes overlooked — but they're worth a visit if you want to avoid a stressful experience after your plane touches down.

At most airports, the signs describing ground transportation never seem to give quite enough information about all the buses,

FROM THE PLANE TO THE TRAIN:
AIRPORTS WITH TRAIN SERVICE

Here are some airports that have pretty good train service to the cities they serve. Some offer more direct or faster connections than others, so check their Web sites for details about routes and prices. During rush hour, you'll be sharing the train with commuters — and some of these connections involve negotiating stairs, escalators, and long walkways — so if you're traveling with a lot of luggage, a train may not be the best choice.

Besides these domestic airports, international gateways with good train connections to the cities they serve include Amsterdam Schiphol (AMS), London Heathrow (LHR) or Gatwick (LGW), Paris Charles De Gaulle (CDG), Rome Fiumicino (FCO), and Tokyo Narita (NRT). Check their Web sites for details.

- **Chicago Midway** (MDW) or **O'Hare** (ORD). Both airports (flychicago .com) connect to downtown and regional subway lines; it's not necessarily the fastest way to get to O'Hare, but for less than the cost of a newspaper and a coffee, you can't beat the price.

- **Minneapolis/St. Paul** (MSP). A relatively new light rail system links the airport (mspairport.com) to downtown Minneapolis — and also the Mall of America, if you've got a long layover and the energy to shop.

- **Newark Liberty** (EWR). The AirTrain (airtrainnewark.com) that runs between Newark's airport terminals and parking lots also connects to the New Jersey Transit railroad, with service to various points in New Jersey and Manhattan's Penn Station.

- **New York John F. Kennedy** (JFK). The long-awaited AirTrain (jfkairtrain .com) at JFK connects to the Long Island Railroad and various subway lines to Brooklyn, Manhattan, and Queens; if you're going to midtown, the LIRR is generally faster than the subway.

- **Oakland** (OAK). You have to take a shuttle bus from the airport to the closest BART station (bart.gov), but from there you can catch a train to various points in Berkeley, Oakland, or San Francisco.

- **San Francisco** (SFO). The Bay Area's BART train (bart.gov) connects Berkeley, Oakland, and San Francisco to the international terminal at SFO; from there, you can walk or take the AirTrain shuttle to domestic terminals.

- **Washington, D.C.** (DCA). Washington National airport links to downtown and surrounding areas via the local metro system (wmata.com).

trains, limo services, taxis, and shuttles you could take. But airport Web sites are usually pretty clear about these details, including schedules and prices. Armed with this information, you're less likely to overpay for a ride into town — or at least you won't be shocked when you're quoted a fare.

Many airport sites also post updates about flight arrival and departure times — useful if you know that your friend is coming in on a flight from Chicago but you can't remember the airline or the flight number — as well as terminal maps and information about hotels and other airport services. So if you know you're going to have a long layover, you can find out where you can grab a Cinnabon (my favorite airport indulgence) or do more practical errands like check your e-mail or get your shoes shined.

You can find airport Web sites pretty easily by searching the Internet for the name of your destination and "airport" or the full name of the airport, if you happen to know it. Worldairportguides .com and Ifly.com also have information about airports around the world — though you'll get more details at the airports' own Web sites.

On that note, many foreign airports have Web sites with English translations, though for some destinations, you may find that you get better transportation advice from a guidebook. Airport sites list all the facts about various options but don't generally tell you that a certain bus stops every four blocks once it reaches the city or that a rush-hour train is impossibly crowded — things a guidebook will usually point out.

Airport parking: Finding a space — and maybe a discount

Another reason to look up an airport Web site is to find out about parking options. Although you probably already know which lots are close to your home airport, it's worth logging on to find out which lots are full or closed (most sites at least give you a phone number to call for an update), not to mention prices for various lots.

A few other sites that take reservations or offer coupons for parking (usually, off-airport) are AirportDiscountParking.com, Long TermParking.com, and ParkingAccess.com. If you usually park at the same lot, you can save money by joining a "frequent parker" program. National chains like Avistar (avistarparking.com), The Parking Spot (theparkingspot.com), and Parking Company of America (parkingcompany.com) give details about these programs on their Web sites — and sometimes, their own coupons.

And if you need to stay near the airport before or after your trip — say, to catch an early-morning flight — some airport hotels offer parking packages that allow you to leave your car at the hotel lot while you're gone. One Web site that lists these specials is Park SleepFly.com, which posts offers at hotels near more than sixty airports.

Preflight Checklist: Checking In, Flight-Status Alerts, Security Lines

Before the Internet turned customer service into self-service, the main thing you had to think about before dashing out the door was making sure that you had your ticket and your wallet. But now that we're all doing the work of laid-off travel agents and airline employees, there's a whole checklist of tasks you should put on your preflight to-do list, at least if you want to avoid stress at the airport.

Checking in

Printing a boarding pass from your home computer used to be a novelty, but these days, that's how lots of passengers routinely check in. Most U.S. airlines now offer Web check-in, at least for domestic flights, and some allow it for international flights, too. The only reason I can think of not to use Web check-in is if you don't have access to a computer and a printer the day before your flight. But there are many reasons you *should* check in on line — number one being that it can save you a lot of time and hassle at the airport.

With airlines pushing passengers to use self-service technology, you often have to wait in line to use a check-in kiosk at the airport (my record: forty minutes), so checking in *on line* is the only way to avoid waiting *in line*. Also, if you use Web check-in, you can change your seat assignment to a better spot before passengers who get their boarding pass at the airport — at which point, all the good seats are usually taken.

You may also get earlier notice about flight cancellations or delays. On several occasions, I've started the Web check-in process only to get a message saying that my flight was delayed or canceled; with that early warning, I called and switched to a different flight hours ahead of time, thereby avoiding the chaos at the airport when everyone else was scrambling to get rebooked.

Web check-in options are difficult to miss on an airline's home page — if it's offered, you'll see it. For most carriers, you can check in between twenty-four hours and one hour before your flight, and you can use Web check-in even if you have to check bags (you can check your luggage at the airport with a curbside agent or use one of the self-service kiosks). And if you happen to lose your boarding pass somewhere between your printer and the airport, you can print another one, using a kiosk, or ask an agent for help.

Flight-status alerts

You can't count on an airline to call and let you know that your flight has been canceled or delayed, but most carriers will send a text message to your cell phone — that is, if you've signed up to receive flight status updates. These messages, which can be sent to a cell phone or other mobile device, typically list the flight's gate number, whether it's on time, and sometimes new departure information if the flight has been delayed. They usually arrive an hour or two before your flight, so you may already be on your way to the airport, but these alerts are especially helpful if you have to change planes. Ideally, once you land and turn on your phone, you'll have a message with details about your connecting flight — including the gate number — so you don't have to wait for an agent to give you this information (though you should double-check the first electronic display you pass by, since gates sometimes change).

Carriers such as American, Continental, Delta, Northwest, Southwest, and United are some of the airlines that offer these services; to sign up, look for a link on the carrier's home page that says "flight messaging," "flight paging," or "flight updates." With some airlines, you have to sign up for these alerts every time you book a flight, but a few carriers let you register once to get updates anytime you fly that airline. You can also use these services to get flight-arrival information — say, if you have to pick up someone at the airport and want to find out if the flight is on time.

Airport security wait times

If you're worried about long security lines at the airport, there's a way to find out whether you have any reason to be concerned: The Transportation Security Administration's Web site has a feature that lets you look up security checkpoint wait times at various airports in the United States. Just stop by waittime.tsa.dhs.gov, choose your departure airport, the day of the week you're traveling, and the time your flight departs. The site displays average and maximum wait times at that airport for the day and time you select, based on data collected during previous weeks (so it's not real-time information).

You can also check the airport's Web site, which may suggest how early you should arrive for your flight. Some airports have more sluggish security checkpoints than others — Las Vegas is notorious for long waits — but you may find backups at other airports when a lot of flights are departing at the same time. So don't assume that arriving an hour early is always enough; if you have to check in, check luggage, *and* know that the security lines are slow, ninety minutes is a safer bet.

Reconfirming your flight

Now, there are two ways to check whether your flight is on time: the Web or the phone. Either way, you *should* get the same information, though sometimes I've found that it's quicker to use my computer, if it's still turned on. Another reason to opt for the Web is that many airlines have adopted voice-response systems that don't work well if you're calling from a noisy area — a detail the designers may have overlooked when they got rid of the option of pressing buttons, forcing us all to shout our flight numbers into the phone.

While you're on line, you can also visit www.fly.faa.gov, the Web site of the FAA's Air Traffic Control System Command Center, which shows a map of the United States with real-time information about any air traffic delays at major airports. That's certainly not something most people would take the time to check before every flight, but if you're an airline buff, it's kind of fun.

Having backup connection plans

This may sound overly pessimistic — and I freely admit that it is — but if your itinerary involves a change of planes, prepare for the worst and look up later flights to your destination just in case you miss your connection. That way, you can go straight to the gate for the next flight once you finally land or at least know what your options are when you talk to an agent to rebook. (I've found that it helps to be able to say to an agent, "Well, instead of waiting three hours for the next flight to LaGuardia, how about if you put me on the flight to Newark that leaves in forty-five minutes?")

Sure, you can look up other flights on the electronic display once you finally land, but if you're trying to get on a standby list for a later connecting flight while you're still waiting for your first flight to take off or you're dealing with an agent who isn't very helpful, you'll have an edge if you know your options.

9 At the Airport

DESPITE ALL THE COMPLAINTS about long lines, bad food, invasive security procedures, and surly employees, I have to admit — I still like airports. I like the hustle and bustle, all the activity on the tarmac, watching the planes take off and land, and the feeling of possibility when you're in transit.

Of course, that romance can fade quickly, usually in about the time it takes for a gate agent to announce, "If you're waiting for flight #487, that plane has not left Denver yet, so at this point, we're anticipating a ninety-minute delay . . ." And unfortunately, those types of frustrations have become more common in recent years, as airlines have cut corners on service and more people are traveling again.

Although there's no way to avoid some of the hassles of air travel (other than not ever getting on a plane), you can at least minimize some inconveniences by knowing the rules of the game. Because when a flight gets canceled or delayed, it's the savvy travelers who get rebooked first or know when the airline has to put them on another carrier — topics this chapter explains.

It also covers how to avoid excess-baggage charges — or theft from your luggage — what it takes to upgrade your ticket, when you can fly standby, and what you should ask before agreeing to be bumped, as well as tips on negotiating the sometimes capricious security procedures we live with these days. As for bad weather, that often comes down to bad luck, so get out your rabbit's foot if the forecast isn't in your favor.

Checking Bags: Avoiding Extra Fees — and Theft from Your Luggage

Seasoned travelers know that the first rule about checking bags is that you should try *not* to check any bags, but of course there

are times when that advice is impossible to follow. If you're traveling with an infant, a toddler, a stroller, a car seat, and clothes for
everybody for a week, it's tough enough to get through the airport
and onto the plane, let alone carry all your luggage the whole way.
And even when you *want* to hang onto your bag, you can't always fit
it in an overhead compartment, no matter how much you push,
prod, or plead with the flight attendant to find some extra space.

But before you let your luggage out of your sight, there are a few
things you should know about the airlines' liability for checked bags
— which may discourage you from packing all your favorite clothes
in one suitcase. And if you aren't traveling light, higher fees for extra, oversize, or overweight luggage may prompt you to put that duffel bag on a diet before it gets on the scale. (For advice on flying with
a pet or checking one as cargo, see the sidebar on page 250.)

Liability limits

Many travelers are surprised to find out that the airlines' liability for
checked luggage is limited to an amount that may not cover all the
shoes, sweaters, and suits most people manage to stuff into one
suitcase, let alone several bags. For domestic flights, that limit is
$3,000 per passenger, an amount determined by the Department
of Transportation. For international travel, the Warsaw Treaty limits
the airlines' liability to $9.07 per pound for checked luggage, which
is at most about $640 per suitcase, given the weight limit for
checked bags on international flights.

But these amounts refer only to the *maximum* you'd be reimbursed: you have to show proof of your loss when you submit a
claim (see page 272 for details). Also, most airlines don't accept
liability for valuables like antiques, cameras, computers, electronic
equipment, fragile items, jewelry, or watches — all things you
shouldn't pack in checked luggage anyway. But if you do and your
bag disappears, you can't include these items in any claim.

Baggage insurance

If these numbers make you nervous about checking your best suit
and a pair of shoes that cost half a paycheck, one option is to buy
excess-valuation insurance when you check in. This extra insurance

costs $1 to $2 per $100 of declared value beyond $3,000, with a maximum value of $5,000 per passenger. You have to pay this fee at the ticket counter each time you check in — in other words, twice for a round-trip ticket — and you can't buy insurance for any of the valuables mentioned earlier, or certain sports equipment.

But before you spring for extra insurance for your luggage, check your homeowner's or renter's policy. It may cover you beyond what the airline will pay if your bag or any of its contents disappear.

To lock or not to lock

Although the chances are pretty slim that an airline will lose your luggage, theft from checked bags has become more of a problem since the Transportation Security Administration started advising passengers to leave their bags unlocked to make luggage searches easier. You can buy special TSA-approved locks that federal screeners are *supposed* to be able to open (see travelsentry.org for details), but these locks sometimes get cut off anyway, and I've had to snip two locks myself because the combination somehow got reset after my bag was searched.

If you return a TSA-approved lock that's been cut, you can get a free replacement, but these days, I mostly use an old luggage lock and figure that if screeners have to remove it, it's cheaper to replace a lock than anything missing from my bag. Another option is to cinch together your bag's zippers with a plastic cable tie, which deters sticky fingers but is easy for screeners to cut if they have to look inside. (Just make sure that you have nail clippers in your carryon so *you* can remove the plastic tie when you land.) You can buy these ties at a hardware store, and baggage handlers sometimes will give them to you at the airport.

But I would never check a bag that someone could get into simply by giving the zipper a tug. Passengers have filed tens of thousands of claims about theft from checked bags since the government started telling travelers to leave their luggage unlocked, and lots of those claims are in limbo because the TSA and the airlines are still arguing about who should pay them (since it's often impossible to determine whether government screeners or baggage handlers are responsible for whatever is missing).

Although theft from checked luggage is not a common occurrence, it happens more than it should. So secure your bag somehow if you're going to send it through the system.

Weight and size restrictions

Another issue that may catch you by surprise is lower size and weight allowances for checked bags. A few years ago, most airlines began limiting passengers to two checked bags on domestic flights (except Southwest, which still allows its customers to check three pieces of luggage without charge). And those bags have to be lighter and slimmer than the airlines used to accept, partly to account for the fact that passengers have generally moved in the *opposite* direction.

Policies vary, depending on the airline, but for most flights, each bag you check can't weigh more than fifty pounds, and the length, width, and height of the bag added together can't be more than sixty-two inches. If your bag is heavier or bigger, you'll have to pay a fee ranging from $25 to $80 each way (see the sidebar on the facing page for details), and most carriers charge at least $80 for any extra bag you check.

There are often more generous allowances for elite frequent fliers and business- or first-class passengers, as well as for some international flights. But around the holidays, some airlines adopt stricter luggage limits to certain foreign destinations, and international carriers may have more restrictive policies, especially low-fare carriers in Europe.

Checked baggage deadlines

If you can't avoid checking a bag, make sure that you hand it over before your airline's stated cut-off time: typically, at least thirty minutes before departure for domestic flights and sixty minutes for international travel, though some airlines specify even earlier time limits for certain airports, like Las Vegas or Denver, or during the holidays.

If you miss the cut-off time and your bag ends up on a later flight, you may have to wait around for it or pay to have it delivered,

CHECKED BAGGAGE: RULES AND FEES

Here are some general guidelines about how many bags you're allowed to check on most U.S. airlines, as well as typical size and weight limits for each bag. If you're not traveling light — or you're planning to check any unusual items, like scuba equipment or a bike — double-check the rules at your airline's Web site, then get out a tape measure and a bathroom scale before you show up for your flight. That way, you can do any necessary repacking while it's still possible to leave a few things behind.

- *Number of checked bags allowed free:* Two on most airlines (Southwest allows three).

- *Charge for additional bags:* $80 for the first extra bag; fee may be higher for additional bags.

- *Weight limit for checked bags:* Fifty pounds per bag on domestic flights; fifty to seventy pounds per bag on international flights (varies by airline).

- *Charge for overweight bags (fifty-one to one hundred pounds):*$25 to $50, depending on the airline and the bag's weight. Most airlines don't accept bags that weigh more than one hundred pounds.

- *Size limit for checked bags:* Sixty-two inches total allowed for free (length plus width plus height).

- *Charge for oversize bags:* $80 per bag. Some airlines limit the size of bags they'll accept; maximums range from 80 inches to 160 inches (length plus width plus height).

since most airlines don't accept responsibility for items checked after the deadline.

Carryon baggage

As for what's allowed inside the cabin, officially you're limited to one "personal item" and one carryon bag. What's considered a personal item is somewhat open to interpretation, but it basically refers to a purse, briefcase, small backpack, or computer bag. This quota isn't supposed to include your coat, any food you're taking to eat on the flight, or newspapers and magazines you picked up at the

FLYING WITH A PET: BEWARE THE CARGO HOLD

If you're thinking about taking your pet with you on a flight, you may want to reconsider that decision — unless Buffy or Bitsy is allowed in the cabin and is small enough to fit in a crate under a seat. Both the Humane Society and the American Society for the Prevention of Cruelty to Animals recommend against transporting a pet in an airline's cargo hold unless absolutely necessary, based on a lack of regulations about how animals are handled. According to some reports, as many as several hundred pets are injured, lost, or killed annually after being checked as cargo, though some airlines dispute those statistics.

To help clarify things, Congress passed the Safe Air Travel for Animals Act in 2000, requiring the airlines to report any loss, injury, or death of an animal to the Department of Transportation, which now publishes that data in the monthly report it compiles about lost luggage and flight delays (look for the "Air Travel Consumer Report" at airconsumer.ost.dot.gov). That data has been made public only since mid-2005, but over time, pet owners will have better information about which airlines have the best track record transporting animals. (Reports about each incident are published along with overall statistics.)

If you can't avoid the cargo hold, try to find out from the airline how your pet will be handled. You have to pay an extra fee to fly with an animal, even if it travels with you in the cabin (it's about $50 to $80 each way), and there are times when airlines won't accept pets in the cargo hold, like during the summer, when temperatures peak. There are also limits on how many animals can travel as cargo or be brought on the plane.

Most airlines post their pet policies on line, but call to get specific information about your flight and to make a reservation. If you're traveling abroad, you should also check what documents or health certificates you might need for your pet and whether the country you're visiting imposes any quarantines — which may be another reason to find a pet sitter instead.

newsstand, but if the gate agent seems to be cracking down, best to consolidate everything before you get in line.

Technically, the size limit for carryons is forty-five inches (length plus width plus height), and the weight limit is forty pounds, but whether these rules are enforced depends more on how full the flight is and the gate agent's mood than any written rules. If your flight is oversold and everyone waiting to board is laden down with bags competing for overhead space, you can expect stricter enforcement of carryon limits. The same goes for flights on smaller planes with limited overhead space.

But if you have to give up a bag before boarding, ask to have it "gate checked," which means that you can pick it up at your arrival gate when you disembark rather than waiting at the baggage carousel. This isn't always possible, but it's worth asking.

Navigating Airport Security: Keeping Up with the Rules

By now, most people who travel frequently have gotten used to stricter security at the airport, automatically removing their shoes and jackets before passing through the metal detector and taking their laptops out of their carryons to send them through the x-ray machine. But if you don't fly that often, some of the routines that road warriors take for granted at the airport can take you by surprise — and judging from the confusion at security checkpoints, plenty of people are still adjusting to the rules.

Security procedures are a moving target, so even frequent fliers can get tripped up by policy changes, like the decision to ban liquids and gels from carryon bags (except in containers that are three ounces or less). And despite the agency's commitment to improving customer service, some screeners are still a bit overbearing at times.

There's not much you can do about an unpleasant situation at the airport, since anything you say pretty much guarantees that you'll be subject to an invasive secondary search, if not detained. But if you feel that you've been mistreated, you can file a complaint later; instructions are posted on the Transportation Security Administration's Web site (tsa.gov).

That's also where you'll find the agency's list of "permitted and prohibited items," if you have any questions about what you can take on the plane. That list is the authority on which items are allowed in carryon luggage or in checked bags, so you can look up things like knitting needles, tweezers, or nail clippers and find out that all three are allowed either on board or under the belly of the plane. (But having sat beside a passenger who clipped and filed her nails during the flight, I would suggest leaving that activity to an area with more space.)

The TSA's Web site also lists general information about security procedures, where to file a complaint if anything is missing from your checked luggage, and average wait times in security lines at major airports (see waittime.tsa.dhs.gov). But if you just want the highlights of the agency's advice, here's a cheat sheet of tips. (For advice on accompanying another passenger through security — even if you don't have a boarding pass — see the sidebar on the facing page.)

Don't put film in checked bags

The machines used to screen checked luggage can damage film, so if you haven't gone digital yet, pack your camera and all your rolls of film in your carryon. Sending film through the x-ray machine at passenger checkpoints shouldn't cause any problems if it happens only a few times, but if you've taken the same film on several trips, you can ask to have your film or camera hand searched instead. (Too many trips through the x-ray can degrade the quality of your pictures.)

Leave presents unwrapped

If you wrap any presents you're taking before your trip, it may be a TSA employee who gets to rip all the paper away to see what's inside. Screeners don't examine every wrapped package, so you can take your chances if you're determined to do your decorating at home, but the agency asks travelers to leave presents unwrapped.

Don't overstuff your bags

One good reason not to fill every nook and cranny of your suitcase is that someone else may have to unpack and repack your bag. If your carryon is searched in your presence, some screeners will let you help rearrange the contents after everything has been pulled out and examined. But if your checked luggage has to be hand searched in the bowels of the airport, it probably won't be repacked

ACCOMPANYING A PASSENGER TO THE GATE

Although you generally need a boarding pass to go beyond the security checkpoint at U.S. airports, it's possible to get permission to accompany a passenger to the gate. If you're dropping off a child, a spouse who's flying alone with the kids, or a parent who needs help getting around, call the airline and ask what you need to do to get permission to accompany another passenger through security. Saying that you want a little more time to say goodbye to your girlfriend probably won't cut it, but if you're dropping off a passenger who legitimately needs help, you should be able to get a pass to go to the gate.

with the care you'd take; also, an overstuffed bag increases the chances that something might get left behind — or taken.

Beware "dense" items

The machines used to screen checked bags for explosives have a high false positive rate, which means that they set off an alarm about 25 percent of the time, though obviously there aren't explosives in all those bags. Some of the items that tend to set off alarms are dense objects like shoes or sneakers with thick rubber soles, books, stacks of paper, and certain foods like chocolate or cheese. You can't always avoid packing these things in your luggage, but the TSA recommends spreading out books or shoes in your bag rather than stacking them together and packing food in your carryon instead.

Prepare to disrobe

One of the more controversial aspects of passenger screening is the arbitrary way rules are enforced about removing your shoes, jacket, belt, and other items of clothing before passing through the metal detector. According to the TSA, you don't *have* to take off your shoes before walking through the metal detector, but if you don't, screeners can subject you to a secondary search, even if you don't set off the alarm. This additional screening can involve a full hand search of your carryon and potentially a more personal pat-down, so it's often easier to just remove your shoes and not risk a delay. (Wear socks if you don't want to walk barefoot where thousands of other feet have passed.) Screeners may also ask you to take off a blazer or suit jacket and send it through the x-ray machine, so if the only thing you're wearing underneath is a skimpy camisole, explain your dilemma and hope for an understanding employee.

Assume that what's personal may become public

Your dirty socks and belly button piercing aren't the only things that may be exposed to a group of strangers at the airport; if screeners have to hand search your luggage, anything you've packed may be pulled out, handled, and repacked. The TSA's tip sheet delicately recommends that you "think carefully about the personal items you place in your carryon baggage," which suggests that screeners have seen a few other things besides boxers, bikinis, and briefs. If there's anything you'd rather screeners be able to see but not touch, the agency recommends packing the item in a clear plastic bag.

Leave the heavy metal at home

Remember, you're going to be passing through a *metal* detector, so this is not the day to pull out all your bangle bracelets or wear an outfit with lots of buckles, zippers, or metal studs. (It seems there's always someone in line who dressed almost to challenge the machine.) And if you typically travel with full pockets, everyone else in line will appreciate it if you empty out all those dimes and nickels before you walk through the metal detector *the first time*.

Put your name on your laptop — and inside your bags

I'm more protective of my laptop than just about any other item I own, so the thought of leaving it behind at a checkpoint or grabbing the wrong computer from the conveyor belt sends chills down my spine. But it happens more often than you'd expect, so if it ever happens to you, you'll have a better chance of getting your computer back if your name is somewhere on the machine. The same goes for your coat and your carryon bags, which people don't usually label. A quick fix: Stick some business cards in the pocket of any items you typically travel with — handy not only if you leave a bag behind but also if you meet a potential client during all that time in line.

Upgrading Your Ticket: What It Takes
to Move Up Front

Travelers accustomed to flying in the back of the plane often wonder how to make the leap from the cramped claustrophobia of
coach to one of those wide, comfortable seats up front. The short
answer: You need status.

By *status,* I mean become one of those travelers who log at least
25,000 miles a year with the same airline, thereby qualifying for
gold, silver, or *platinum* status in an airline's frequent flier program
(each tier is based on how many miles you've flown). These elite
passengers earn various benefits, including complimentary upgrades, but lately, even they have had to compete with one another
for scarce seats in the front cabin.

Besides getting a free upgrade, you can use frequent flier miles
to upgrade a ticket you've purchased or use upgrade coupons that
some airlines sell. But even then, an airline's elite customers are
usually given the chance to upgrade before everyone else.

Following are some general guidelines about all these options,
but keep in mind that the rules vary, depending on which airline
you're flying, how much you paid for your ticket, where you're going, and, of course, your status. These policies change frequently,
so check with your airline for specifics. (For more advice about flying first or business class, see the sidebar on page 257.)

Qualifying for a complimentary upgrade
Most of the major U.S. airlines still offer free upgrades to elite-level
frequent fliers and sometimes passengers traveling on full-fare
economy tickets — but these days, even if you have elite status, you
may not qualify for an upgrade unless you've purchased one of the
more expensive coach-class fares.

So how do you get elite status? Each airline has different rules,
but you generally have to fly at least 25,000 miles in a calendar year.
All those miles you earn by using your credit card don't count as
EQMs (elite qualifying miles), but airlines occasionally have promotions that can fast-track the process. It's not a lifetime appoint-

ment — you have to earn your elite status every year — and many frequent fliers have been grumbling that the airlines have made it more difficult to qualify. And of course, it's not enough simply to cross the threshold into the elite circle: You want to be in the top level of elites, usually platinum, though some airlines also have secret levels you have to be asked to join.

Complimentary upgrades are based on availability and are usually confirmed shortly before travel according to a complex formula that boils down to this principle: People who fly more and spend more will be given first dibs, though when you purchase your ticket also factors into the equation.

Using frequent flier miles to upgrade

If you don't have elite status, using frequent flier miles to upgrade is another option. But here's the catch: Even if you're using miles to upgrade, some carriers will let you do so only if the paid ticket you're trying to upgrade is one of the more expensive coach fares. Other airlines let passengers upgrade some discount fares but charge an extra fee on top of the miles you need (about $250 to $450 each way).

For instance, if you buy a full-fare economy ticket on American to go to Europe, you can *try* to upgrade that ticket for just 20,000 miles round trip (remember, upgrades are based on availability, so there are no guarantees). But if you want to upgrade a discounted economy-class ticket, you'll need to give up 50,000 miles *and* pay a $500 fee.

Continental is another airline that allows passengers to use miles to upgrade some discounted fares but charges a fee plus the miles you need for the upgrade. On Delta, Northwest, and United, you have to buy a more expensive coach-class fare to use miles to upgrade your ticket, though on most carriers, having elite status sometimes lets you bypass these rules.

In any case, if you plan to use miles to upgrade, ask before you buy your ticket whether the fare qualifies for that option — especially if you're flying on a partner airline — and whether the carrier will confirm your upgrade at the time of purchase. Some airlines will do this, but others don't let you know whether you got an up-

MORE ADVICE ABOUT FLYING UP FRONT

If you really want the inside track on getting upgrades or earning the elite status that's key to flying in the front of the plane, one of the best sources for advice is Flyertalk.com, an on-line community dedicated to discussions about miles, points, and perks. The travelers who hang out on Flyertalk's message boards know the secrets to getting upgraded — often people who fly a lot for work but whose companies don't spring for business-class fares.

Also worth looking into is FirstClassFlyer.com, a subscription newsletter that covers tips and strategies on upgrading or finding more affordable business and first-class fares. A one-year subscription is about $100, but there's also a monthly plan.

But before you get too mired in the minutiae of upgrading a coach ticket, it's worth checking what it would cost to simply buy a business-class seat. Business-class fares have come down to earth in recent years, so that may be a cheaper option than buying a full-fare coach ticket — often, the only type of ticket you can upgrade — and that way, you're guaranteed a seat up front.

grade until shortly before your flight, meaning that it's a real gamble to buy a more expensive ticket and hope that you can use miles to move up front. If your upgrade request is denied, flying economy is going to be even more miserable.

Purchasing an upgrade

At least four airlines — American, Delta, United, and US Airways — also sell electronic upgrade coupons, which you can use to upgrade some of the more expensive coach-class fares. (If you have elite status, some carriers will let you use paid upgrades with a wider range of fares.)

Upgrade coupons are sold in five-hundred-mile increments, so you'd need ten of them to upgrade a round-trip ticket from New York to San Francisco. American charges $25 for each five-hundred-mile upgrade, United charges $81, and US Airways charges $50, which works out to between $250 and $810 to upgrade a cross-country flight. Delta uses a different system, charging between $50 and $150, depending on the length of the flight.

Paid upgrades are generally managed electronically, so an airline's computer system awards passengers an upgrade depending on space availability, how much each customer paid for a ticket, and the customer's frequent flier status — giving priority to elite fliers and travelers on expensive tickets. (Once the upgrade is approved, the credits are deducted from your electronic account.)

But before you buy into these e-upgrade programs, read the fine print. Paid upgrades can't be used on some international routes or with all fares and in some cases expire if you don't use them within a year.

Flying Standby: When It's Free, When It's Not, and When It's Worth a Try

Most airlines charge a hefty fee if you have to make any changes to your ticket, but one time a change in plans usually won't cost you is if you fly standby on a different flight the same day as your original reservation. So if you're scheduled to take a 6:00 P.M. flight but your meeting ends early or if you find out that a snowstorm is expected later in the day, you can head to the airport early and try to get on a flight leaving sooner — if seats are available.

If I have a tight connection, I often fly standby so I can get to the connecting airport sooner and not risk missing my other flight or if the only cheap ticket I could buy was the redeye but I really wanted to fly earlier in the day. And sometimes, flying standby isn't a choice: If you miss a connection and your airline can give you a confirmed seat only on a plane leaving five hours later, you can try to go standby on an earlier flight.

How standby travel works
If you're hoping to fly standby, call your airline before you leave for the airport to find out whether your ticket allows standby travel and whether there's space on the flight you want to take. Most agents will help you gauge your chances of getting a standby assignment: If the flight is overbooked by ten people, it's probably not worth going to the airport early, but if the plane is only half full, you can pretty much count on getting a seat.

Once you get to the airport, ask an agent to put you on the standby list for the flight you want *as* you're checking in. (Some airlines let passengers request a standby flight when checking in on line or at a kiosk, but this is one time I prefer to deal with an agent, since computers don't answer questions very well — or bend the rules.) If the flight you want has plenty of space, the agent may issue you a new boarding pass on the spot, but you'll probably have to check in for your original flight, then go to the gate for the earlier flight to put your name on the standby list.

And that's when flying standby starts to get tense. Once everybody else has boarded, the gate agent will assign any remaining seats to passengers on the standby list, to some degree in the order you signed up, but elite frequent fliers or people who bought more expensive tickets get first dibs on any open seats. If your name isn't called, you can either try to go standby on another flight or resign yourself to taking your original flight (you'll still have a confirmed seat).

Because standby travel is so iffy, it's a better option if you're traveling alone or with just one other person and if you're not checking any bags. It gets more complicated if you're a family of four — especially if you need seats together — or you've checked any luggage, since your suitcase may end up on the flight you were originally scheduled to take. And if you're making a connection, you may have to go through the standby process all over again, though some airlines will change your connecting flight when you're assigned a seat for the first leg of your trip.

Which airlines allow standby travel
American, Continental, JetBlue, and United are among the U.S. airlines that allow free standby travel for most domestic fares. The main exceptions are if you purchased an unpublished fare — say, through Priceline, Hotwire, or a consolidator — or if you're traveling abroad, since standby travel isn't allowed on many international flights.

Besides standby travel, a few airlines charge a fee if you want to switch to a different flight on your scheduled departure day. For instance, Delta offers a "same-day confirmed" option that allows you to change your ticket to a flight leaving within three hours for a $25 fee; with this option, you're confirmed on the new flight, so you don't have to wait at the gate to find out whether there's space on the plane. But if there's more than a three-hour time difference between the time you call or check in and the flight you want, you have to pay Delta's standard change fee. (For more about ticket changes, see page 100.)

US Airways also charges $25 for its "move up" option, which gets you a confirmed seat on any flight leaving on your scheduled travel day, if space is available. Although Northwest doesn't allow free standby travel, its FlyNow option allows you to pay $25 to change your ticket to a different flight leaving within three hours — the difference being that you get a confirmed reservation rather than having to queue for a seat at the gate. American, Continental, and United offer passengers a similar option for the same price.

Because Southwest doesn't charge a fee for ticket changes, you can switch to an earlier or later flight without paying a fee, though you'll have to pay the difference between the fare you purchased and the lowest fare available for the new flight. Some other carriers allow standby travel, too, but this is one of those airline policies that's subject to change, so before you head to the airport early, call and double-check the rules.

Getting Bumped: What to Know About Those "Free Ticket" Coupons

For some travelers, the moment when a gate agent asks for volunteers willing to be bumped is music to their ears — though they don't necessarily join the rush to the ticket counter, because true experts get their names on the list even before an announcement is made. Others are sent into a frenzy trying to decide whether to volunteer, not realizing that eight other people have already beaten them to the punch.

The reason airlines sometimes bump passengers is that most carriers sell more tickets than there are seats on the plane, assuming that some people won't show up. But if everyone *does* show up, the airline has to coax a few passengers to take a later flight. If you're not in a hurry to get to your destination, you can earn a free ticket or a voucher worth several hundred dollars off a future flight by giving up your seat, which is why some people make a habit of getting bumped.

But the airlines aren't as generous as they used to be in compensating bumped passengers, and some of the "free tickets" they hand out come with restrictions that make them difficult to use. Here's what you need to know before you volunteer and how to increase your odds if your goal is to get bumped.

How to get bumped

If you really want to get bumped, you should start thinking strategically when you book your flight. Your best chances to get bumped are peak travel times, like the Wednesday before Thanksgiving or the Sunday after and similar busy days around other holidays. If you're not traveling on a holiday, you'll find more overbooked flights on Fridays, Sundays, and Mondays and in the summer, when planes tend to be full.

The day before your trip, you can gauge your chances of getting bumped by calling the airline and asking whether your flight is overbooked — or check the seat map for your flight on line. If there are twenty empty seats, the airline probably won't need volunteers to stay behind, but if your flight is overbooked, plan on showing up at the airport at least ninety minutes before your flight. At smaller airports, you can tell the agent when you check in that you're willing to be bumped, but usually you have to do this at your gate — and then you want to be the first person to volunteer.

The airlines generally take volunteers in the order everyone's name was added to the list, but a few things can hurt your chances. You'll be less likely to get picked if you've checked any bags, since pulling your luggage from the plane will delay the flight. And if you're a party of five, you have to be willing to split up; even when the airline bumps that many passengers, it's easier to rebook five people traveling to three different destinations than a family all going to the same place. Finally, if you go up to the counter every ten minutes and ask how things look, you may get passed over in favor of someone less high-maintenance.

What to ask about compensation

If your name is called, now is the time to start negotiating. Some airlines offer bumped passengers a "free domestic ticket" in exchange for giving up their seats, but what they don't tell you is that these tickets come with some significant restrictions. The biggest drawback is that they can only be used for the same seats designated for frequent flier awards — which are few and far between — and flights booked using free-ticket coupons generally don't earn miles.

So you should always ask for a monetary credit instead, which can be used to pay for any ticket, and your flights will earn miles. Some airlines give you the choice between a credit or a free-ticket coupon — but if not, ask. (Both have to be used within a year.) A voucher good for $300 off a future flight is pretty typical, but you may get a lower or higher amount, depending on the airline and how long you have to wait for the next flight.

If you're giving up a seat on an international flight or you have to stay overnight — in which case, the airline should give you a hotel voucher, too — you should get more than $300 for the inconvenience of staying behind. This is one of those "you get what you negotiate" situations, so if it's Christmas Eve and you're the only volunteer, try for a better deal. (You can get a sense of what various airlines offer bumped passengers if you visit BumpTracker.com.)

You should also make sure that you have a *confirmed* reservation on a later flight — and don't feel like you have to take the first option the agent offers. If the next flight your airline has space on doesn't leave for another five hours, ask to be booked on a different carrier leaving sooner, or if the flight requires changing planes, find out whether a nonstop is available. You should also ask for a meal voucher if you have to wait around the airport for a while.

If you don't like your options, there may be time to back out — but act quickly. Once the agent hands someone else a boarding pass for your seat, it's too late to change your mind.

When you're bumped against your will

There's also a chance that you might get bumped from a flight even if you don't volunteer to give up your seat. That's a rare occurrence, but it happens to about one in ten thousand passengers (the Department of Transportation keeps statistics on these things). That's called being "involuntarily denied boarding," and if it does happen, the government has rules about how the airline has to compensate you. (Airlines are required to give you a copy of these rules if you ask.)

If you're rebooked on another flight that lands between one and two hours after your original arrival time — between one and four hours for an international flight — the airline must pay you an amount equal to the one-way fare to your destination, up to $200. The amount of that compensation doubles, up to $400, if you have to wait longer than two hours for the next flight (or more than four hours for international travel).

But if the airline can get you to your destination within an hour of your original arrival time, it doesn't owe you anything, and this rule doesn't apply if you're bumped from a flight with fewer than sixty seats. You also don't qualify for any compensation if you didn't board the plane within the time frame stipulated by the airline (usually, at least fifteen minutes before departure); in that case, the airline is free to give away your seat.

Surviving Flight Delays and Cancellations: Know the Rules — and Your Rights

The only thing worse than finding out that your flight has been delayed is hearing that it's been canceled, although sometimes a cancellation actually puts you out of your misery. You can go back home and collapse on the couch, instead of pacing the airport while a one-hour delay stretches into six.

What you can do about either situation depends mostly on the reason the plane isn't taking off as scheduled — bad weather, a mechanical problem, air traffic control, or delayed inbound crew. But as long as you're not dealing with a hurricane or a snowstorm that has closed half a dozen airports, there's often *something* you can do to get yourself on another flight sooner rather than later. The first step is knowing what the airline is required to do for you if your flight is canceled or delayed; then it's a matter of helping yourself when a crowd of frustrated passengers is clamoring for attention from one or two equally frustrated agents.

The rules and your rights

When you buy a plane ticket, the airline doesn't make any promises to get you to your destination on time — or even within any particular time frame. What that means may not really sink in until you've missed a connection and are told that the next available flight is three days later (which happened to me one Christmas) or you've booked a trip to a remote island for a long weekend, and the only flight there is canceled two days in a row (which happened to a friend).

The *contract of carriage* that outlines the terms of every ticket purchase describes the airline's responsibilities and your rights in such situations — look for it on your airline's Web site, but you can also ask for a copy at the airport (no promises the agent will have one handy). The provision relevant to missed connections, cancellations, or travel delays is loosely known as *Rule 240*, though in each airline's contract, these policies may appear under a different number or name — and the terms may vary slightly from the general rules described here.

When the airline is at fault . . . Although the contract of carriage exempts an airline from liability for failing to operate a flight on schedule, it does say that if a flight cancellation, delay, or missed connection is caused by the airline, it must rebook passengers on a later flight — which most airlines routinely do — or if there isn't space on another flight within two hours, arrange transportation on an alternate carrier — which many airlines don't offer to do unless you know to ask.

It's possible that there isn't another airline with empty seats on the route you're traveling or at least not before the next flight your own carrier has available, but you should always ask the agent to check for flights on other airlines if you can't get a timely alternative on your own carrier — but remember, this is an option only if the airline is at fault for the delay.

If your airline can't arrange another flight that's acceptable, you can request a refund of the unused portion of your ticket — for instance, if it would be quicker to rent a car and drive to your destination instead or if you decide to abort your trip. Just make sure that the return leg of your ticket doesn't get canceled if you plan to use it to get back.

If you're delayed overnight *and it's the airline's fault,* most carriers stipulate in their contract of carriage that they will make a "reasonable effort" to put you up at a nearby hotel, but that promise is based on availability. If lots of passengers are stranded by the same event, there may not be any room at nearby inns — which is why you should contact nearby hotels on your own and request a "distressed passenger" rate. (You can make a reservation, then queue for a hotel voucher from an agent.)

Since the airlines negotiate special rates with nearby hotels, you can't just book a $250 room and expect to get reimbursed for the full amount. If rooms are scarce, take any room you can find and argue about compensation later, but if you're one of only a few passengers stuck overnight, you can save yourself that headache by working with the gate agent to make your hotel arrangements.

Besides a hotel room, most carriers will pay for your transportation to the hotel (if there isn't a free shuttle) and give you a meal voucher. Though again, this is only if the airline caused the delay.

When the airline is not at fault. If the delay is caused by forces outside the airline's control — like bad weather, a strike, government action, a labor shortage, or air traffic control — the airline's only responsibility is to refund the unused portion of your ticket. However, in practice, most airlines will reschedule you on a later flight, and some carriers do make this promise in their contract of carriage.

When the delay isn't the airline's fault, most carriers will not pay for a hotel, even if you're stranded overnight. That said, you may be able to talk your way into getting a hotel voucher — it helps if you're a valued customer, traveling with two small children, or walking with a cane — but probably the most relevant factor is whether you're dealing with a sympathetic employee.

In either case . . . Regardless of whether the airline is at fault, your carrier is *not* required to reimburse you for other expenses you incur because of a flight cancellation or delay — for instance, if you arrive at your destination a day late but had to pay for the missed hotel night or if you had to rent a car to drive to your destination. If you're a valued customer, you *may* be able to plead your case and get some type of compensation for your pain and suffering or out-of-pocket expenses — most likely, some frequent flier miles or a voucher for a credit toward a future flight — but these types of complaints are handled on a case-by-case basis, and being persistent is key.

Tactics for managing flight delays

Besides knowing the rules, it helps to know how to work the system if your flight is canceled or delayed — because Darwin's theory about the survival of the fittest definitely applies when dozens of passengers are scrambling to get seats on other flights. Here are some tips on helping yourself when your original flight plan goes astray.

Don't assume that you can't abort your trip if the outlook isn't good. If really bad weather is looming, the airlines often waive their change penalties and let passengers rebook on flights leaving a day or two later; sometimes, you can even reschedule your trip over the phone and avoid a mess at the airport. So if you're not desperate to get to your destination, it doesn't hurt to ask whether you can change your ticket to a later date — the airline may be glad to get you out of its hair.

Start planning early if a missed connection seems likely. If your outbound flight is delayed and you're likely to miss your connection, call the airline or ask a gate agent for details about other connecting flights headed to your destination later that day. Although your airline should automatically rebook you on the next flight if you miss a connection, this sometimes doesn't happen until you actually miss the plane, so you can jump-start the process when things start to look dicey by asking the airline to "protect" you on the next available flight to your destination. That means your original reservation will be held in case you make it, but you'll have a backup reservation on the next flight if you don't.

Call — don't wait in line. Whether you need to get rebooked or just want information about a flight delay, you'll often get faster service by calling the airline's toll-free number instead of waiting in a long line at your gate. (A good reason to travel with a fully charged cell phone, or at least remember to pack your charger in your carryon.) When lots of passengers are stranded, seats on other flights are reassigned on a first-come, first-served basis — though elite frequent fliers get priority over the masses — so acting quickly is key. Even if you just want an update about the status of your flight, I find that you often get more up-to-date information over the phone, since gate agents always seem to be the last people to hear what's going on.

Try an agent at a different gate. If you rebook your flight over the phone, you'll still need a new boarding pass to get on the plane. If the line at your gate is long, ask an agent at a different gate to print your boarding pass. Some agents might tell you that they can't do that, but they can, so politely explain that you've already rebooked by phone and only need your boarding pass printed.

Ask to be double-booked. If it looks as though another flight might leave before the one you're on that's delayed, ask the airline whether you can be "double-booked" — meaning that you'd have a reservation on both flights and could take whichever one left first. This is one of those gray areas that some agents might tell you isn't allowed, but if you're persistent and the other flight isn't overbooked, it should be possible to at least be put on the standby list for the other flight. Things get tricky if the two gates are far apart and the flights' estimated departure times start to converge — at that point, you'll have to pick one to stand near and hope it's the right bet.

Check flights to alternate airports. If you're flying to a city with more than one airport, ask whether any flights are leaving sooner going to another airport — say, Newark instead of LaGuardia or JFK. Some agents will automatically check all your options, but often you have to ask. If a gate agent tells you that switching airports isn't allowed on your ticket, call the airline's toll-free number and see whether you get a different answer. In many cases, it *is* allowed for certain airports — as long as there's space on the other flight and you haven't checked any bags.

Don't queue without a clue. Although most U.S. carriers have adopted customer service policies that promise to give passengers more timely information about flight delays, I'm continually amazed at how infrequently announcements are made in the gate area — which only causes more people to line up at the counter to ask the same questions. Rather than wait in line, I've learned to hover near the agent and eavesdrop; usually, someone else asks what I'm wondering about long before I would've made it to the front of the line.

Call and check the status of your plane. One of the most maddening things about delays is that they're often *creeping delays* — meaning thirty minutes becomes forty minutes and then an hour and then an hour and a half — and if you knew it would be that long in the first place, you could have gotten something to eat. One way to figure out how long a delay might *really* last is to call and check the flight's inbound status — whether it's left whatever airport it's coming in from. If not, you have time to buy some magazines or a slice of pizza. But if your plane is at the gate waiting for crew or for a mechanical problem to be fixed, don't wander too far, because the flight could start boarding while you're reading celebrity gossip ten gates away.

Don't hesitate to try an emotional appeal. I'm not suggesting that you lie to the gate agent — that's just bad karma — but if you're desperate to get to your destination, don't hesitate to make your case. "My grandma is in the hospital" is always going to sound fishy — even if it *is* true — partly because so many people lie about sick relatives. But if you're going to try an emotional appeal, detail is key. For instance, one Christmas when I was stuck at a connecting airport, I happened to team up with a woman who had such an elaborate tale about missing dinner with her fiancé's parents, whom she was meeting for the first time, that a sympathetic agent finally overrode some standby rule and booked us both on the next flight. (When he looked at me and asked, "And you?" I just said, "I can't top that.")

10 What to Do If . . .

PROBLEMS THAT COME UP on the road tend to fall into two categories: what you might call speed bumps, like a delayed flight or getting lost, and the travel equivalent of a ten-car pile-up — when your trip gets derailed by something a bit more serious, like you have an accident in a rental car or you end up in a foreign hospital with an ill-timed kidney stone. Because previous chapters address how to handle many minor mishaps, this chapter focuses on some of the more worst-case scenarios you might encounter during your travels. Among them: you get sick or injured and need a doctor far from home, the airline loses your luggage, your passport or wallet gets stolen (or lost), or you have a problem with your rental car.

There's also advice about what happens if your airline, cruise line, or tour operator goes out of business — maybe not so unlikely in the current travel climate. And the last section covers what to do if the service you paid for doesn't measure up — in other words, how to complain effectively, not just loudly, when something goes wrong.

But the point is *not* to suggest that travel is fraught with all sorts of bad things that can happen if you venture out into the world — you could spend a lifetime traveling and never need any of this advice. But if you do, I hope these tips will help you get out of a bind or salvage your trip while there's still time left to enjoy it.

You Need a Doctor: How to Find Medical Help Far from Home

Getting sick while traveling is one of the quickest ways to ruin a vacation, which is why most advice about travel and health focuses on *preventing* anything from going wrong. But if you log enough miles in far-flung locales, at some point, you're bound to break out in a mysterious rash or come down with an illness you can't treat with a good night's sleep and whatever over-the-counter remedies you brought along. In other words, a situation that requires a doctor — preferably, one who speaks a language you understand.

My worst travel sickness was an intestinal bug that hit me in a remote town in northeastern Brazil; I still don't know what I had, because the only doctor nearby was a visiting obstetrician who kept asking me, in Portuguese, whether I was pregnant (no). But at least I got some antibiotics, and after a few weeks, I was able to eat solid food again — and that episode is nothing compared to some of the horror stories I've heard.

But despite all the worry about illnesses — ranging from your basic Montezuma's revenge to more modern threats like SARS — plain old injuries are the main reason travelers seek medical help abroad. So whether you cut your foot on a broken bottle at the beach or wake up in the middle of the night with a high fever and the chills, here are some options you can try to find a doctor, clinic, or hospital nearby.

Call your own doctor or insurance company

If you have a regular doctor at home who is reachable in a pinch, it's worth calling to get advice about what to do and possibly a referral to someone local. But if your fever strikes after hours, you may find that your insurance company is more accessible around the clock or has better access to lists of physicians around the world. While you've got your provider on the line, you can get any approval you may need to file a claim later on. (See the sidebar on page 272 for advice on that topic.)

Ask your hotel for a referral

Some hotels have a doctor or two on call, while others at least keep a list of physicians you can contact, some of whom make "hotel calls." High-end hotels are more likely to have a relationship with a local physician, so if you're staying somewhere more budget-minded or the front desk isn't very helpful, call a more expensive hotel nearby. Even if you're not a guest, they may be able to refer you to a doctor, though some hotels don't make medical referrals at all, because of liability concerns.

Look in the phone book
Although it may sound dodgy to find a doctor using the same method you'd use to find a paint store, if you just need a prescription for some antibiotics or someone to look at a swollen ankle, you can often find a walk-in clinic listed in the phone book; look under "urgent care," "physicians," or "hospitals." You can also let your fingers do the walking to find specialists, dentists, and pharmacies, though in some cases — or places — an urgent-care clinic may be your best bet, since they're often cheaper than seeing a doctor in a private practice and less chaotic than going to an ER.

Call a U.S. embassy or consulate
If you're overseas, call the nearest U.S. embassy or consulate; most maintain lists of English-speaking doctors in the area, and some even post these lists on their Web sites. To find contact info for U.S. embassies abroad, check the State Department's Web site (see travel.state.gov). But if you're stuck somewhere far from a diplomatic post, especially in a developing country, ask whether anyone knows any foreign aid workers in the area, who are likely to know where to find medical help. (A good tip one traveler shared with me: Ask for the *best* doctor or hospital in the area, not just the closest one.) And if your symptoms suggest a potentially serious problem, get yourself to a big city before you're too sick to travel.

Call your credit card company
American Express, MasterCard, and Visa all offer various travel benefits to cardholders, including a referral service for doctors and hospitals. One advantage of these services is that they're usually staffed around the clock and often accept collect calls, so it's worth trying the customer service number for your credit card company — especially if you're traveling abroad.

PAYING THE BILL

Got health insurance? Not necessarily outside the United States, since many plans don't cover policyholders who venture beyond U.S. borders (see page 71 for details). Even if you *are* covered wherever you're traveling, you'll probably have to pay your bill on the spot and submit a claim to your insurance company, unless you see a doctor who's in your network. Some clinics, especially abroad, may even expect you to pay cash, so try not to show up at a hospital or doctor's office with an empty wallet. In certain situations, the quality of the care you get may depend on what you can pay, so that's not a time to be caught short.

Look on line

If you have access to the Internet, a few Web sites offer directories of physicians you can search. WebMD (webmd.com) has a pretty comprehensive database of doctors in the United States; in a big city, you'll get lots of results, which you can narrow down by choosing a specialty or a neighborhood. The International Society of Travel Medicine (istm.org) and the American Society of Tropical Medicine and Hygiene (astmh.org) both offer directories of travel medical clinics in the United States and abroad. Listings include contact information, languages spoken, and services offered, but most clinics are located in urban areas, and this is a better option for minor illnesses. And if you join the International Association for Medical Assistance to Travelers (iamat.org), you'll get a directory that lists participating doctors, clinics, and hospitals in 125 countries. The physicians all speak English and have agreed to a set payment schedule.

The Airline Loses Your Luggage: How to Track Your Bag — and File a Claim

Nothing gets a trip off to a bad start quite like that sinking feeling you get when you're waiting for your luggage to show up on the baggage carousel and the steady stream of bags coming out of the chute slows to a trickle and finally the conveyor belt grinds to a halt. Your bag is a no-show — now what?

Filing a claim

First, don't spend too much time waiting around the baggage claim area, searching in vain for your suitcase; find the luggage office for your airline and get in line. If your bag has been delayed, chances are it wasn't the only one, and the only thing more aggravating than having to file a lost-luggage claim after a long flight is waiting in line for forty-five minutes to fill out the paperwork.

It's always best to file a claim while you're still at the airport. But if you absolutely have to dash off, many airlines require you to submit a lost-luggage report within twenty-four hours of your flight's arrival in order to qualify for any compensation (you usually have a few extra days for international flights).

Sometimes, airline personnel can check the computer and tell you on the spot where your bag is — more often than not, it ended up on a different flight. There's a chance it may have even arrived *before* you did, especially if you were rerouted or your flight was delayed. If that's the case or the computer doesn't know where your bag is, politely ask the baggage attendant to check the luggage room — or check it *just one more time* (then smile and explain how attached your daughter is to the PJs in your suitcase).

If you're at a smaller airport, the luggage-storage system may be somewhat haphazard. I was once trying to track down a missing blue duffel bag, and the agent I was speaking with kept insisting that it hadn't arrived . . . until another employee passed by and said, "Yeah, it did, I just saw that bag." (Yet it still took fifteen minutes to find it.)

Negotiating delivery

If your bag is coming in on the next flight, the baggage attendant may encourage you to wait around for it, usually by telling you that the airline can't guarantee how soon it will be delivered ("We're really backed up . . ."). If you've flown in to your home airport or you don't need anything in your luggage that desperately, don't feel pressured to kill two hours at the airport — especially if you can't verify that the plane your bag is on will arrive on schedule. The airline is responsible for getting your luggage to you, so unless you're a shareholder, don't feel obligated to save the company the delivery expense.

But if you're boarding a cruise or driving to a cabin four hours away, you may be better off cooling your heels rather than taking a chance that your luggage doesn't catch up with you in a timely manner. In that case, don't be shy about asking the airline to compensate you for the inconvenience (see page 287 for tips on how to make your case).

Tracking your bag

Before you leave the airport, make sure to get a printout of your claim and a phone number you can call to check the status of your bag. Some airlines (among them Continental, Delta, and Northwest) also have tools on their Web sites that let you track your bag on line, much like you can track a package through FedEx. I've found these tools surprisingly reassuring when I've used them — at least you can see that your bag is in Tulsa, even though you flew to Los Angeles.

The airlines claim that more than 95 percent of all delayed bags are reunited with their owners within twenty-four hours, so if you can see where your luggage is, you can be pretty sure that you'll get it back. But don't throw away your ticket receipt, your checked-baggage stickers, your boarding passes, or any other paperwork, just in case you have to file a claim.

Interim expenses

Although most airlines will reimburse you for some expenses if your luggage is delayed while you're away from home, the amounts are rather limited and usually have to be approved in advance. Some airlines say that they'll approve only up to $50 in expenses for the first day of a delay and $25 per day thereafter, up to a limit of about $250 — but this is one of those situations when you get what you negotiate, despite whatever policy is stated in the airline's contract of carriage.

So don't assume that you have to accept whatever amount the airline first offers, especially if your golf clubs were circling the globe the entire weekend you were in Pebble Beach. But you'll have a much better chance of collecting if you work out a deal with the airline before you go on a spending spree. And be reasonable: Your airline isn't going to pay for a new set of golf clubs if you ultimately got yours back, but the company should reimburse you for whatever you paid to rent a set for two days. (No promises, though — the airlines aren't exactly flush with cash they're looking to give away.)

When all really *is* lost

There's no set time when a delayed bag is officially considered lost, but the airlines typically transfer the case to a central luggage service department if your bag hasn't turned up after four or five days. At that point, your suitcase may still surface, but as time passes, that likelihood starts to fade.

Whenever you decide to give up hope, you'll have to file another claim for the value of whatever you lost. Don't let too much time pass, because some airlines require you to submit a formal claim within a few weeks after your flight (time limits vary, so check with your airline). But before you start itemizing your losses, keep in mind that the airlines' liability for checked luggage is limited to $3,000 per passenger for domestic flights and $9.07 per pound for international trips. And you don't automatically get a check for the maximum amount — you have to prove the value of your loss. (To find out where some lost luggage ends up, see the sidebar on page 276.)

I've always gotten my luggage back, but I've talked to travelers who spent months haggling with an airline over the value of items in a missing bag. That's because the airlines often expect you to come up with receipts for whatever you lost, and then they depreciate the value of anything you've owned more than a year. Be persistent, and hold your ground.

If you don't get what you feel you're owed from the airline, you can try filing a secondary claim through your homeowner's or renter's insurance, which may cover lost or stolen items outside your home. Some credit card companies also offer lost-luggage benefits

WHERE DOES LOST LUGGAGE GO?

Well, some of it ends up in Scottsboro, Alabama, home to Unclaimed baggage.com, a company that purchases items the airlines were never able to reunite with their owners and it then sells to the public. Its store has become a tourist attraction in its own right, selling clothing, electronics, sports equipment, jewelry, and of course, an assortment of luggage. You can also shop on line, but the items posted on the Web site are only a fraction of what's available in the store.

Despite the flow of inventory to Alabama, some of the things passengers lose along the way do end up in a lost-and-found, so if you left your jacket in the overhead compartment or your child's blankie on a seat near gate B9, don't assume that a call to the airport or your airline is a waste of time — they may be able to track it down. I've heard tales of travelers who got back all sorts of lost possessions, though the odds of recovery are better if whatever you left behind isn't something everybody else wants — say, an iPod.

to cardholders (more likely if you have a premium card, and you must have used it to pay for your plane ticket). And if you purchased travel insurance for your trip, comprehensive travel policies usually offer some coverage for lost or delayed luggage — though the limits on this coverage are pretty minimal (see page 71 for more about travel insurance).

Damaged luggage

Most airlines don't accept liability for "normal wear and tear" on luggage — like minor cuts, scratches, dents, or broken handles — or damage resulting from overpacking. But if your bag shows up on the carousel with a six-inch gash in the side or was left out in the rain and all your clothes are soaked and stained inside, by all means, submit a claim. (Claims for damage are subject to the same monetary limits described earlier.)

Missing items

Things get dicey when anything is missing from your bag. If government screeners had to open it to search it by hand, they're supposed to leave a note inside, but in that case your claim may get caught in the ongoing game of hot potato between the Transportation Security Administration and the airlines, which have been arguing over who should pay claims when anything is missing from a checked bag. You can file a claim with both your airline and the TSA, but you may get quicker action if you choose one over the other — in which case, I'd go with the airline.

Your Travel Company Goes Out of Business: What Happens When a Company Folds

With so many airlines declaring bankruptcy in the past few years but continuing to sell tickets and fly planes, it's easy to forget that bankruptcy can ultimately lead to a total shutdown, sometimes overnight. Remember National Airlines? Pan Am? Tower Air? TWA?

In fact, more than a dozen airlines have disappeared in the past two decades, as have tour operators, cruise lines, and travel agencies, and the number of companies operating on financial thin ice suggests that at least a couple other logos may soon be retired. Of course, the travel industry has had to deal with more than its fair share of challenges in recent years — the aftermath of the September 11 attacks, war, high fuel prices, recession, hurricanes, and outbreaks of illnesses like the Norwalk virus and SARS. But the fact is, when a company finally goes under, travelers often get left in the lurch, stuck at airports scrambling for a way to get home or holding tickets for a tour or a cruise that isn't going to depart.

Whether you can get any of your money back depends on the situation, but you usually have some recourse to at least try, not to mention find another way home if your airline leaves you stranded in the middle of your trip. Here are some of your options if a company you're traveling with suddenly pulls the plug.

Protection for plane tickets
In late 2001, Congress passed a law requiring U.S. airlines to provide transportation to passengers holding tickets on another mestic carrier that ceases operations — originally a short-ter

quirement that has been extended several times. At first blush, that seems like a pretty solid safety net, but the legislation has some holes.

For starters, other airlines have to offer stranded passengers a seat only if space is available, which some carriers have interpreted as same-day standby travel. So if your airline goes out of business but your flight isn't for another month, you may have to wait until the day you're scheduled to travel to find out whether you can get a seat on another airline. There also has to be another U.S. carrier flying the same itinerary as your original ticket (this law doesn't apply to foreign carriers), which may not be the case if you're traveling through a small airport or abroad. And it's not clear whether this rule covers tickets booked with frequent flier miles. (For more about what happens to your frequent flier miles when an airline folds, see the sidebar on the facing page.)

Also, you have to pay a fee to the carrier that bails you out. At first, Congress didn't stipulate how much other airlines could charge to accommodate passengers left holding worthless tickets, but the Department of Transportation later set a limit of $25 each way, which was increased to $50 each way in 2005. You also have only sixty days after your original airline folds to make arrangements with another carrier, so you should start making inquiries right away, even though you may not get a confirmed seat until the day you're scheduled to travel.

Despite these protections, other glitches can occur. For instance, when National Airlines stopped flying in late 2002, the company also shut down its Web site, literally overnight. So travelers holding e-tickets who didn't have a copy of their receipt couldn't access their reservations to prove they had purchased tickets on National. The lesson learned: Make sure you print a receipt after you purchase a ticket, and also get a copy sent to you by e-mail, which is easier to forward.

Credit card chargebacks

Another option — not only for airline tickets but also for cruises, tours, and hotels — is to try to get a refund through your credit card company, assuming you used one to pay for your travel. Under the

WHAT HAPPENS TO YOUR FREQUENT FLIER MILES IF AN AIRLINE FOLDS?

That's the million-dollar question, and the answer is that no one knows. According to the fine print of all frequent flier programs, the airlines have the right to change or even discontinue these loyalty programs without any advance notice to members, and other airlines aren't required to honor unused miles if a competitor closes its doors.

That's why some frequent flier pundits recommend using up miles on airlines that have declared bankruptcy or at least switching your loyalty to another carrier. To be extra cautious, book your award tickets on a partner carrier if you can get seats (see page 117 for more about airline alliances); that way, you can avoid the unpredictability of holding an award ticket on an airline that may stop flying. Then again, most of the major carriers are having financial troubles, so it's not like any of them are a completely safe bet right now.

There's always a chance that another airline will take over the frequent flier program of a competitor that goes under — American Airlines adopted TWA's frequent flier members and their miles, and Delta did the same thing for Pan Am. But with so many airlines struggling to stay afloat, and travelers already complaining about scarce award seats, it's less certain that a frequent flier takeover would happen in today's travel climate — especially when cultivating customer loyalty isn't the airlines' top concern.

Fair Credit Billing Act, you're entitled to a refund if you purchase goods or services that aren't delivered, but you have only sixty days after the bank mails your statement to dispute a charge on your bill.

However, some credit card companies have said that they won't issue chargebacks in a bankruptcy situation — a position that may or may not withstand public pressure or a legal challenge. So it's worth trying to get a refund if you'd rather buy a new plane ticket instead of taking a chance flying standby or if you've been left high and dry by a cruise line or a tour operator. But your credit card company may balk at giving you one.

Travel insurance coverage

If you purchased travel insurance for your trip, you may be able to get a refund through your policy, but in some cases, supplier default isn't covered. For instance, most travel insurance providers specifically exclude coverage for companies that are operating un-der bankruptcy protection or whose financial situation seems precarious; you can usually find a list of excluded companies on the insurer's Web site.

In order to get coverage for supplier default, you have to buy travel insurance within two or three weeks of paying for your trip, and it's best to buy travel insurance from a third party, not your tour operator or cruise line, since those policies won't do you any good if the company closes shop. (See page 71 for more about travel insurance.)

Bankruptcy court claims

Another option is to submit a claim through the bankruptcy court, but this is a last resort, because the process can take a long time, and chances are you won't get much money back — if anything at all. When it comes to bankruptcy proceedings, the phrase *get in line* is apropos, and individual creditors are always behind all the suppliers and lenders the bankrupt company still owes.

Other options

If you purchased a trip from a member of the United States Tour Operators Association, you may be able to get some money back by filing a claim with that organization, whose members are required to post a $1 million bond to cover refunds in case they close shop (see ustoa.org for details). That's not a guarantee you'll get all or even some of your money back, because you'll be competing with lots of other customers — not to mention hotels and other companies the tour operator owes — but it's certainly an option worth exploring.

If you were a resident of California when you made your purchase, you may be eligible to get a refund from the state's Consumer Restitution Fund. Any agency that sells travel to California residents has to pay into this fund, so if the company goes out of business, customers are eligible to get a refund up to $15,000. Other states may offer similar protections, so check with your attorney general's office or a state consumer protection group to find out.

You Lose Your Passport or Wallet: Coping with No ID and No Money

You probably don't need to be told what to do if your wallet is lost or stolen — something that can happen even if you don't wander far from home. But getting separated from your ID, credit cards, or passport while traveling raises a few extra issues to sort out — starting with how to get through security if you have to fly. (At least with plane tickets going electronic, that's one less thing you have to worry about leaving behind.)

Following are some tips to help you deal with unexpected losses — as well as some advice about what you can do to minimize the hassle of a robbery or your own forgetfulness in case bad luck strikes.

Flying without ID

When my mom's wallet was stolen a few years ago, somewhere between leaving my apartment and arriving at Newark airport, her first concern wasn't canceling her credit cards — but how to get on the plane without ID. In that case, she was told to get a police report to prove that her wallet was stolen; also, she happened to have in her pocket a few business cards that have her photo, and she still had her ticket receipt.

If you find yourself without ID before a flight, call your airline and ask what you need to do — or ask an airline agent if you are already at the airport. (The airlines are responsible for verifying passengers' identities, so they hire the staff that checks your driver's license before you pass through security.) It's not that uncommon for travelers to find themselves in a panic midtrip, searching for ID that's disappeared, so the airlines have other ways to confirm your identity.

Preparing for the worst: Keep a copy of your driver's license in your suitcase or another piece of photo ID, like a gym club card or a company badge, somewhere besides your wallet. In a pinch, having some backup identification will help get you on the plane more quickly than if you have no other ID.

Replacing a passport

If you lose your passport overseas, you'll have to make a detour to the nearest embassy or consulate to get a temporary replacement. That process will go a whole lot more smoothly if you have a copy of your passport or at least know your passport number. But if you don't have any other identification with you, you may have to enlist someone at home to send you a copy of your birth certificate, a social security card, or whatever ID the embassy staff tells you is acceptable. Once you get home, you'll have to apply for a new passport, since the government only issues temporary replacements overseas.

Dealing with a lost or stolen passport in the United States is much easier; you can download forms and instructions from the State Department's Web site (see travel.state.gov). You're supposed to file a report as soon as you discover that your passport is missing, so the government can prevent anyone else from using it to travel; that also protects you from a potential identity-theft scenario.

Preparing for the worst: You've probably heard this advice a dozen times: You should always keep a photocopy of your passport separate from the real thing in your luggage. But if that hasn't motivated you to follow through every time you travel abroad, another solution is to store a copy of your passport on line. All you have to do is make a digital scan of the first page of your passport and send it as an attachment to an e-mail account you can access away from home (use an account that stores your messages on line). That way, you can print it from any computer with Internet access if you're ever in a bind. While you're at it, e-mail that same account a copy of your driver's license.

Getting emergency cash and new cards

If you lose your credit cards, your ATM card, and your cash all in one fell swoop — or swipe — little things like buying dinner or paying for a cab can suddenly become a problem. Your best bet is to borrow some cash from a traveling companion until you can get a new card; a more upscale hotel might also lend you some spending money and charge it to your bill. Another option is to take advantage of the emergency cash-advance services American Express, MasterCard, and Visa offer, but before you do, make sure that you understand exactly what service fees and finance charges are involved.

Visa and MasterCard work with Western Union to get cash to cardholders stranded without any funds, but you'll probably have to pay the fees Western Union charges to wire money (which aren't negligible). Your bank may also hit you with a finance charge that starts accruing the day you accept a cash advance, even if you pay your bill on time, so this can turn out to be a very expensive way to fill your new wallet.

As for replacing your credit cards, it may take a couple of business days to get a new card if you're traveling overseas, but within the United States, your bank should be able to deliver a new card or arrange for you to pick one up within twenty-four hours — unless you're somewhere remote, in which case it may take longer.

Preparing for the worst: It's certainly a good idea to keep phone numbers for your bank and credit card company somewhere besides your wallet, but you can also find emergency contact numbers for Visa (800-VISA-911), MasterCard (800-MC-ASSIST), and American Express (800-333-AMEX) in phone books, on their Web sites, through directory assistance, or in some guidebooks. You can also ask your hotel's front desk. (If you're overseas, you'll need a number you can call from abroad.)

If you report your card lost or stolen, you're not liable for any fraudulent charges, and the same goes for your ATM or debit card. But one issue to consider is that some debit cards are also linked to a credit card network, so it's possible for a thief to use your card to make purchases without having your PIN number — potentially draining your checking account before you notice the charges. Banks are required to redeposit withdrawals reported as fraudulent within forty-eight hours while they investigate, but in the time it takes you to discover them, some of your checks or automatic payments might bounce. That's why I asked my bank for an ATM card that's *not* linked to a Visa or MasterCard network — an option most banks offer (you have to call and ask for a new card).

There's a Problem with Your Rental Car: What to Do, Who's Responsible

Having an accident with a rental car is the travel scenario I dread the most, probably because I live in New York and rarely drive, so getting behind the wheel feels like being sixteen all over again — maybe even more tense, when you add jet lag and a busy highway to the picture. So far, I've been lucky (knock on wood), but I've talked to lots of people who have had problems with rental cars, ranging from lost keys, a flat tire, or engine trouble to a break-in, a fender-bender, or questionable charges for damage.

Looking into these situations, it turns out that having a toll-free number you can call for "emergency assistance" is sometimes more reassuring in theory than in practice, especially if you're calling in a panic from the side of the road. So don't assume that anyone is going to race to your aid or that whatever service you do get is included in the price of your rental — you'll often have to pay or wait for help.

Of course, the response you get depends on the company you rent from, what happened, and where you are when trouble strikes. But you'll probably get better service if you're a frequent renter or at least a member of the company's loyalty program, which is a good reason to sign up (see page 202 for details).

Breakdowns or flat tires
If the car you rented starts making funny noises or a warning light comes on or it simply won't start, first try calling the location you rented from (the phone number should be on your rental agreement); if you can't reach a local office, try the company's toll-free customer service number. When there's an obvious mechanical problem, the company *should* deliver a replacement vehicle to you, at no charge, though how quickly that happens depends on whether you're in the middle of a big city or truly getting away from it all.

Things get a little murkier if you get a flat tire, the battery dies, or you lock your keys in the car. Although some companies might offer you free roadside assistance, you'll probably have to pay for any service you receive or deal with the problem yourself. For instance, some friends got a flat tire in Berkeley, California, and the car rental company told them to change the tire themselves, then drive back to Oakland airport to get a new car — which was where they rented the car but not the closest rental office.

A different company or location might have been more help-ful — there's a lot of franchising in the industry, so service varies widely — but it's not uncommon for companies to expect custom-ers to deal with a flat tire or other minor problems. If you ever feel like you're being left high and dry by a local franchise, contact the parent company and see whether you get a more helpful response.

Lost keys

When some friends were swimming in South Africa, everything they left on the beach was stolen while they were in the water, in-cluding the keys to their rental car. In that case, the company did send help — a good thing, since they were locked out with nothing but their bathing suits — but the agency didn't have an extra key, so they had to break a window to get in, and my friends were charged to replace the key and the window.

Most rental companies don't have extra keys for their cars, so you can expect to pay about $75 if you lose yours (though that fee might be higher, since it's gotten more expensive to have keys made for newer cars). You may also be charged a fee to tow the car back to the lot.

So if you're issued two keys when you rent a car, leave one in your hotel room or give the spare to your traveling companion, which can at least save you from being stranded if you lose a key somewhere inconvenient — like on a beach in South Africa.

Another option: AAA

If you're a member of AAA, you can take advantage of its roadside assistance services even if you're in a rental car. As long as you have your membership card with you, you qualify for AAA's benefits whether you're the driver or a passenger in someone else's car, so that may be a better option than relying on the company you rented from (call 800-AAA-HELP).

Benefits vary, depending on which local club you belong to, but you can generally get help changing a flat tire or a jump-start for free and an emergency fuel delivery if you run out of gas (you'll have to pay for the gas). If the car needs to be towed, there's no charge for a short trip (about three to seven miles, depending on the club); for longer distances, you'd have to pay a fee of $2 to $7 per mile.

You can even get help from AAA if you've lost your key or locked yourself out of your car, though you generally have to pay for any locksmith services that exceed $50. (See aaa.com for details and information about joining.)

Accidents, theft, or damage

If you have an accident in a rental car or the vehicle or anything inside is stolen, call the car rental company as soon as possible and do your best to file a police report. (In some countries, you may find the police reluctant to get involved in minor crimes, like a suitcase stolen from your trunk.) You should also call your own auto insurer and ask what you should do if you plan to file a claim, or your credit card company if you'll be relying on any coverage your card offers.

If another car is involved in the accident, be sure to get the other driver's license number, insurance information, and license plate number, and make your own notes about what happened. The jacket of your rental agreement may also have instructions or a form the company expects you to fill out. But be careful about what you put in writing, because it could qualify as evidence if there's any dispute about who's responsible for the accident or the cost of repairs. And if you're at fault in a serious accident that causes injuries to anyone else, try to get in touch with a lawyer — or the closest U.S. embassy if you're in another country — before you make a statement about what occurred.

What charges you're responsible for, if any, depends on your insurance situation and whether the accident was your fault (see page 199 for details about insurance coverage for car rentals). If you opted for the loss damage waiver most car rental companies offer, you shouldn't be responsible for any expenses to repair the car, unless you were driving recklessly or otherwise violated the terms of your contract. But if you caused damage to someone else's car or property, that's not covered by the loss damage waiver; those repairs would be covered by the car rental company only if you bought supplemental liability insurance.

If you didn't opt for coverage through the car rental company, you probably have some coverage for a damaged or stolen vehicle through your auto insurance provider or credit card company, each of which will have its own process for submitting a claim. But if you have to pay any expenses yourself, make sure that you're not being overcharged. For instance, if you're billed for "loss of use" (to cover lost revenue while the vehicle was out of service), you have a right to see evidence that all the company's other cars were rented while the damaged car was in the shop. You can also ask for proof of actual repair expenses, which you can challenge if they're much higher than quotes you get from other body shops in the area.

Unscrupulous charges

If you're ever billed for damage you didn't know about or you're sure you didn't cause — not a likely scenario but one that happens from time to time — you should definitely dispute the charge (see the next section for advice). Your best defense against a trumped-up damage report is to make sure that you note any damage before you leave the lot (most companies give you a form to fill out), and if the car has more than minor scratches or dings, try to get a company representative to acknowledge the problem in writing or give you a different car. If you want to be extra cautious, ask the agent to sign off on the condition of the car when you return it, but at least keep a copy of the form you originally filled out until you've paid your bill.

You Have a Complaint: Dealing with Problems — on the Road and Once You're Home

In an ideal world, every flight would take off on time, hotel rooms would look like they'd been styled for a photo shoot, and cruises and tours would always deliver the picture-perfect vacations they advertise. Not that anyone really wants to travel in that kind of utopia — after all, the best anecdotes often start with a bad choice or a wrong turn. But sometimes, a trip falls so short of what was promised or the service is so bad that it's not unreasonable to expect someone to fix the problem or at least compensate you for your trouble.

The trick is knowing whom to talk to when something goes wrong and how to make sure that your complaint doesn't end up in the electronic version of the circular file: a form e-mail with a generic apology, an assurance that the company is *absolutely* committed to providing the best service possible, and a promise to do better next time. My favorite touch? Text at the bottom of the e-mail telling you not to bother replying to that address, since it's used only for outbound mail.

Here are some strategies to help you register a more effective complaint — both during and after your trip — and what to do if the first response you get isn't the reaction you'd hoped for.

Speak up right away

If you booked an ocean view room and the bellhop takes you to a room facing the parking lot or if you can see only a sliver of water from the window in the shower, don't hesitate to speak up. If you check in late at night, all the best rooms may be taken, but if you arrive at 3 P.M. and are stuck across the hall from a noisy ice machine, go back to the front desk and ask to be reassigned. (Someone once told me that when he checks in to a hotel, he says, "Instead of giving me the room you're about to send me to, how about if you put me in the room you'll assign me when I come back downstairs and tell you the first one is unacceptable?")

The same goes for problems on a cruise, at the airport, at a car rental agency, or even in a restaurant: It weakens your case considerably to call after you get home and admit that you didn't say anything while the company could have addressed the problem. You may not get the response you want, but at least you'll have brought the matter to someone's attention when there was an opportunity to do something about it.

Talk to the person in charge

Front-line employees aren't always empowered to deal with problems, so if you feel like you're getting nowhere with the clerk at the front desk or an agent at an airline ticket counter, don't waste too much time spinning your wheels. But try to avoid saying, "Can I speak to your supervisor?" — which pretty much guarantees that it will take twenty minutes to track down another employee, who may not have any more authority; you're better off asking for someone else by title.

At a hotel, that's the general manager; if he or she isn't in the building, ask who's next in line if your problem needs an immediate response. On a cruise, you should speak to the hotel manager about issues with your cabin, the maître d' about the dining room, or the purser about any other complaints. If you're at the airport or dealing with a rental car — or you're not sure who's in charge — try "the manager on duty." That's somewhat less confrontational than "your supervisor," which implies, "Now, I'm not just going to complain about the smell in my room — I'm going to complain about *you*."

Get contact information to use later

If you're not getting anywhere with the staff on site or there's no one higher ranking you can talk to, ask how you can contact a manager or the company's customer service department by phone (or by mail, if you can't get a phone number). In some cases, you may have no choice but to take up your case later with someone else, and it's not worth ruining your trip arguing over a minor issue, especially if it's clear that no one is going to do anything about it.

The trick is knowing when to walk away and when to stand your ground. If you're trying to get credit toward a future flight because you've been inconvenienced by a cancellation, that's something you can do later by phone, especially if forty other people are in line waiting to be rebooked. But if you're arguing about a voucher for a hotel because the airline caused you to miss your connection, refusing to budge from the counter may actually help your case. If not, you can always pay for the hotel yourself and try to get reimbursed after you get home.

Get everything in writing

Make sure that you have a paper trail — advice that actually applies *before* something goes wrong with your trip. When you make a reservation, print out the confirmation page and take it with you; that way, if a hotel has no record of your reservation or you booked a minivan and none are left on the lot, you have proof to back up your claim. (I'm always a bit suspicious of people in line at a hotel who say, "But I have a reservation!" yet they don't have a confirmation number or anything on paper.)

Then, if you have a problem, take notes during every discussion you have about the issue, including the name of the person you spoke with, when you had the conversation, and what that person said. When you call back a month later and say that someone promised you five thousand frequent flier miles that never showed up in your account, I guarantee that the first question you'll be asked is, "Who did you talk to?" Also, try to get a direct phone number or extension for anyone you speak to by phone; otherwise, you'll have a tough time tracking down "Sam" through the company's 800 number if you have to call back.

Take photos

If there's mildew on the shower curtain, cigarette burns on the carpet, and stains on the bedspread, don't just make a note of it — get out your camera. It's more difficult for a company to dismiss your complaint or accuse you of exaggerating if you can produce evidence. Photos are also useful for getting attention from the media or pursuing legal action, should you have to escalate things to that level.

Read the rules

Before you get too far along with a complaint, make sure that you understand what you're up against. Most travel companies outline detailed rules in some type of contract you either signed (like a car rental agreement) or implicitly agreed to when you made your purchase (like an airline's contract of carriage or a cruise line's ticket terms). For instance, cruise lines typically reserve the right to change an itinerary, skip a port, or substitute a different ship for the one you booked, so if you plan to take issue with any of those types of changes, you'll be facing an uphill battle. Also, most travel companies have written policies about things like changes and cancellations, so make sure to read all these terms and conditions so you know where you stand.

Of course, you can still contest something covered in a written policy. For instance, even though airlines reserve the right to cancel flights, a carrier may give you some extra frequent flier miles or a credit toward a future flight if you're a valued customer and a delay really messed up your plans. And these types of contracts aren't necessarily legally binding; in some cases, travelers have successfully argued in court that they weren't given adequate notice about the rules, so just because the fine print says it's so doesn't mean that a court will agree.

File a written complaint

If you're not satisfied with the response you get during your trip, the next step is to follow up when you get home. At that point, I'd start with a phone call (ask for the customer service department); if that doesn't get you anywhere, you can either hang up and call back — hoping that someone more helpful picks up the phone — or ask for an address where you can send a letter. Try to find out who runs the customer service department (you can call corporate headquarters and ask), since it's easier to follow up on a letter you sent to someone specific.

These days, many companies refer customers to a form on their Web site to submit a complaint, but I'd try to avoid that. I've seen lots of e-mail exchanges between travelers and employees tasked with responding to digital inquiries, and they're often a frustrating back-and-forth that never results in any action. If you can get an e-mail address for a person at the company, that's a different story; otherwise, skip the Web form unless you can't find any other way to make contact.

Another reason to submit a complaint in writing is that many travel companies stipulate a time frame customers have to file a claim about service (once again, this is usually stated somewhere in the fine print of your ticket terms). Those time limits vary, but don't wait more than a month to send a written complaint, especially if you're considering legal action.

Keep your cool

Before you send a three-page letter ranting about the loud construction at your hotel or the awful food on your cruise, imagine that
you're the person reading it: If a total stranger would think, "This
person is a nutcase," go back and turn off the caps lock key, and de-
lete all those exclamation points. Companies respond differently if
they think they're dealing with someone reasonable, so best not to
sound angry or threatening. Remember, you want the person who
reads your letter — or takes your phone call — to sympathize with
your problem and want to help you.

Try to keep your letter to a page, or two at the most, briefly stating
what happened and what you want the company to do for you (for
example, give you a refund of x dollars or a coupon for a free hotel
night). If you're a member of the company's loyalty program, have
some type of elite status, or stayed at that hotel six times in the past
ten years, by all means mention that, but don't go overboard or resort to petulant playground threats like "I'm going to tell everyone I
know not to fly on your airline." Many travel companies are struggling, and employees are worried about their own jobs, so customer
service isn't the priority it used to be. You'll get much farther with a
rational, concise argument than by threatening to e-mail all your
friends.

Dispute the charge through your credit card

If you don't get a satisfactory response from the company, you may
be able to get a refund through your credit card, assuming that you
used one to pay for the service you're challenging. Under the Fair
Credit Billing Act, you're entitled to a refund if you purchase goods
or services that aren't delivered or don't live up to what was advertised or agreed on. But when it comes to travel purchases (as opposed to, say, a sweater you ordered that never arrived), there's kind
of a gray area surrounding the types of issues you can dispute.

If you can prove that you didn't get what you paid for, like the
pool touted on a hotel's Web site was closed for maintenance, or you
paid for three scuba lessons but the dive shop canceled your last
class, it's worth submitting a claim. Your credit card issuer will investigate the matter and determine whether you're entitled to a

chargeback, and you don't have to pay the charge while the bank looks into the case. But you have only sixty days after the bank mails your statement to dispute a charge on your bill, and a chargeback isn't really an option if you just thought that the service was terrible or you were disappointed by your hotel.

Take your complaint elsewhere

If you're getting stonewalled, another option is to contact a third party, like a trade association, a government agency, or the media; it may help your case to notify an organization that has more influence. For instance, many travel companies are members of industry groups, like the United States Tour Operators Association (ustoa.org), the American Society of Travel Agents (astanet.com), the Cruise Lines International Association (cruising.org), or the American Hotel and Lodging Association (ahla.com). Those groups probably won't get involved in minor complaints about their members, but if you experienced a really egregious breach of service, they might try to help you out.

In cases involving serious harm, fraud, or some law being broken by the company, you can also try alerting a state consumer protection agency, the district attorney's office, or a state attorney general, but government agencies are more likely to investigate cases where there's a pattern of wrongdoing or lots of customers involved. For problems with an airline, you can submit a complaint to the Aviation Consumer Protection Division of the Department of Transportation (see airconsumer.ost.dot.gov), though that division mostly tracks complaints rather than responds to individual problems.

Trying to get press coverage is another way to spark action from an unresponsive travel company, if you can interest a journalist in your story. Several travel publications have regular columns that investigate some of the more shocking or headline-worthy breaches of customer service (see page 5 for a list of publications that cover travel), and television news programs often have reporters who cover consumer affairs. But these journalists get lots of inquiries from people seeking help, so it takes a pretty compelling incident to get their attention. Another route worth trying is posting a message at an on-line travel community (see page 14 for examples); your fellow travelers may have ideas about what to do or where to turn, and some of the bigger travel companies monitor these message boards, so that's another way your situation might get noticed.

Legal action

As a last resort, you can always take your case to the courts. Filing a lawsuit is complicated and expensive — though perhaps worthwhile, depending on what happened and your financial resources. But if your claim is minor, you may want to consider small claims court. In most states, the maximum you can collect is $3,000 per person, but the filing fee for these types of claims is usually $10 or less, and a court clerk can help you navigate the paperwork.

One wrinkle with small claims court is jurisdiction: The company must be located in the same county as the court in order to file a claim. With airlines operating in so many locations, jurisdiction usually isn't a problem, but it can prevent some claims against tour operators, cruise lines, or hotels that aren't in your area. The Department of Transportation's Web site offers a publication about small claims court — "Tell It to the Judge" (see airconsumer.ost .dot.gov) — but the court itself will also have instructions about how to file a claim.

Let it go

It seems inappropriate to end this book on a litigious note — because this is, in fact, the end — so I'll close by saying that sometimes, you're better off putting a bad experience behind you. Travel is unpredictable, and much as this book is about trying to make sure that you get the most out of your trip, there are some things you just can't control. At least some of those mishaps make great stories. (After all, whose fishing trip would you rather hear about: the guy who caught a two-hundred-pound marlin or the one who fell out of the boat?) And there's always another trip you can start planning — which is what I'm going to do, now that I'm finished telling you how to plan yours.

Acknowledgments

Writing a book does not have a whole lot of what I'd call "Rocky Balboa moments" — you know, when Sylvester Stallone pumps his fists at the end of a pre-dawn run, "Gonna Fly Now" playing in the background, or when the crowd roars as he takes to the ring — no one applauds when you sit down at your computer, or for that matter, type the last word.

But in some ways, writing and boxing are similar endeavors: They're both mostly solitary pursuits, but to succeed at either one you need people in your corner. And with a book like this, there were many, many people who taught me all the tips and tricks collected in these pages, or propped me up when I was on the ropes. (OK, that's it for the boxing analogy.)

First, I'd like to thank everyone who has shared their expertise with me during the years that I've been writing about travel. This book is actually a collection of all the knowledge and advice I've gathered through literally thousands of interviews with travel company executives; their publicists; industry analysts; people who run travel Web sites; fellow travelers I've accosted on planes, in airports, or on cruise ships; rank-and-file employees working in the travel industry; and friends who casually mentioned a good (or bad) travel experience and who I insisted tell me more. There's no way I could mention everyone by name, but I hope you all know how much I appreciate your time and input — which I hope will benefit someone else who reads this book.

Much of the research that ended up in this book first appeared in articles I wrote for the *New York Times*, which not only gave me my first print byline but also something of a crash course in reporting. Thanks to all of the editors who have given me assignments and shaped my work along the way, as well as those who weren't ever my editor but as a boss, friend, or consigliere offered support and encouragement.

To those who read some of these chapters when the text was still very much in draft form—Adam, Cath, Jenny, Justine, Margi, Matt, Pia, Todd, Will, my dad, and especially my mom, who slogged through every unpolished word — I promise it's much better now, thanks to your input. Besides pressing friends and family into reading drafts of these pages, I also solicited advice on countless decisions that came up. Thanks to everyone who endured all of my e-mails and phone calls, especially Kim, for wise counsel on book publishing, and my sister, for advice on everything else (even if I often ignored it).

I'm also grateful to those who gave me a place to work when it became apparent that having a room of one's own didn't quite cut it amidst the noise and distractions of New York. So thanks to Gail and Anne for the spare keys, and most of all Amy, who loaned me her ID so I could use the libraries at Columbia University — and then didn't mind that it got confiscated when I was busted. (For the record: getting caught sneaking into a library with a borrowed ID is far more humiliating than being thrown out of a bar when you're twenty.)

To Wendy Lazear, Kate Travers, and everyone at Houghton Mifflin: Thank you for seeing that there was a need for this book and for giving it so much attention and support, as well as having patience with *my* attention to details that other authors might have happily left alone.

To my agent, Will Lippincott: I'm still holding out for the house in Aspen, but otherwise you've gone above and beyond. Thank you most of all for seeing who I could be, even before I could see it myself . . . and then not running for the hills when it became clear that writing this book in six months was not, in fact, going to be "fun."

On that note, I did sort of run for the hills — or at least a lake in northern Michigan — toward the end of this editorial journey, and as always, my parents opened their doors. I wouldn't have finished this book without your support, not to mention your cinnamon rolls, your porch, and your cherry scones, which proved, once again, that often the most valuable thing we gain by going away is appreciating what we left at home.

Index

for flight cancellation, 266
for future flight, 103, 289
with getting bumped, 261, 262
credit card
  and car rental insurance, 197,
    200
  consolidator tickets, 108
  doctor referral service, 271
  fees on foreign charges, 229
  frequent flier miles with use, 111,
    115, 255
  house rental, 149–150
  lost, 282–283
  and lost baggage, 275–276
  overseas validity, 215
  refund chargebacks, 278–279,
    292–293
  safety, 227, 228
crime. See theft; unscrupulous tactics
Cross-Cultural Solutions, 51
crowds, avoiding, 23, 24
cruise bookings
  and discounters, 55, 173, 174
  last-minute, 80, 82–83, 176–177
  overview, 175–176, 177–178
  by travel agency, 83–84, 172, 175,
    176, 177, 181
Cruise Brothers, 177
Cruise.com, 177
CruiseCompete.com, 178
CruiseCritic, 17, 183, 184, 185
Cruise Direct, 177
Cruise411, 177
cruise lines
  bankrupt. See out-of-business
    companies
  complaints against, 287–294
  luxury, 163–164
  mass-market, 159–161

premium, 161–163
  specialty, 164–165
Cruise Lines International Association, 185, 293
CruiseMates, 17, 56, 183, 185
cruises
  airfare, shore excursions, and
    land tours, 178–179
  bookings. See cruise bookings
  cabin selection, 55, 82, 168–169,
    171–172
  classes on, 46, 163, 168, 173
  and airline connections, 178–
    179
  cruise line selection. See cruise
    lines
  deposits, cancellation policies,
    and refunds, 180–183, 278–
    280
  on-line cruise forums, 17
  other guests aboard, 25
  pre- and post-cruise tours, 180
  questions to ask, 166–167
  ship and itinerary selection, 159,
    165–168
  shore excursions, 179–180
  solo travelers, 54–55, 56
  spas on, 42, 161, 162, 174
  stereotype vs. reality, 158
  tall-ship, 57
  upgrades, 172
Cruises 'N More, 177
Cruises Only, 173
Cruise Value Center, 177
Cruise West, 165
Crystal Cruises, 163
CSA Czech Airlines, 120
CSA Travel Protection, 73
culinary adventures, 45–48
Cunard Line, 160, 162